COMPARATIVE LAW
LAW, REALITY AND SOCIETY

COMPARATIVE LAW
LAW, REALITY AND SOCIETY

BY

ALAN WATSON

VANDEPLAS PUBLISHING
UNITED STATES OF AMERICA

Watson, Alan

Comparative Law: Law Reality and Society

Published by:

Vandeplas Publishing
May 2007

801 International Parkway
5th Floor
Lake Mary, FL. 32746
USA

www.vandeplaspublishing.com

ISBN-13: 978-1-60042-018-4
Library of Congress Control Number: 2007927257
© Alan Watson 2007

Printed in the United States of America

To the two men who shaped my life:

James Walker Watson, railway booking clerk in a small Scottish town, and a dedicated poet.

David, Daube, refugee from Hitler, a great scholar in various fields, and a wonderful teacher.

With love,

Alan

Table of Contents

PREFACE

Comparative law provides unique insights into law in general, the forces behind legal change, law and society.

Rulers are interested in keeping power, not in making satisfactory law (Chs. 1,2); when they make law they often borrow from a foreign system, from a different time (chs. 4, 6, 11); law making is often left to subordinates who are not given power to make law (chs. 8,10); neglected law has unforeseen and far-reaching consequences (chs. 2,3,4,5,9,10); law survives for a very long time, even in very different places, in very different circumstances (chs. 2, 4, 6); law is everywhere, in everyday life, and is often not noticed (ch. 4).

It is often said that I exaggerate and set out to shock. Not so!

This book is compiled largely from previous writings of mine, and was intended as the course book for the class of Comparative Law at the University of Auckland, when I was to be Visiting Professor in April, 2007. Unfortunately, I was unable to hold the classes.

I am deeply in the debt of Cindy Wentworth who typed many versions of this volume. My other great debt for this book – I have many debts – is to the staff at the Law Library of the University of Georgia. They give me unstinting help and unfailing encouragement.

Alan Watson,
Athens, GA
February, 2007

Chapter 1

Law in Books, Law and Reality:
a Comparative Law Perspective

I consider myself a comparative legal historian and range widely over time and space. My interest is in private law. My general conclusions, developed over years, on law in society are three and are interconnected and are as follows:

1) First Conclusion: Governments are not much interested in developing law especially not private law. They generally leave this to subordinate law makers to whom, however, they do not grant power to make law. For instance:

(a) The great Roman jurists from the second century B.C. to around 235 A.D. to whom modern private law owes so much were as such private individuals even though many, for instance Julian, Paul, Ulpian and Papinian, were top public officials. Others, such as the obscure jurist Gaius famous for his elementary textbook, were not. Much of their works formed Justinian's Byzantine *Digest* (533 A.D.) and thus lived on into the modern world.

(b) The great figures in the early and fundamental Reception of Roman law from the 11th century onwards, the Glossators and Post-Glossators such as Irnerius, Accursius, Baldus and, most famous of all, Bartolus, were University professors.

A pattern is already beginning to emerge: law lives on long after the death of the law maker, and in territories distant from his place of business. And it continues to thrive even in very different circumstances and even though misapplied. For instance, the *Ordenaçoes Filipinas* promulgated by Philip II (of Spain) for Portugal under Spanish domination, and confirmed by

João IV in 1643 gave subsidiary validity to the opinions of Bartolus. The *Ordenaçoes* applied to the Portuguese colonies and remained in force even when Brazil became independent in 1822.

(c) The development of English law which was mainly the work of judges whose task was supposedly to find the law, not to make the law, is equally unthinkable without the *Commentaries on the Laws of England* (first edition 1765-1769) of William Blackstone, composed when he was the first Vinerian Professor at Oxford from 1758.

The reception of English law in the U.S.A. after Independence is equally unthinkable without these *Commentaries*. There were, of course, numerous American editions with significant changes -- which must not be minimized – but Blackstone remained Blackstone.

The accessible structure of Blackstone's *Commentaries* has been the subject of lively debate but the issue is simply resolved. The *Commentaries* follow the slightly flawed reconstruction of Justinian's *Institutes* by Dionysius Gothofredus (1549-1622). Gothofredus tabulates the arrangement with connecting lines. Blackstone does the same. Another example of extreme borrowing.

Perhaps an even more telling example for survival is William Geldart's celebrated *Introduction to English Law* [first edition, 1911; latest edition, 1995]. This also follows the structure of Justinian's *Institutes*. Thus:

Chapter 1, Statute law and Common law;

Chapter 2, Common law and equity;

Chapter 3, Other bodies of English law; = *J.* 1.1-2:

Chapter 4, Persons and personal relations; = *J.* 1.3-26; (end of *J.* 1.).

Chapter 5, Property = *J.* 2.1-25; 3.1-12;

Chapter 6, Contracts = *J* 3.13-29; (end of *J.* 3).

Chapter 7, Torts = *J.* 4.1-5;

J. 4.6-17 on procedure have no equivalent in Geldart;

Chapter 8, Crimes = *J.* 4.18; (end of *J*.4).

Even within a chapter the order may follow that of the *Institutes*. Thus,

Geldart's Chapter 5 begins with the conception of property, then ownership and possession and ends with succession. *J* 2.1-3.12 begins with the division of things and ends with a final point of succession.

Western law is unimaginable without the input of scholars writing without governmental authority.

(2) *Second Conclusion*: Even when famous legislators emerge, they are seldom much interested in inserting a particular social message or even certainty into their laws.

(a) Moses and the Ten Commandments. Moses is a leader in serious trouble with his own people who are on the verge of revolt. Moreover, his own father-in-law has just told him that he is wearing himself out deciding lawsuits, and that with God's help he should concern himself with weightier matters (Exodus 18.13ff). God comes to Moses' aid and gives him the Ten Commandments or Ten Words (Exodus 20. 1ff.) Significantly, God insists that Moses be given the laws in private, and far from the people. (Exodus 19.10ff.).

The secular legal provisions are banal in the extreme: no murder (or killing) (Exodus 20.13), no adultery (Exodus 20.14), no theft (Exodus 20.15). What society – apart from ancient Sparta and theft – would fail to have such rules? More to the point, these offences are not defined. But what amounts to murder, theft or adultery? Some precision is needful, but is not given. But if no precision is to be given, what is the point of stating no adultery and no theft? After all, they are certainly covered by the last Commandment. Adultery and theft are the strongest cases of coveting a neighbour's wife or anything that is your neighbour's.

Even the religious commands leave much to be desired. No work on the seventh day (Exodus 20.8ff). But work is not defined. What amounts to work? We are not told. The resulting endless debates of the Pharisees and rabbis can be no surprise. Exodus 20.8 tells us that on the Sabbath "you shall not do any work – you, your son or your daughter, your male or female slave, your livestock, or the alien resident in your town." There is a glaring omission: "Your wife." Is she permitted to work on the Sabbath? It would be very convenient if she were! Someone is needed to interpret the Commandments, but no one is appointed.

(b) Justinian's enormous codification, the *Corpus Iuris Civilis*. The *Corpus Iuris Civilis* is in four parts: the *Institutes* (533 A.D.) is the elementary textbook, with the force of statute law, for first year law students; the *Digest* (533) is a vast collection of selected texts from the classical jurists; the *Code* (second edition 534) is a collection of imperial rulings; and the *Novellae*, a collection of subsequent Justinianic legal pronouncements.

A dominant concern in Justinian's time, and of Justinian himself, was religion. Which form of Christianity was to be accepted, which doctrines were heretical, the treatment of Jews. Yet in the whole body of the *Institutes* and *Digest* there is not one mention, not one, of Jesus, of the apostles or saints or fathers of the church. God is mentioned only once in the *Institutes*, in the very last text, *J.* 4.18.12. Justinian has given a very brief outline of public prosecutions which will be amplified, he says, *deo propitio*, with subsequent study of the *Digest*. The *Digest* has twelve mentions of the word 'god', but in none can we tell whether the god is that of the Christians or an old pagan deity. The *Code* has more of Christianity (and anti-semitism). But there is a wonderful twist. The *Institutes* were the subject of first-year study, the *Digest* of the second, third and fourth years. The *Code*, as an object of study, appears only in the fifth year. And even if by then the students' minds were not fixed, the fifth year was optional!

Justinian has not brought up-to-date the law of the pagan Latin-speaking jurists of classical Rome to reflect the Christian Greek-speaking lawyers of the very different Constantinople. And economic conditions had varied greatly from time to time. And if the *Digest* had been in Greek, not Latin, it could never have had much impact in western Europe.

One further example out of many. The ancient Roman law code of 451-450 B.C., the *Twelve Tables*, contained a provision *Si aqua pluvia nocet*, "if rain water does damage." This was the subject of intense discussion by jurists from at least the second century B.C. to the third century A.D., and it is the subject of a *Digest* title, *D.* 39.3. One issue was settled: an action did not lie when the flow of water onto a neighbour's land was diminished; it was not the water but its lack that caused loss. But what work on your land that increased the flow onto my land could give rise to an action to restore the *status quo ante*? The jurists mightily disagreed. No legislation was forthcoming, the juristic disputes were not settled, not even in the time of Justinian in the very different climatic conditions of Byzantium. Indeed – and this is why I have chosen this example – it was taken over in France. Robert Pothier (1699-1772) took it over in its entirety and cites no other source in his account. Odder still, it was not until the final revision of the draft French *code civil* of 1804 that any fundamental change was made.

3. Third Conclusion: Legal Transplants. Borrowing is the name of the legal game and is the most prominent means of legal change. That this is so often overlooked can only be explained by extreme prejudice brought about by notions such as that "Law is the Spirit of the People" or that "Law reflects the Power Structure of the Ruling Class." But in the previous two main topics in this chapter transplants have appeared in almost every situation discussed. So true – and obvious – is this that I will limit myself to only two, more detailed, examples.

But before I come to these, I would like to insist on the intertwining of the factors shaping law in society. Much has already emerged about this intertwining:

A. The lack of interest on the part of government in making law, especially private law.

B. The fundamental role of subsidiary law makers who are not given power to make law.

C. The longevity of legal rules whether in the same or a different context, whether in the same or a different state. There has been no need to set this out under a distinct heading. It is self-evident.

Law, as we know it, is inconceivable without these factors. To come at last to the two examples of legal transplants which also inevitably throw still more light on the intertwining of the factors of legal development.

For Frederick the Great of Prussia it is enough to call attention to the first fruits of his attempts to codify the law. *Das Project des Corpus juris Fredericiani, d.h. S.M. in der Vernunft und Landes verfassungen gegründetes Landrecht, worin das Römisches Recht in eine natürliche Ordnung und richtiges Systema nach denen dreyen Objectis juris gebracht,* which was published at Halle between 1749 and 1751. The very title is instructive; "The Project for the Corpus juris Fredericiani, that is, the Territorial Law of His Majesty, Founded in Reason and the Territorial Constitutions, in which Roman Law Is Brought into a Natural Order and Right System in Accordance with Its Three Objects of Law." That is to say, it gives the *ius commune,* and it is in fact arranged in the order of Justinian's *Institutes.* No attempt is made to compose afresh a law peculiarly suited to the Prussian territories. Indeed, some paragraphs of the preface, particularly 15,22,23, and 28, make it plain that for the drafters the impetus for the *Project* was not dissatisfaction with the substantive *ius commune* but with the difficulty of ascertaining the law because of the poor arrangement of Justinian's *Corpus Juris Civilis* (apart from the *Institutes*) and of the multitude of writings on it by subsequent jurists. In the second section of part 1, book 1, Frederick claims it is only to be regretted that the German emperors when they received Roman law did not always systematize it. Frederick's primary intentions – at least as they were perceived by his famous chancellor, Samuel Cocceii – ought best be revealed by the main thrust of this first production. The fact that, because of the Seven Years' War, it never came into force (which is regarded, for instance, by Franz Wieacker as rather fortunate) is not of consequence here. For later attempts at codification, ultimately crowned with success, with rather different aims, Frederick was indebted to a new generation of lawyers and philosophers.

The other example is Atatürk, who wished to reform and modernize Turkish life in so many ways (and was very largely successful). He promulgated in 1926 the Turkish Civil Code, the *Türk Kanunnu Medenîsi*

(*TKM*), which contained virtually all of the two Swiss codes, the *Schweizerisches Gesetzbuch* (*ZGB*) and the *Obligationenrecht*. Turkey in the same year issued its commercial code, which was a compilation of at least a dozen foreign statutes, and issued in 1929 its code of the sea, which is a translation of book 4 of the German Commercial Code (*Handelsgesetzbuch*).

The Turkish Minister of Justice of the time, Mahmut Esad Bozkurt, on the occasion of the *Festschrift* of the Istanbul Law Faculty to mark the civil code's fifteenth birthday, explained the reasons for the codification. First, the Turkish legal system was backward and primitive. Three kinds of religious law were in force, Islamic, Christian, and Jewish, each with its appropriate court. Only a kind of law of obligations, the "Mecelle," and real property law were common to all. (If I may interject a comment, I do not see why it is backward to have separate rules with separate courts to decide on family law and succession. In practice, families with a choice in a unitary system opt for the structure that fits their beliefs). Second, such an odd system of justice, with three kinds of law applied through three kinds of courts, could not correspond to the modern understanding of the state and its unity. Third and most important, each time Turkey had demanded the removal of the capitulation terms of the First World War by the victorious Allies, the latter refused, pointing to the backward state of the Turkish legal system and its connection with religion. When as a result of the Lausanne Peace Treaty the capitulation terms were removed, the Turks took it upon themselves to form a completely new Turkish organization of justice with a new legal system, new laws, and new courts. Bozkurt said that in one word the system was to be "worldly," The duties undertaken by the Turks under the Lausanne treaty had to be accomplished as quickly as possible. During the First World War commissions were already set up in Istanbul to prepare laws and they had started work. The results were examined in 1924. After seven or eight years the Turks had completed only two hundred articles on a law of obligations; the sections on succession, guardianship, formation of marriage, and divorce, of a civil code; and between seventy and eighty articles of a criminal code; and even the code of land transactions was only a torso.

Consequently, after various systems had been looked at, the two Swiss codes were adopted virtually in their entirety.

Although the motivation was different from most earlier receptions – drastic modernization of society rather than the filling of gaps in the law – the Turkish reception was otherwise similar. Because the creation of new autochthonous law is difficult, it is much easier to borrow from an already existing, more sophisticated system that can be used as a model – above all, where the donor system is accessible in writing. By this time, of course, various excellent codes would have provided a model; notably the French, German, and Swiss were all greatly admired. Why was Swiss law chosen? Various answers have been given, but three strike me as most important: the Swiss laws were the most modern; Switzerland had been neutral during the war, whereas French law was that of a former enemy and German law was that of a defeated ally; and Bozkurt had studied law in Switzerland, so Swiss law was most familiar to him. Hirsch, a German scholar who was a professor of commercial law at Istanbul and Ankara between 1933 and 1952, emphasizes what was to him the overriding importance of the last factor. In any event, there is no reason to think that somehow Swiss law was more adapted than was French or German law to the society that Turkey wanted to become.

The Turks did not accept some Swiss rules at all and changed others. For instance, whereas the legal regime in Switzerland for spouses' property is community property (*ZGB* 178), in Turkey it is separate property (*TKM* 170); the surviving spouse's right to a usufruct is smaller in Turkey (*TKM* 444 §2) than in Switzerland (*ZGB* 462 §2); the judicial separation of spouses may in Switzerland be pronounced for an indefinite time (*ZGB* 147 §1); desertion as a ground of divorce in Switzerland must have lasted at least two years (*ZGB* 140), but in Turkey at least three months (*TKM* 132); the minimum age for marriage in the former is for males twenty, for females eighteen (exceptionally eighteen and seventeen), in the latter for males eighteen, for females seventeen. Other rules would be accidentally mistranslated and the final result need not be that of the donor nation. Others were deliberately given a different value in the translation. Still others remain a dead letter because they have no counterpart in Turkish conditions. The Turkish courts in giving flesh to the rules through interpretation may, as they usually but not always have done, follow the interpretation of the Swiss courts. Again, many rules have a different societal value in the two countries, such as those on a minimum age for marriage or on the requirements for a divorce. Finally, such a reception, as fast as Atatürk wanted it to be, will, like that of Roman law and of other systems, be a slow process, and the speed and the extent of its success – never complete – will vary with circumstances. Any new law resulting from a massive transplantation has to be learned by judges and lawyers as well as by the people before it becomes effective. In the case of Turkey, where the new legal system was so different from what had gone before but was so closely attached to European models, the solution was to import foreign professors from Germany and Switzerland, notably Andreas B. Schwartz and Ernest E. Hirsch, to teach the new law, and to send budding lawyers and law professors to study law in Europe. Also, aspects of traditional social life, such as marriage, respond only slowly to the pressures of new law, especially in country districts. Significantly, essays in a collection published to mark the thirtieth anniversary of the Turkish codification stress the extent to which the reception had not "taken," whereas those in another collection to mark the fiftieth anniversary accept the reception but emphasize its continuing nature and the fact that it is not, nor will be, complete. In 1956 Kurt Lipstein could describe the extent of acceptance of compulsory civil marriage as "disappointing, to say the least." In 1978 June Starr reported that in a particular village that she had studied, she found little evidence "that villagers are lax in obtaining state marriage licenses."

The success or partial success of the transplanting of Swiss legal ideas into Turkey gives many insights into what happens when a less "modern" or less "developed" system comes into powerful contact with a sophisticated modern system. These insights become almost blinding when we notice that Eugen Huber, who virtually alone was responsible for the *ZGB*, said that "the law must be delivered in speech out of the thought of the people. The reasonable man who reads it, who has pondered the age and its needs, must have the perception that the law was delivered to him in speech from the people" And Virgile Rossel declared that "in particular if one could say of the Code Napoléon that it was 'written reason,' we intended to work according to the sense of the national spirit, raising the moral level of our law so far as possible, and we would be happy if it was said one day of the Swiss civil code that it is, to some extent, the written internal moral sentiment". Yet the same Virgile Rossel was well aware that the differences in the laws of the various Swiss cantons could not be explained on the basis of religion, economy, language, or "race."

Thus, the Swiss codification was intended by those who worked on it to be the written moral consciousness of the Swiss people. The arbitrary rules of cantonal law were to be remedied by federal law appropriate to the conditions of the Swiss. The "Swissness" of the codification is stressed. Yet the Swiss codification could be taken over, almost in its entirety, some years later by Turkey, a country with a vastly different history, legal tradition, religion, culture, economy, political setup, and geographical and climatic circumstances. Turkey under Atatürk is a prime example not only of legal transplants but of revolution in law. Substantive alternative alterations were few and minor. But what is striking is that the two Swiss codes were regarded by their creators as particularly Swiss and in accordance with the Swiss national spirit and moral consciousness. Yet, writing in the context of Turkish marriage law, N.U. Gürpinar can claim that "in addition, after the revolution in Turkey it was urgently necessary to create a law corresponding to the principles of the young Turkish republic. This for civil law was the Turkish civil code taken over from Switzerland." And in a more general context, after explaining the need for a modern Turkish code, B.N. Esen writes:

That was the situation of fact. Now, Switzerland always was and is the land of democracy par excellence. As a land with a long democratic past Switzerland was quite especially called to serve as a model for the civil code. Turkey did not hesitate a single second. And in 1926 the Schweizerisches Gesetzbuch and the Swiss Obligationenrecht were taken over with minor alterations as the statute law of the state. If those codes of foreign origin have been used in Turkey for a quarter century without the slightest difficulty, then it is on this account, because they mirror exactly the spiritual inclination of the social milieu, that they reflect the idea of law and justice of the place in which they are interpreted and used.

Thus, insofar as private and commercial law are concerned, a revolutionary leader seeking democracy in Turkey could find almost precisely what he needed in codes framed for very different conditions in Switzerland. I do not entirely agree with Esen. The making of a civil code for Turkey was proving difficult. So a model was borrowed. Swiss law was not easily accepted in practice. I do not believe that the Swiss code mirrored exactly what was wanted or needed.

For me, one personal example of the practical significance of my arguments is the translation into Serbian of my book, *Legal Transplants* (2000). This work is now a third part of a compulsory first year course at the University of Belgrade on introduction to law, of which the other two parts are from Theodor Mommsen and Sir Henry Maine. A Belgrade law professor, Sima Avramović, wrote to me that in the end examination most students wrote an answer on my work. He asserted that this was very important because the Belgrade students would soon become the top judges and legislators in Serbia. There was, he wrote, a general feeling that to borrow law from elsewhere was a sign of inferiority and that there was a consequent hesitation to borrow. But, he claimed, I had shown that to borrow law was virtually a universal phenomenon, and therefore wholly respectable for Serbia.

It will, of course, be claimed that legal borrowing is highly selective, and, hence, that borrowed law still reflects society. I would, of course, agree that borrowing is selective. But this selectivity is not to be equated with a search for the most satisfactory rules for the social, economic, political conditions of the borrowing state. Often law is borrowed because it is there. Factors include: (1) Imposition of law by an occupying force, and the law remains even when occupation ends. (2) Accessibility of the foreign law because it is in a language that is well-understood, or is available in a usable form such as Gaius' *Institutes*, Justinian's *Institutes* and the subsequent numerous local *Institutes*. (3) The search for legitimacy of some kind whether by legislators who seek to bolster their power by a reliance on esteemed models or by judges and jurists who desperately need authority but local authority is lacking. (4) Chance; for example, when Serbia won its independence from the Turks and sought a new legal system it turned first to the French *code civil* but the translator proved incompetent and recourse was had to the Austrian civil code.

Indeed, even love can make a mess out of law. I give two examples. First the Roman senate passed a decree to enable the unfortunate Emperor Claudius to marry his brother's daughter, Agripina, but it still remained incest to have sex with a sister's daughter (*G.* 1.162), and the rules are still recorded for Ulpian, killed 223 by the praetorian guard (*Coll.* 6.1.1). Secondly, the great Justinian who wanted to marry Theodora who had been an actress or worse, had his uncle Justin issue a ruling in 530 that allowed him to do so. The constitution in question, *C.*5.4.23, is full of pious moralizing.

I hope that I have shown that the commonly-made distinction between law in books and law in action is too simple. The distinction is valid, but law in books must be subdivided. Much law in books reflects the conditions, needs and desires of the society in which it operates. But likewise much is accepted because it was borrowed often without much thought, and often without the intervention of any government. History shows that borrowed law, foreign law, is not necessarily to be regarded as unsatisfactory law. It may be as satisfactory as indigenous law.

Law to me is a mystery and to understand law it must not be deprived

– brutally – of its mystery. The mystery must be gently unraveled.

(I have not given references for my examples which are taken from previous works of mine. Besides, the purpose of this chapter is to set the scene for what follows).

Chapter 2

Moses and the Ten Commandments

In the first chapter I set out my general conclusions on the development of law, and the relationship of this law to the society in which it operates. The conclusions were not based on abstract theory but on observation of what actually has happened in various societies at various times and places. I believe the conclusions from the numerous specific examples which follow in this book can be generalised.

Now I want to take a closer look at Moses and the Ten Commandments and their place in understanding legal development. But I will begin with an introduction and end with an appendix.

Yahweh directly gave the Ten Commandments to Moses on Mount Sinai.[1] Apollo, through the Delphic oracle, gave Lycurgus the laws of Sparta,[2] Zeus gave the Cretans their laws,[3] and Hermes gave the Egyptians theirs through Mneves.[4] The significance for us of these traditions is that the fiction of a gift of god heightens the laws' authority and makes their acceptance and maintenance easier. As Plutarch says: 'Thus the law code of Zaleucus found favour with the Locrians not least, it is said, because he asserted that Athena had constantly appeared to him and had in each case guided and instructed him in his legislation, and that nothing he proposed was of his own invention or devising.'[5] Nothing could illustrate better man's need to have his laws as authoritative as possible in order to ensure that they are

---

[1] Exodus 20; Deuteronomy 5. Probably within biblical times the whole Pentateuch was regarded as so given.

[2] Cf., e.g., Herodotus, *Historiae*, 1.65; Plutarch, *Lycurgus*, 5.3; Plato, *Laws*, I (p. 624); Diodorus Siculus, 1.94.

[3] Plato, *Laws*, I (p. 624); Diodorus Siculus, 1.94.

[4] Diodorus Siculus, 1.94.

[5] *De se ipsum citra invidiam laudando*, II: cf. Scholiast in Pindar, *Olymp.* 10. 17. See also for the laws of Numa in regal Rome, Dionysius of Halicarnassus, 2. 61.

obeyed.[6]

Secondly, it is striking how often codifications are produced for, or demanded by, national heroes, despots, and military leaders. Thus, the king Lipit-Ishtar who "procured the freedom of the sons and daughters of Nippur, the sons and daughters of Ur, the sons and daughters of Isin, the sons and daughters of Sumer and Akkad upon whom slaveship had been imposed"[7] is the king responsible for one of the earliest known legal codes, probably of the early 19th century B.C. And Hammurabi, king of Babylon in the 18th century B.C. is as famous for his conquests as for his code. Moses, who led his people out of bondage in Egypt, also acquired for them the Ten Commandments. Both Julius Caesar[8] and Pompey the Great[9] wished to codify the law of Rome. Justinian, who did so successfully from Constantinople between A.D. 529 and 534, also reconquered Africa, Italy and part of southern Spain. In more recent times, the impetus for the first modern European codification, Prussia's *Allgemeines Landrecht,* came from Frederick the Great, and Napoleon was responsible for the *code civil.* The phenomenon is complex and has several causes, one of which is the conqueror's desire to be remembered as a wise man of peace since a main benefit of peace is law and justice. There is also the wish to be the initiator of a new era. Another cause is undoubtedly the man of action's impatience with the convolutions and ambiguities which invade any legal system, and especially one which has developed without overall planning. What *he* wants is a system which is its own authority, one in which an answer to every problem exists, and can be quickly found by the interested parties. The speed and certainty of the answer is more important to *him* than its subtlety or absolute quality.[10] There is a link

[6] See also, H.H. Cohn, 'Secularization of Divine Law', *Scripta Hierosolymitana,* xvi (Jerusalem, 1966), pp. 55ff.

[7] From the prologue of the Lipit-Ishtar Law code, translated by S.N. Kramer in J.B. Pritchard, *Ancient Near Eastern Texts Relating to the Old Testament,* 3rd edit. (Princeton, 1969), pp. 159ff).

[8] Cf. Suetonius, *Divus Iulius,* 44. 2; Isdorus, *Orig.* 5.1.5.

[9] Cf. Isidorus, *Orig.* 5.1.5

[10] Some of these leaders, notably Napoleon and Frederick the Great, were

here with transplants which owe much of their popularity to the ease with which the rule can be acquired even when it is not wholly appropriate in its adoptive society.

The central role in law of authority – as contrasted with quality – is thus emphasized.[11] Law should be its own authority; for some people (including legislators) it has sometimes seemed more important that the law be easily known than that it have objectively excellent rules.[12] Again a law is often adopted because of the reputation and authority of its model or promulgator; hence, in part, the reception of even less than adequate rules. Finally, law is maintained by the authority of the government, and even gods are invoked; questioning, examining of quality is reduced to a poor second best.

The Ten Commandments are beyond doubt the most celebrated collection of laws in the western world. They also have a very high approval rating for their quality. Yet they are extremely peculiar. I believe it is possible to understand them better if we approach them from the general understanding of law making that I have just sketched. But first I must set out some of the obstacles to our comprehension.

There is widespread but not universal scholarly opinion that they are not the work of Moses.[13] But, then there is no agreement as to the precise

---

extremely interested in the quality of the rules of their codification. But always they wanted a decision made as to what the law on a point was; and always they wished to end discussion, controversy and doubt.

[11] On the significance and effects of an authoritative tradition see, e.g., M.P. Gilmore, *Argument from Roman Law in Political Thought 1200-1600* (Cambridge, Mass, 1941).

[12] Cf. the Roman tradition of the plebs' demand in the 5th century B.C. for codification – which led to the XII Tables – because they did not know what the law was: Livy, 3.9. 1 ff.

[13] For a brief introduction see C.J.H. Wright, 'Ten Commandments,' in *The International Standard Bible Encyclopedia*, 4, ed. Geoffrey W. Bromiley, (Grand Rapids, 1988), pp. 786 ff.; see also Brevard S. Childs, *The Book of Exodus*

dating of the laws or the historical circumstances in which they were made. Or even if they were originally laws at all. It is by no means certain that they were the work of one leader at one time. It can be plausibly argued that they are a collection from various materials and were never established at one time. If so, can one reasonably talk of a common purpose? Again, in Exodus the account of them is immediately followed by judicial laws and by ceremonial laws, both ostensibly given to the Israelites by God through Moses. Should we see the Ten Commandments as one part of a trilogy? Again a rather different version of their origin is given in Deuteronomy. What are we to make of this?

My approach will be to assume that there were standard – more than one, but connected – traditions about God giving laws to the Israelites. These traditions were formed into the accounts in Exodus and Deuteronomy. Those responsible for the final version of the traditions made choices, but they were limited in their options by the traditions themselves.

On this basis, I will treat the Ten Commandments in Exodus as a unit – ignoring for the time being the judicial and ceremonial laws. I will not be concerned with the historical accuracy of God delivering the laws to Moses. My concern will be with the nature of the tradition. Historical or not, the tradition should reveal much for the understanding of the factors in law-making, not only of the belief of the redactor, but also of the people from whom it derived and for whom it was intended.

On this basis I wish to address some of the peculiarities of the Commandments. The relevant passages of Exodus 20 read:

1. Then God spoke all these words:

2. I am the Lord your God, who brought you out of the land of Egypt,

(Philadelphia, 1974), pp. 385 ff.; Reuven Yaron, 'The Evolution of Biblical Law,' in *La formazione del diritto nel Vicino Oriente Antico* (Rome, 1988), pp. 77 ff., especially pp. 90 ff.; Reuven Yaron, 'Social Problems and Policies in the Ancient Near East,' in *Law, Politics, and Society in the Ancient Mediterranean World*, edd. Baruch Halpern and Deborah W. Hobson (Sheffield, 1993), pp. 19ff.

out of the house of slavery;

3. you shall have no other gods before me.

4. You shall not make for yourself an idol, whether in the form of anything that is in heaven above, or that is on the earth beneath, or that is in the water under the earth.

5. You shall not bow down to them or worship them; for I the Lord your God am a jealous God, punishing children for the iniquity of parents, to the third and the fourth generation of those who reject me,

6. but showing steadfast love to the thousandth generation of those who love me and keep my commandments.

7. You shall not make wrongful use of the name of the Lord your God, for the Lord will not acquit anyone who misuses his name.

8. Remember the Sabbath day, and keep it holy.

9. Six days you shall labor and do all your work.

10. But the seventh day is a Sabbath to the Lord your God; you shall not do any work – you, your son or your daughter, your male or female slave, your livestock, or the alien resident in your towns.[14]

11. For in six days the Lord made heaven and earth, the sea, and all that is in them, but rested the seventh day; therefore the Lord blessed the Sabbath day and consecrated it.

12. Honour your father and your mother, so that your days may be long in the land that the Lord your God is giving you.

13. You shall not murder.

14. You shall not commit adultery.

15. You shall not steal.

16. You shall not bear false witness against your neighbor.

17. You shall not covet your neighbor's house; you shall not covet your neighbor's wife, or male or female slave, or ox, or donkey, or anything that belongs to your neighbor.[15]

---

[14] Is the omission of the wife significant?

[15] The translation is that of the *New Revised Standard Version*.

A first peculiarity to notice is that the provisions are remarkably non-threatening. A glance at other ancient codes or laws will point the difference. Thus, the first section of the Code (or Laws) of Hammurabi (of, at the latest, the early 17th century B.C.) reads:

> If a man has made allegations against another man, and he has laid a charge of homicide against him but is unable to substantiate his guilt, the one who made the allegations against him shall be killed.[16]

In contrast, penalties are noticeably absent from the Ten Commandments. Mention of punishment occurs only in three, two of them among the religious rules, and they are non-specific. Thus, for bowing down to other gods, God will punish the children for the offence of their parents down to the fourth generation (20.6). The precise punishment, however horrible it might be, is not expressed. For wrongly using the name of God He will not acquit (20.7). The remaining mention of punishment scarcely deserves that name: you should honour your parents "so that your days may be long in the land that God is giving you." (20.12). The provision on honouring parents might be regarded as transitional. The rule of human kindness is interpersonal, but the "penalty" involves God. It might be suggested, moreover that this "penalty" is a much later addition: as such it does not appear in the corresponding text of Deuteronomy 5:16:

> Honour your father and your mother, as the Lord your God commanded you, so that your days may be long and that it may go well with you in the land that the Lord your God is giving you.

Here the supposed penalty appears as a reward. Indeed, in Jewish tradition the Commandment in Exodus is regarded as a blessing.

---

[16] Translation of M.E.J. Richardson, *Hammurabi's Laws* (Sheffield, 2000), p. 41.

Again the Commandments are split into two very distinctive parts: behaviour toward God, behaviour toward other humans. And the parts are distinctly unequal. Duties toward God are much more prominent. It is not just that these rules come first. They are much more detailed. For example, prohibitions against work on the Sabbath are spelled out to apply not only to the male head of the family, but also to his sons, daughters, male slaves, female slaves, even his animals and visitors. In contrast, for inter-human law we have, for instance, simply "you shall not kill". There is a translation difficulty: "kill" or "murder"?[17] No matter for the moment. Not only is the penalty not set out, but the offence is not defined or described. Yet the offence cries out for clarification.

But there is much more. The rules about behaviour to other humans are socially necessary but banal in the extreme: no murder, no theft, no adultery, no false witness. Why did God bother with these? Why was He needed? Not even the penalty is spelled out.

Then the two interpersonal commands that are not just framed "You shall not _____" are framed in a more complex manner. Thus, a reason for honouring father and mother is given, and it scarcely seems to have a legal content.[18] It is also expressed more directly: "Honour _____." The last command, "You shall not covet _____" concerns mental activity, not physical action, and can scarcely give rise to a law suit. And there is a third peculiarity in the tradition – though this time not in the substance of the Commandments – in the role of Aaron. And Aaron's role is pivotal.

These peculiarities in the tradition must be explained and, for me, the explanation must lie within the tradition itself.

[I am well aware that some readers will reject this chapter as giving too few references to standard scholarship. I understand. But my concerns are not with the precise meaning of individual provisions, nor with the

---

[17]See, e.g. Childs, *Exodus*, pp. 419 ff.

[18]For a convincing explanation of the formulation of this commandment and its position in Exodus immediately before the prohibition on murder, see above all, Calum Carmichael, *The Spirit of Biblical Law* (Athens, GA 1996), pp. 94 ff.

historical provenance of our accounts in Exodus and Deuteronomy, nor even with Deuteronomy. All I set out to do is to understand the tradition in Exodus in the context of the place of legislation in the history of legal development.][19]

Legislation is a very particular form of law making – the only source of law that rulers keep under their direct control. And the only necessary talent of rulers is to remain in power. Moses is a leader in trouble. Indeed, for him, one problem follows another. It was God who appointed Moses as the Israelites' leader, and who performed miracle after miracle to keep Moses in power. Defeat for Moses would be defeat for God. And Moses always had a prospective rival in the wings, his elder brother Aaron. Aaron is prominent in Moses' leadership from the very beginning, and is also a leading figure in the Israelites' rebellion against God, in the making of the golden calf. Just before God gave the Commandments to Moses his sympathetic father-in-law told Moses he was wearing himself out in deciding law suits. Moses has to keep his authority and God's authority. Legislation is his solution. God is Moses' authority, and the legislation must stress God's authority for the Israelites. The control of legal relations between humans is of little concern. These can be dealt with by lower officials.

Moses murdered an Egyptian and fled to Midian (2.11ff.). God appeared to Moses and told him He would send him to Pharaoh to deliver the Israelites from bondage (3.7f.). Moses protested, but God insisted (3.11ff.). God emphasized that the Egyptian king would not let them go, but that He would smite the Egyptians, and the Israelites would be allowed to leave (3.19ff.). Moses continued to protest and God showed him miracles (4.1ff.).

---

[19] It has been suggested to me that the structure is exactly what one should expect if God actually gave the Commandments to Moses. The interpersonal laws would be familiar, and would need no detail. Yet for me, detail would still be needed -- as we find in other ancient legislation -- and the sanctions should be set out.

Moses continued to protest, claiming that he lacked eloquence (4.10ff.). God was angered and replied that his brother Aaron (who was coming to meet Moses) had fluency and would act as his mouthpiece (4.14ff.). "He indeed shall speak for you to the people: he shall serve as a mouth for you, and you shall serve as God for him" (4.17).[20] Moses left for Egypt with his wife and sons (4.18ff.). God told Aaron to meet Moses, and Moses told Aaron of God's miracles and what He had said (4.27f.). Moses and Aaron assembled the Israelite elders (4.29). "Aaron spoke all the words that the Lord had spoken to Moses, and performed the signs in the sight of the people" (4.30). The people believed (4.31). Moses and Aaron went to Pharaoh and told him God wanted them to celebrate a festival in the wilderness (5.1ff.). But Pharaoh answered: "Moses and Aaron, why are you taking the people away from their work? Get to your labours" (5.5). Note that Moses and Aaron are treated as equals before Pharaoh. Pharaoh increased the work load of the Israelites who blamed Moses and Aaron (5.20ff.). God spoke to Moses, promising freedom (6.1 ff). "Moses told this to the Israelites: but they would not listen to Moses, because of their broken spirit and their cruel slavery" (6.9). God told Moses to tell Pharaoh to let the people go, but Moses protested that Pharaoh would not listen because he was a poor speaker (6.10ff.). God then gave Moses and Aaron His orders (6.13). We are again told that God ordered Moses and Aaron to bring the people out of Egypt (6.26), and they spoke again to Pharaoh (6.27). God spoke again to Moses who again protested he was a poor speaker, and that Pharaoh would not listen.

---

[20]At 4.10, Moses says literally that "he is not a man of words." It has been suggested that his difficulty was not lack of fluency, but that he was a foreigner in Egypt. But: (1) apart from his stay in Midian he had spent his whole life in Egypt; (2) After his childhood Moses was treated as a son by an Egyptian princess (2.10). (3) In Midian the daughters of Jethro thought he was an Egyptian (2.19). (4) Aaron would have the same problem with speech; (5) Pharaoh is reported as speaking Hebrew. Another late version is that as a child Moses burned his tongue with a coal of fire; for sources see Louis Ginsberg. *The Legends of the Jews* 2 (Philadelphia, 1923), pp. 272 ff.

God said "See I have made you like God to Pharaoh, and your brother Aaron shall be your prophet. You shall speak all that I command you, and your brother Aaron shall tell Pharaoh to let the Israelites go out of his land." (7.1f). Then comes the biblical treatment of the ten plagues inflicted upon Pharaoh by God for failing to let the Israelites leave (7.14-12.32).

The chapters reveal a fascinating dichotomy. God speaks primarily to Moses, with Aaron very much Moses' helpmeet. Yet Moses' weakness is very much stressed. In contrast, in their interaction with Pharaoh Moses and Aaron appear very much on the same level. If we can assume, as I believe is reasonable, that, when Moses and Aaron were before Pharaoh and his officials, members of the Israelite elite were to be regarded as also present or at least knew of the meeting, Aaron would be regarded by them as very close to being Moses' equal.

But a side issue then arises. If God can work so many miracles, why does He leave Moses with such a defect that he needs Aaron's constant help? The issue, I think, is significant.

While the Israelites were still in Egypt, God gave Moses and Aaron instructions for the first Passover (12.1 ff.), but it is Moses who communicated them to the Israelites (12.21 ff.). Yet again, God gave Passover instructions to both Moses and Aaron (12.43 ff.). And the people followed their instructions (12.50). God told Moses to consecrate all the firstborn to Him (13. 1f) and Moses did so. In these fundamental legal matters Moses is basically his own spokesman.

God told Moses to camp before the Red Sea (14.1 ff.); Pharaoh prepared to attack (14.5 ff.), and the people blamed Moses vehemently for what seemed an approaching disaster (14.11ff.), but, through the agency of Moses, God destroyed the Egyptians (14.15 ff.). The miracle of the Red (or Reed) Sea is the climax of the Exodus, and Aaron is not mentioned. 14.31 records "So the people feared the Lord and believed in the Lord and in his servant Moses." According to the tradition in the Passover Haggadah (section 'The Plagues'), the number of plagues inflicted on the Egyptians at the sea was vastly greater than the ten plagues in Egypt.

Later at Marah the water was bitter and could not be drunk and the people blamed Moses (15.23 ff.). In the wilderness the Israelites complained against both Moses and Aaron (16.1ff.) And God told Moses he would rain manna from Heaven (16.4), and Moses and Aaron gave instructions to the people (16.6ff.). Moses then told Aaron to say to the people "Draw near to the Lord" (16.9). Moses gave further instructions to the people about manna, but not all of them obeyed (16.5ff.). Further on, again the people disobeyed (16.27ff.). God told Moses that some manna should be placed before the covenant for ever, and Moses so instructed Aaron (16.31 ff.). The people quarreled with Moses because they had no water, and Moses told God that the people were almost ready to stone him. God told Moses to strike a rock with his staff and water came forth (17.1ff.). God enabled Moses, with the help of Aaron and Hur, to defeat Amalek (17.8 ff).

Again a clear pattern emerges. God had chosen Moses to be the leader of the Israelites. For God, Aaron is definitely Moses' subordinate , and Aaron acted as Moses' intermediary with the people. Time and again God saved the Israelites in distress with a miracle performed through Moses. Yet time and again when the people were in distress, they quarreled with Moses. Despite his authority from God, Moses did not have the confidence of his people. His control was shaky.

Perhaps more immediately in the present context, Moses was wearing himself out with hearing lawsuits all day long. His father-in-law had come for a visit, saw Moses judging all day, wearing himself out (18.13), and he advised him to teach the people the statutes and instructions. He also advised that Moses should appoint judges to hear minor cases, but should hear major cases himself. Moses agreed. He summoned the people and they agreed to do whatever God said (19.7). Shortly thereafter, God delivered the Ten Commandments. Thus, a leader in trouble received authoritative legislation.

I need not record the steps by which God ensured that only Moses would see Him and speak with Him (19.9ff.). Nor is it important to discuss the laws that God subsequently gave orally to Moses (20.22-40.38). Whether they come from a different time in history need not concern us. But three points about them should be mentioned:

First, the rules on behaviour between humans do not confirm the widely held view that the Ten Commandments cover all the law in short compass.[21] The Commandments contain nothing about slavery, violence less than murder, the law of torts and restitution; all these are matters treated in the Book of the Covenant. These rules in the Book of the Covenant again indicate the lack of interest in 'secular' law in the Commandments.

Secondly, the rules on religious ceremonial matters are very much more detailed than those on interpersonal law. Again the authority of God and the importance of reverence toward Him are stressed. They are of supreme importance to Moses as leader.

Thirdly, much is made of Aaron and his sons being appointed priests, their vestments, the ephod, and of a splendid breastplate for Aaron, other priestly vestments for the sons and their ordination, their tending of the lamp (27.20-29.46). God, or Moses, needs to keep Aaron loyal to the service of God, and hence to Moses. [It may be worth noting that rabbinic tradition emphasizes that Moses and Aaron were of equal worth.[22]]

A little more should be said about the distinction made between the Ten Commandments and the judicial and ceremonial laws which existed – as Philo shows[23] – as early as the time of Jesus. The Ten Commandments, it is often claimed, were addressed to all, the other laws only to the Jews. Not so. The Ten Commandments are expressly addressed to the Jews. Exodus 20.2 reads: "I am the Lord your God who brought you of out the land of Egypt." A further distinction often drawn is that God gave the Ten Commandments directly, the other laws were mediated through Moses. This distinction seems

---

[21]For this view see, e.g., G. Henton Davies, *Exodus* (London 1967), pp. 167 ff.

[22]Shir Ha-shirim Rabbah 4.5. See Ginsberg, *Legends* 4 (1925), p. 424 n. 152.

[23] See his distinction in his books (*De Decalogo* and *De Specialibus Legibus).*

arbitrary. The real difference seems to me that the ceremonial and judicial laws could never be acceptable outside of a small Jewish section.

When Moses descended from Mount Sinai the worst had happened (32.1ff.). The Israelites had made a golden calf, a new god, who was asserted to have brought them out of Egypt (32.4). Thus, God was denied, and so was Moses' authority. Aaron is not reported to be the ringleader of the revolt, but only as much involved from the start. The people said to Aaron: "Come, make gods for us, who shall go before us." (32.1). Aaron's reported response was: "Take off the gold rings that are on the ears of your wives, your sons, and your daughters, and bring them to me." (32.2). Aaron actually made the calf-god (32.4) and instituted a festival for it (32.5f.).

At this point I would like to respond to a friendly criticism from a Christian fundamentalist who believes God did give the Ten Commandments to Moses. He says with respect to the final Commandment: "God, but not man, would care about coveting".[24] I disagree. Moses, a leader in trouble, has supreme interest in coveting. His job! It is at risk. The behaviour of Aaron is revealing. When Moses left for the mountain, Aaron has not yet made his move, but he will. No one should underestimate the vigour with which political figures protect their job. I can understand that God *might* oppose coveting but I see no compelling reason for Him to legislate. But in the tradition Moses has a strong positive interest.

Another point should be made. The prohibition against coveting makes superfluous the rules against stealing and adultery. Both involve coveting.

My conclusions about the history of the tradition behind the Ten Commandments in Exodus are as follows:

---

[24]See, e.g., Childs, *Exodus*, pp. 425 ff.

1) Of the four sources of law only legislation is under the direct control of governments.

2) The lesson of history is that in general most governments at most times are little interested in legislating in many areas of law.

3) The sole necessary talent of governments and rulers is remaining in power. Hence the paucity of legislation in many areas of law. Rulers have better things to do (for themselves) with their time.

4) Legislation is accordingly always or usually political: its raison d'être is to keep the government in power.

5) According to the tradition of Exodus, the Ten Commandments are no exception.

6) Moses became leader of the Israelites who were under the subjugation of the Egyptians; on the basis that he was elected by God. Moses, we are told, was reluctant to accept the office, because of his lack of fluency in speech, but God insisted and appointed Moses' brother Aaron to be his helpmeet.

7) Moses' authority before the people was based precisely on the belief that he was the elect of God.

8) Through miracles of God Moses did obtain the Israelites' release from slavery in Egypt.

9) Moses' authority continued to rest on his unique position from God. Whereas God kept Aaron in a clearly subordinate position, Aaron's status among the Israelites seems, in contrast, almost like that of Moses.

10) When great hardships befell the Israelites during the Exodus they continually blamed Moses for their plight. This inevitably entails a diminution of faith in or respect for God on whose authority Moses' power depended. Aaron was less criticized. Despite God's miracles the Israelites repeatedly showed a lack of confidence in Moses' leadership, and hence in God. Moses' authority was under siege. Hence, he could not afford to seem too threatening.

11) Moses was under great strain not only from this but also because he was spending his days in judging. A solution was proposed by his father-in-law, significantly not an Israelite but a Midianite.

12) God intervened, and provided laws for the Israelites but under specific circumstances. a) The people were told that God would legislate with no input from the people. b) The laws were given directly by God to Moses, but to no one else. c) Indeed, God was to be absolutely hidden to others.

13) As is to be expected, if my first four conclusions are correct, the laws of God very much bolstered the authority of Moses. The stress is precisely on religious laws, hence on the authority of God, hence on the authority of Moses. Laws with a secular impact were little considered. This is why they are banal.

14) The people were still not impressed by Moses' leadership and during his absence on Mount Sinai they worshiped as god a golden calf, thus attacking God's first Commandment (which they still did not have), hence God's authority and thus Moses' authority.

15) If not the instigator, Aaron, the second in command, was prominent in the revolt, even suggesting where to obtain the material for the calf and making it. As often, the second-in-command is eager for the leading role. In Exodus the talent of Aaron is presented above all as the power of persuasion. Given that fact, it seems plausible that at one stage in the tradition (now unrecorded) Aaron appeared as the instigator of the revolt. As often in history, then, Moses would have coopted Aaron, and used him against his followers.

16) Thus, God had been eager to encourage or placate Aaron by giving favours. In vain. (Aaron's resentment against Moses is brought up very sharply in Numbers 12. It is part of the tradition. God weighs in in favour of Moses.)

17) Moses ultimately triumphed through the power of God. Aaron easily submitted to him.

18) The role of Aaron is essential to the tradition. Moses must have weaknesses for the story to unfold. He must have a helpmeet. Moses must

have great problems with the people, and the people must have an alternative power-figure. For the authority of God fully to emerge this figure must in the end fail miserably.

I will not dwell here on the subsequent history of the Ten Commandments ripped out of context. It is enough to note that "Honour your father and mother" survives in the French *code civil* of 1804, art. 371, though it has almost never been applied. And the reason given for it has disappeared. And the debate over the placing of the Commandments in U.S. court houses continues to this day.

Appendix:

The short appendix to this chapter relates to the often repeated, but groundless, claim that "the United States Constitution is a Judaeo-Christian document." It is nothing of the kind. There is no mention of God, nor of Jehovah or Moses, nor of Jesus or Paul. There is nothing in the Constitution that would point distinctively to Judaisim or Christianity. The mainsprings are Humanism and more especially the eighteenth century Scottish Enlightenment, above all David Hume and even more, Thomas Reid. A very direct influence was John Witherspoon, President of the Presbyterian Princeton University, born and educated in Scotland. The Declaration of Independence was signed on his appeal to the representatives . Six of the signers of the Declaration were students of his at Princeton, as were President James Madison and Vice-President Aaron Burr. Two of the signers of the Constitution were born in Scotland.

Of course, in the various constitutional debates before, during and after the U.S. Constitution, biblical references were very common.[25] That in itself cannot surprise for it was the one work known to all, and best known to all especially to the Presbyterians. Paul was the biblical writer most often cited especially for the passages in Romans concerning authority and

---

[25] For figures see, e.g. Donald S. Lutz, *The Origins of American Constitutionalism* (Baton Rouge,1988), pp. 136 ff.

obedience. Given the history of the Revolution that is only to be expected. To make a point they would naturally use Scripture. It would make a good argument. The frequency of references to Montesquieu on separation of powers is also not remarkable. But it is to be noted indeed that Montesquieu's views on separation of powers differ from those the framers in that he pays little attention to control of the executive and legislative branches by the judiciary.[26]

---

[26] For the argument see Alan Watson, *The Making of the Civil Law* (Cambridge, Mass., 1981), pp. 154 ff.

Chapter 3

Two Gospel Vignettes: Jesus and the Samaritan Woman; Jesus and the Adulteress.

One of my legal heroes is Rudolf von Jhering, and one of my best-loved law books is his *Law in Everyday Life* .[27] Law is everywhere, and usually not noticed. A favourite example of mine is law in the Gospels: Jews do not read the New Testament, Christians ignore rabbinic law.[28] [29]

Here I wish to bring forward two vignettes, beloved episodes from the Gospels. In both, rabbinic law is necessary to understand what is going on. In the first it is usually not noticed, in the second it is underplayed and misunderstood.

I.

Jesus and the Samaritan Woman

Jesus' meeting with the Samaritan Woman, recorded in John 4.4-30, seems straightforward. Still, when we take the episode at face value we encounter several peculiarities.

Jesus is resting about noon beside Jacob's well, while the disciples have gone to the town to buy food. He is alone. A Samaritan woman comes

---

[27] First published in 1870 as an Appendix to his *Civilrechtsfälle ohne Entscheidungen*, then subsequently in many editions: translated into English by Henry Goudy under the title *Law in the Daily Life* (Oxford, 1904).

[28] See, e.g. Alan Watson, *Jesus and the Jews* (Athens, GA., 1995); *The Trial of Jesus* (Athens, GA., 1995); *Jesus and the Law*, (Athens, GA 1996).

[29] There are exceptions: see above all, *New Testament Judaism: Collected Works of David Daube*, edit. Calum Carmichael (Berkeley, 2000). See also E.P. Sanders, *Jewish Law from Jesus to the Mishnah* (Philadelphia, 1990); J.D. Derrett, *Law in the New Testament* (London, 1970).

to draw water. This is surprising because the time to draw water is the early morning and in the cool of the evening,[30] and the timing of a visit to the well is important because it is the occasion for female sociability. Moreover, when a time is mentioned in John, it is usually significant. Still stranger, as commentators stress, there were springs between the woman's town -- if it is to be identified, as it usually is, with the modern 'Askar[31] – and the well. "Why," asks Marcus Dods, "should a woman have come so far, passing good sources of water supply?"[32] Jesus asks her for a drink, a perfectly natural request in the context[33], except that, as we are told, Jews did not drink from the same vessels as Samaritans.[34] She responds, "What! You, a Jew, ask water from me, a Samaritan woman?" Is this response to be seen as expressing surprise or rudeness? Or is it flirtatious, the beginning of a wider conversation?[35] Certainly, Jews did not use vessels used by Samaritans,[36] but Jesus is a thirsty man, and there is no one else to give him water. Moreover,

---

[30] Genesis 24.11; see also W.E. Hull, in *The Broadman Bible Commentary*, p. 9, p. 250; W.F. Howard, in *The Interpreter's Bible*, 8, p. 521; J.A. Gossip, in *The Interpreter's Bible*, 8, p. 521. For this whole episode see the detailed account in Craig S. Keener, *The Gospel of John,* 1, (Peabody Mass., 2003) pp. 588 ff.

[31] See, for example, Herman L. Strack and Paul Billerbeck, *Kommentar zum Neuen Testament aus Talmud und Midrasch*, 2, 4th ed. (Munich, 1965), pp. 431f.: C.K. Barrett, *The Gospel According to St. John*, 2 ed. (Philadelphia, 1978) p. 231.

[32] Marcus Dods, in *The Expositor's Greek Testament*, 1, ed. W. Robertson Nicoll (Grand Rapids, 1974). Cf. Howard, *Bible*, 8, p. 521; John Painter, *The Quest for the Messiah*, ((Nashville, 1993), p. 200.

[33] A parallel request is that of Abraham's servant to Rebecca in Genesis 24.17-20.

[34] A translation such as that of *The New English Bible* is inaccurate: "Jews and Samaritans, it should be noted, do not use vessels in common." Only the Jews were exclusive, and that is expressed in the Greek.

[35] I am not persuaded by David Daube's suggestion (in an otherwise convincing paper) that she was expressing surprise at his kindness in being willing to drink from her vessel: "Jesus and the Samaritan Woman: the Meaning of συγχράο" *Journal of Biblical Literature 69 (1950);* pp.137 ff.

[36] For this as the meaning of συγχράο see Daube, "Jesus and the Samaritan Woman"; cf. Barrett, *St. John*, p. 232.

the great majority of Jews were AmHaaretz, scarcely observing, and the woman would have no reason for believing that Jesus was otherwise.[37] Jesus replies that if she knew who he was, she would have asked him, and he would have given her living water. What is the Samaritan supposed to make of this? Jesus has no water. What is she supposed to understand by "living water"? Often "living water" is used to mean spring water, usually better tasting than well water.[38] But an offer by Jesus of spring water, rather than well water, makes no sense here precisely because Jacob's well was a spring.[39] The Samaritan woman has access to her own spring water! Jesus seems to be offering her nothing she does not already have. And the problem remains that he has not the implements to provide her with any water. If we, from our vantage point, interpret "living water" as something like eternal life, how was the Samaritan supposed to know that? Jesus appears to be playing games. After her obvious response, she asks how Jesus can give her living water. He does not answer the question but says he can give her water after which she will never thirst again. The woman's response is still odder: "Sir, give me that water, and then I shall not be thirsty, nor have to come all this way to draw." The reply is nonsensical, if taken at face value. On the wording, the woman understands Jesus as talking quite simply about water.[40] Otherwise, she could not say that she would never again have to come to draw, which shows she is not talking about eternal life. Yet she does not act as if Jesus were behaving like a madman which would have been reasonable behaviour

---

[37] See, for example, Raymond E. Brown, *John I-XII,* (New York, 1970), p. 325; Davies, *Invitation,* p. 33.

[38] Strack-Billberbeck, *Kommentar*, 2, p. 436.

[39] John 4.6.

[40] Rudolf Schnackenburg's treatment is revealing: *The Gospel According to St. John* (New York, 1980), 1, p. 428. For him, the "woman is moved by Jesus' words but has not grasped their profounder meaning. Hearing Jesus' offer of 'living water' she misunderstands it as a promise of something earthly and natural . . . . She is interested in the 'living water' but can only think of the water in the well of Jacob. Still, she now addresses the stranger respectfully as 'sir,' and asks him 'whence' he can procure this water without a vessel to draw it in."

on her part because, in truth, the fact remains that he does not have the means to provide her with water. Moreover, she would still have had to come to the well to draw water -- if not for herself to drink, then for her household needs. The issue is acutely brought out by John Ashton:

> It is easy to see that many of Jesus' utterances in the Fourth Gospel have the flavour of a riddle... "If you knew...who it is that is saying to you, 'Give me a drink,' you would have asked him and he would have given you living water" (4.:10). Living water -- ὕδωρ ζῶν – the first meaning of this phrase is *running* or *flowing* water. How could the Samaritan woman be expected to know that Jesus was going to understand the word literally (*living water*) and apply it to his own revelation?[41]

How indeed? Jesus next asks her to fetch her husband, she replies that she has none, and Jesus acknowledges this. It emerges that the Samaritan has led a less than respectable life, has had five husbands, and is living with a man to whom she is not married. A woman was expected not to marry more than two or three times.[42] A further surprising feature in the text is that the disciples, on their return, are "astonished to find him talking with a woman" (4:27). Why?

I would like to suggest that much light may be cast on the episode in the first instance if we consider Proverbs 5.15-20:

> Drink water from your own cistern and running water from your own spring; 16. do not let your well overflow into the road, your runnels of water pour into the street; 17. let them be yours alone, not shared with strangers. 18. Let your

---

[41]   John Ashton, *Understanding the Fourth Gospel* (Oxford, 1991), p. 190; cf. p. 219.

[42]   See Strack-Billerbreck, *Kommentar*, 2, p. 437.

fountain, the wife of your youth, be blessed, rejoice in her, a lovely doe, a graceful hind, 19. let her be your companion; you will at all times be bathed in her love, and her love will continually wrap you round. Wherever you turn, she will guide you; when you lie in bed, she will watch over you, and when you wake, she will talk with you. 20. Why, my son, are you wrapped up in the love of an adulteress? Why do you embrace a loose woman?

The sexual implications of the passage are well known. "The joys of sex at home with one's own wife are set in contrast with the bitter and disastrous results of loving a 'strange woman,'"says Marvin E. Tate. "The sexual pleasures of a wife are commended in vv. 18-19," he continues.[43] In the symbolism of verse 15, the words *cistern* (Hebrew, *bor*) and *well* (Hebrew, *beér*) – "metaphors for the lawful wife," according to *The Jerusalem Bible*[44] – refer to her genitalia. Such a verbal usage is common practice and -- even in an age that eschews euphemisms -- will be found in American novels of the recent past.[45]

If we return now to John, we may suspect a subtext. The woman, perhaps flirtatiously as an opening gambit to more conversation, asks why Jesus requests water from her. Jesus responds by saying he could give her living water. However this may be intended, the woman covertly takes this as a hint of a sexual advance. She takes "living water" in the sense of semen. What liquid could be more alive? She responds: "You have no bucket and this well is deep," or "You have no dick and this (my) cunt is deep." The woman uses *well* with the meaning we saw in Proverbs. In a different

---

[43] In the *Broadman Bible Commentary*, 9, p. 24.

[44] (New York, 1966), p. 939 n. c. Sexual symbolism is, of course, extremely common. For examples from Latin, see J.N. Adams, *The Latin Sexual Vocabulary* (Baltimore, 1982), pp. 82 ff.; for visual examples from Dutch painting, see Simon Schama, *The Embarrassment of Riches* (Berkeley), 1982), pp. 433 f., 473 f.

[45] See, for example, Jean M. Auel, *The Plains of Passage* (New York, 1990),

context, *bucket* might also we used of a vagina, but with respect to the well it means a penis: that enters the well and goes up and down. Sexual innuendo by a willing woman implying that she is too much woman for the male who comes too close is a common come-on trick. We shall see an example from Apuleius later in this chapter. When Jesus says whoever drinks the water that he can give will never thirst again, she demands it. She takes his words as hinting that he will give her such a stupendous orgasm that she will never need sex again. She wants such good sex. It is on this basis that she wants Jesus' "living water" so that she will never need it again. Nor to have to come so far to draw! From her very first words she has been testing Jesus out.[46]

Jesus backs off from the direction in which the conversation is going by telling her to fetch her husband. She responds by stating that she has no husband. She is a free agent!

This approach to the episode enables us to go still further. We now see why we are told the woman is not respectable.[47] She goes to the well at an unusual time when other local women would not be there, either because she has been (as many believe) ostracized or (as I believe) in the hope of meeting a man, perhaps indeed a stranger as Jesus is. In fact, she behaves exactly as she should have done if she wished to meet and entice a male stranger. A well beside a roadway at the heat of noon is precisely where and when she could expect to find a stranger relaxing[48] and no local inhabitants. The alternative would have been for her to wait at a crossroads, a favourite spot for prostitutes to find passing clients.[49] But in my view the alternative was

p. 59.

[46] Calum Carmichael also notices the sexual overtones in the episode, but he gives the whole encounter a spiritual meaning: "Marriage and the Samaritan Woman," *New Testament Studies* 26 (1979): 332ff.

[47] See, for example, Strack-Billerbeck, *Kommentar*, 2, p 437; Hull, *Commentary*, 9, p. 250; Gossip, *Bible*, 8, pp. 521f. Gossip also suggests that she "was a trachled, futile creature always behindtimes."

[48] The heat of noon is the time of rest and also of dalliance: cf. Song of Songs 1.7.

[49] See, for example, Genesis 38. 13-21.

out of the question. The woman is not a professional -- there is no sign of that in the texts -- and at the crossroads there could have been no pretense. Likewise, we understand why the disciples are "astonished" to find Jesus talking with a woman. A woman at that time and place could not possibly be respectable.

(It might be objected that my thrust is misdirected. After all, Jacob did meet Rachel at a well at high noon (Genesis 29.6ff.). Still, sexuality is not absent from that encounter. Jacob asks Laban, Rachel's father, for her in marriage (Genesis 29.18).)

We can now begin to answer a question that has troubled commentators: why does the woman go to this well when there are streams between it and her town? There are, I suggest, three reasons. First, the well is beside a highway; therefore, she is more likely to meet a passing stranger. It is precisely because the road is nearby that Jesus stops there. Secondly, simply because there is running water between her village and the well, the chance of her being caught out by neighbours is diminished. Any woman who ran out of water would go to a nearby stream and not venture so far as the well. Thirdly, Jacob's well was deep, with a shaft of 106 feet.[50] No passing stranger would have the equipment to draw water. With her bucket, the woman of Samaria could be assured that any male stranger would enter into conversation with her.[51]

The preceding paragraph requires expansion or qualification. There is some doubt as to the whereabouts of the town that is called Sychar in almost all of the manuscripts (4.5). No traces of a town with that name have been found in Samaria. The most common view is that it is modern 'Askar, which lies about one mile northeast of the well. Raymond Brown, who actually gives Shechem as his translation, objects that this site is mediaeval. Yet he seems more troubled by the fact that if the woman was from 'Askar she had come so far. Shechem was only 250 feet from the well, he says, and if Shechem is the correct reading, "everything fits." But, no, it does not fit.

---

[50] Cf. Schnackenburg, *Gospel*, 1, p. 424.

[51] See, for example, Howard, *Bible,* 8, p. 520.

Brown has to admit: "Probably Shechem was only a very small settlement at the time."[52] But "a very small settlement" does not fit John's description of the Sychar as πόλις, a city (4.4, 28, 30), and that "many" of the Samaritans believed because of the saying of the woman (4.39), and "many more" believed because of Jesus' own words. (I do, of course, accept G. E. M. de Ste. Croix's argument that in the New Testament πόλις corresponds more to our notion of a village than to the Greek notion of πόλις.)[53] Shechem as a city was destroyed in 128 or more probably in 107 B.C. by John Hyrcanus, who ruled the Jews as ethnarch and high priest. If small villages clustered around modern Balâtah,[54] and the woman was from one of these, her distance to Jacob's well would still not be inconsiderable. But even if Sychar were very close, the thrust of the argument in my paragraph would stand. The woman could still hope to meet a stranger resting at the well and avoid seeing neighbours at that time of day. Even if by some unfortunate chance a neighbour appeared, she had lost little. Further activity was needed before there could be a scandal.

My explanation is strengthened by some parallels in Apuleius, *Metamorphoses*, 2.3. Lucius comes upon Fotis cooking and stirring the pot. He says: "O Fotis, how prettily, how merrily you stir the pot, wiggling your hips. What a sweet sauce you prepare. Happy and even blessed would he be whom you permit to dip his finger in." Here *pot (ollula)* is used, as was *well*, with the meaning "vagina." The symbolism is the same. Fotis replies: "Leave me, wretch. Go as far as possible away from my fire. For if my tiny fire should blaze forth even a little, you will burn up inside, and no one can put out your heat but I alone who with dainty seasoning know how to shake both pot and bed." Fotis is very willing and, as I have suggested for the

---

[52] Brown, *John I-XII*, p. 169

[53] In *The Class Struggle in the Ancient Greek World* (Ithaca, N.Y., 1981), p. 428, de Ste. Croix describes Sychar as "a mere village, of course." He has in mind, I believe, the English notion of a village – not all that tiny.

[54] See, for example, *The Biblical World*, ed. Charles F. Pfeiffer (Grand Rapids, 1966), p. 522.

Samaritan woman, seeks to entice the male further, suggesting that she is too much for him.

To this point, I have said as little as possible about Jesus' role in all this. But that must now be examined. The woman has widened the conversation by expressing surprise that a Jew would ask a Samaritan for water. There is more to the issue than that Jews do not use vessels that Samaritans have used. David Daube has pointed out with his usual acumen that, for Jews, Samaritan women were to be deemed unclean.[55] A regulation supposedly of A.D. 65 or 66 declared that "the daughters of the Samaritans are menstruants from the cradle,"[56] and this view would have been held by the more rigid for a considerable time before. Moreover, since Samaritan purification rites were different from those of the Jews, strict Jews would regard Samaritan women -- and their men through contact with them -- as always unclean. Thus, Jesus' offence against rabbinic teaching is even greater. As Daube observed, this explains a detail previously thought inexplicable: after the disciples returned, "the woman put down her water jar and went away to the town" (4.28). John is emphasizing the nature of Jesus' behaviour: he will drink again from the unclean vessel.[57] I would add that the detail might also suggest that the woman's need for water from the well was not that urgent in the first place.[58]

---

[55] Daube, "Jesus and the Samaritan Woman," p. 137; cf. Painter, *Quest*, p. 199.

[56] Mishnah Niddah 4.1. A.D. 65 or 66 is the date supported by Daube. The regulation was certainly before the destruction of the Temple in 70: Babylonian Talmud, Shabbath 13b, 16b. The date is quite uncertain, but it is after the division of the schools of Shammai and Hillel: cf. 1. Epstein, *Babylonian Talmud: Seder Móed,* 1 (London, 1938), p. 54 n.i.

[57] It should be noted that, though he does not say so, Daube's treatment of the woman leaving her pot behind presupposes a source such as I am suggesting. The realistic detail has a real meaning and direct relevance to the story, yet it has nothing to do with John's theological message.

[58] Of course, the significance of the detail is not just that the woman left her pot behind but that John treats the detail as worth recording. For Schnackenburg there is no need to see anything in the detail except that she wants to return home

42

At this point we should go back to yet another detail that is overlooked but that cries out for explanation. As they come to Jacob's well, Jesus is tired out by his journey (4.6). But what about his disciples? They go into Sychar to buy food (4.8). How many disciples are there? By my calculations there are at least two from John the Baptist (1.37), plus Peter (1.41f), plus Philip (1.43), plus Nathaniel (1.45), thus five, but there may be more who are not mentioned. All would have been tired. But five out of six tired men -- the sixth being Jesus -- set off to Sychar to buy food for lunch for six. Why are so many needed to bargain and to carry back? They aren't. Yet they go. Not one stays to keep Jesus company. Five go off to carry back the lunch pail of six, leaving the master alone.[59] Why? Oddly, Schnackenburg writes that "we must not ask why they all went off together.[60] The easiest answer is that their absence from Jacob's well is necessary for the episode. Again, why? Their absence is not needed if Jesus is going to reveal he is the Messiah. But it is necessary if the Samaritan is going to make sexual advances to Jesus. The presence of third parties, I suppose, would have been a deterrent.[61]

When the Samaritan expresses surprise that he asks her for water, Jesus replies that if she knew who he was she would have asked him and he would have given her living water. At this stage, she cannot understand Jesus as meaning eternal life, and the meaning, "spring water," which is the obvious, innocent meaning, has to be excluded from her understanding.

---

quickly and unimpeded: *Gospel*, 1, p. 443.

[59] But at 13.29 some disciples thought Jesus was sending Judas by himself to buy food for thirteen.

[60] Schnackenburg, *Gospel*, I, p. 424.

[61] The significance of the disciples' absence is not noted, for instance, by R.K. Bultmann, *The Gospel According to John: A Commentary* (Philadelphia, 1970), Barrett, *St. John*, or Brown, *John I-XII*, though Bultmann (p. 178) and Barrett (p. 231) stress that it was natural for Jesus to be tired at that time of day. Barrett calls the removal of the disciples "a stage direction," and some scholars see 4.8 as an insertion by John into the episode. But if it were natural for Jesus to be tired, why not also the disciples?

"Living water" has to suggest something else. Jesus seems to be deliberately encouraging the woman to go further. She does. Jesus leads her on: after the water he can give, she will never want more. After she asks for it, Jesus stops the course of the conversation. She realizes that he is a "prophet." For her then, and for later generations, Jesus' words are understood in their spiritual sense.

Indeed, the whole encounter, as told by John, now takes on a deeper spiritual meaning, as we shall see. Still, the episode reveals a previous layer, an earlier source. For the spiritual point of the story, the woman's sexual advance and Jesus' ambiguous response are quite unnecessary. But they are prominent and must originally have had a purpose. John has not succeeded in removing all traces of the earlier source. I suggest that, in the original, Jesus was shown as again offending against Jewish law -- indeed, the text emphasizes this directly, by having the Samaritan bring it up. Jesus was also portrayed as less than perfect by his ambiguous response.

But John endows the episode with spirituality. Jesus is shown as dealing with the lowest of the low, a Samaritan, a woman outcast even by her own people, who is even inciting him to sin. He does not condemn or insult her. Rather, he goes along with her, perhaps humours her, and then reveals his true power and nature. She is won over and persuaded, all the more perhaps because of her previous improper conduct. Jesus is to be seen here taking his message at an early point of time to a non-Jew. And he has chosen as the recipient of the news, not the best and most powerful, but the sinner and the powerless.

My interest is law but religion is also involved. The episode with the Samaritan woman is one of four which occur only in *John*, and which show Jesus behaving in a way that seems not entirely perfect. The others are the wedding feast at Cana, the raising of Lazarus, and the scenes involving Nicodemus. My explanation is that they derive from a Pharasaic source which was so well known in the community where John wrote that he could not ignore it. John incorporated the episodes but added a spiritual message in each to defang it.[62]

Appendix to Jesus and the Samaritan Woman

When I first taught this subject I was received with skepticism and even anger. So I produced a spoof piece under the pseudonym Sandy Jardine: my full name is William Alexander Jardine Watson, and 'Sandy' is the Scottish traditional abbreviation for 'Alexander'. With Jesus removed from the story, none of my students doubted the idea of a sexual encounter. I reproduce the coda below:

A Monk's Musings
A *Coda* by Sandy Jardine
(Afterword by Alan Watson)

Editor's note:

In the *Infortiatum* volume of what we now call the *Corpus Iuris Civilis*, published at Venice in 1590, I found a folded vellum folio sheet. This contained musical notes accompanied by large letters:

Laudate eum in cymbalis sonantibus

Laudate eum in cymbalis tinnientibus

Omne quod spirat laudat Dominum.

It is, thus, the final page of a manuscript psalter, and the hand appears to be Italian of the early 15th century. Beneath appear in a minuscule script the musings that I have translated below. The hand appears to be of similar date to the main text. No provenance can be established. The point of the musings is not clear: are they historically accurate, or purely fictitious? Is there a reminiscence of a much earlier true event? Is the monk disillusioned, affected by the suspicions against him of heresy? Why did he write at all?

The folio leaf was removed from the psalter. But by whom? Was it the writer of the musings, perhaps anxious over what he had done? Or was it

---

[62] Watson, *Jesus and the Jews, passim.*

by someone else, who found the page offensive? In either event, the conclusion must be that the removal was shortly after the monk mused. Not very much later the growing popularity of printing would make reading and excision of a manuscript page unlikely (except for stuffing and binding of a printed book).

Nor can I discover how the manuscript page came to be placed in this volume. The book was purchased some years ago from the celebrated dealer in early law books, Libreria Petrarca of Arezzo, but its ownership could not now be traced further back. The edition was a cheap one for its time, quarto not folio, full of abbreviations, unlikely to be owned by anyone prominent as a jurist or in social life. Various owners (presumably) have left their signatures on all five title pages of the set, but none of these is known to history.

The Latin of the musings is simple but without distinction, and I have not thought it necessary at the present time to present it or proffer an *apparatus criticus*.

Sandy Jardine

Manuscript Text:

My lord abbot with five monks (of whom I was one and the youngest) was traveling through Sienese territory during a period of calm. We came to the famous deep spring well of Santa Lucrezia. It was noon and my lord abbot was tired so he sat at the well-head while we five went to the village to fetch food. A serving woman came to the well to draw water. My lord abbot asked her to give him a drink. She said, "Why do you, a lord abbot from Florence ask drink from me, a Sienese serving woman?" For Florentine lord abbots do not drink from the cup of Sienese serving maids. To her he replied, "If you knew the gift of God, and who he is who asks you for a drink, you would have asked me first, and I would have given you living water." The woman replied "you have no bucket and the well is deep. Where will you get this living water?" My lord abbot: "Whoever drinks this water will be thirsty again. But whoever drinks the water that I will give shall never thirst again. It will be a well of water springing up forever." The woman replied, "Give it to me, so that I never thirst again." My lord abbot told her to fetch her husband, she told him she had none; he knew that (he said), because she had had five husbands and was now living with a man to whom she was not married. This made her think he had second sight. At this point we came back, and were astonished that my lord abbot was with a woman. She departed hurriedly, leaving her pot behind.

I am, I am told and believe, naive, but at that time I had not long been a monk. There were so many questions I wanted to put to my brothers but did not dare in case they laughed at me. But why did my lord abbot send all five of us to fetch food for us six? Did he not want our company? Did he want to be alone? But why did he not want an entourage? And why did this woman come to the well in the noontime heat? On our way to the village we passed fresh rivulets. Why did she not fill her jug at one of these? It was rather beneath my lord abbot's dignity to ask a strange serving woman for water. Could he not have waited until we returned with utensils? And what did he mean by asking "If you knew the gift of God, you would have asked me first for water"? I believe there is a saying that some men think they are God's gift to women but my lord abbot was not talking in that sense. Was he? But what on earth could he mean by "living water"? How would this well up in her that she would not be thirsty again? In any event, she would have to come back for water for her household. And how was he to get water anyway? Why did my lord abbot say he was interested in meeting her husband? And why was he interested in her background? We were, of course, astonished at seeing him chatting to a strange woman. But what really stirs my curiosity is that she left her pot behind. Had she come this distance when she did not really need the water? Why was she there?

In the end I could not restrain my curiosity, and I asked my mentor, Fra Giacomo (now of blessed memory), one question. "What," I asked, did my lord abbot mean when he offered to give "living water" and how to an unreasonable statement could the woman reasonably respond "You have no bucket and the well is deep"? Fra Giacomo told me that in the Holy Scriptures of the Jews 'well' is sometimes used to designate those parts of a woman that are shaded, are frequently wet, and sometimes overflow. I was no wiser. "What is the bucket and what is my lord abbot's living water"? I insisted. Fra Giacomo replied that it was good to know everything, but not to seek to understand.

Much later, I think I may understand Fra Giacomo. But I am a staunch upholder of what I know are the true Franciscan values, of poverty and chastity. I am suspected of heresy, and of my youthful experiences I prefer not to speak.

Editor's comment:

The musings raise many questions. The reader will have noticed parallelisms with the holy, mystical account of Jesus' meeting with the woman of Samaria at Jacob's well that is found in the Gospel of John. If the monk is recalling a true episode, was the abbot engaging in a suggestive discourse with the maid, using the imagery of Our Lord? Or was the encounter of Jesus only in the subconscious of the abbot's mind? One thing, I believe, cannot be denied if the monk is recalling a factual event: the episode has overt sexual implications for the abbot and the maid. It is easy to imagine how Boccaccio would have reveled in the story. If the monk's musings have no substance in fact then we can guess at his fevered imagination. I showed the musings to my colleague -- though scarcely friend -- Alan Watson, who had written a scandalous account of Jesus' meeting at the well.[63] His response, iconoclastic as ever, took me no further. He insisted on the importance of context. The meaning of the monk's musings, he said, fictitious or not, was clear: sexual advances were being made with obvious innuendoes. The same, he claimed, was true of the episode in John. The details were the same; only, because Jesus was a participant, readers would not accept the obvious. He also added his opinion that the monk's musings were fictitious. One argument that he gave -- unattributed as is Watson's wont, but I suspect deriving from John Cairns -- is that the monk could not

[63] *Jesus and the Jews: The Pharisaic Tradition in John* (Athens, Ga., 1995), pp. 29ff.

know what happened at the well in the monk's absence.

Appendix by Watson. I have set out this *coda* by my close relative and colleague with some reluctance. My reluctance has nothing to do with the quality of the piece. But Sandy is insistent. He is keen on advancement within his law school. Publications are needed. But no Law Review would be interested in this; it is too short, and has not enough footnotes.

My reluctance to deal with Sandy's *coda* increased because it contains no law. Yet it is precisely that which brings out the importance of the episode of Jesus and the Samaritan woman in the Gospel of John. For the Gospel episode is full of law. The woman was Samaritan, and therefore always unclean and should not have been touched by a Jew. Her water pot was presumably made of pottery and would therefore partake of her uncleanliness and pass it on to Jesus. The Samaritans who sold food to the disciples would be unclean through contact with Samaritan women. Moreover, it was wrongful for religious Jews to buy food that had not certainly been tithed to the Temple, and this food had certainly not been tithed because Samaritans did not accept the Temple. Law in everyday life is found in many contexts but is often unnoticed. This is especially true for the Gospels: Jews do not read the Gospels, and Christians do not read Jewish legal works. But the Gospels, especially Mark and John, are full of law in action but are largely ignored by comparative lawyers and legal historians. Yet knowledge of law adds a further dimension to such episodes, and the episodes add a further dimension to our understanding of law. Law in action is often different from law in books.

II.

Jesus and the Adulteress

John 7.53: Then each of them went home, 8.1. while Jesus went to the Mount of Olives. 2. Early in the morning he came again to the temple. All the people came to him and he sat down and began to teach them. 3. The scribes and the Pharisees brought a woman who had been caught in adultery; and making her stand before all of them, 4. they said to him, "Teacher, this woman was caught in the very act of committing adultery. 5. Now in the law Moses commanded us to stone such women. Now what do you say?" 6. They said this to test him, so that they might have some charge to bring against him. Jesus bent down and wrote with his finger on the ground. 7. When they kept on questioning him, he straightened up and said to them, "Let anyone among you who is without sin be the first to throw a stone at her." 8. And once again he bent down and wrote on the ground. 9. When they heard it, they went away, one by one, beginning with the elders; and Jesus was left alone with the woman standing before him. 10. Jesus straightened up and said to her, "Woman, where are they? Has no one condemned you?" 11. She said, "No one, sir." And Jesus said, "Neither do I condemn you. Go your way, and from now on do not sin again."

The opening verses of chapter 8 of John (with 7.53) present one of the most puzzling episodes in the New Testament. There is widespread agreement that the pericope was not part of the original Gospel. It is missing from the earliest manuscripts.[64] In the manuscripts in which it does appear it is usually in this position, sometimes after John 8.36 or John 8.44, or even after Luke 21.38. The language also seems not to be consistent with the general pattern in John.[65] In presenting a new interpretation of the pericope I

---

[64] For the manuscript history see Ulrich Becker, *Jesus und die Ehebrecherin* (Berlin, 1968).

[65] See J. Duncan M. Derrett, *Law in the New Testament* (London, 1970), pp. 156f.; C.K. Barrett, *The Gospel according to St. John*, 2d ed. (Philadelphia, 1978), pp. 589 f.; P. Perkins in *The New Jerome Biblical Commentary*, ed. Raymond E. Brown et al. (Englewood Cliffs, 1990), p. 965; Leon Morris, *The Gospel according to John* (Grand Rapids, 1995), p.p.778f. A particularly fine account of the problems of origins, canonicity, and meaning of the periscope is Raymond E. Brown, *The Gospel according to John I-XII* (New York, 1966), pp.332 ff. See also Keener, *John*, 1, pp.

will leave open its genealogy.[66] My concern is with its meaning. It is not related to the four episodes mentioned in the Appendix to part 1 of this chapter.

I believe it would be generally accepted that the episode has never been adequately explained. I should like to begin with listing the troubling features.

II

1. The woman is accused of adultery, we are told she was caught in the act (v.4), yet she has not been tried for the crime, nor apparently will she be. Jesus asks if no one has condemned her (v.10), and she replies "No one, sir." (v.11).

2. Although she has not been tried or condemned, Jesus accepts that the woman is guilty. "Go your way, and from now on do not sin again," he says (v.11).

3. We are not told of the evidence for this adultery. Adultery, with its penalty of stoning to death, was very difficult to prove. Two eye-witnesses were required who could testify to the unequivocal nature of the act, to the time when and the place.[67]

4. The witnesses are remarkably absent from the scene: they do not appear in front of Jesus, and according to Jesus (and contrary to Scripture) it is not they who should cast the first stone.

5. Where is the adulterer? If the woman was caught in the very act of adultery, the man would also have been caught. And the man was equally

---

735ff.

[66] I do agree, of course, that meaning and context are much intertwined. But since I am proposing a fresh interpretation I prefer not to complicate matters by offering a hypothetical genealogy for the pericope. Still, see the final section of this chapter. Some commentators on John leave the whole pericope out of account: e.g. John Ashton, *Understanding the Fourth Gospel*.

[67] Susanna (Chapter 13 of the Greek Daniel, mid-second century); Mishnah Sanhedrin 5; Babylonian Talmud Sanhedrin 30a. For an extreme analysis of the difficulty of proof see Derrett, *Law*, pp. 160ff.; cf. Morris, *John*, p. 781.

liable to the death penalty; Leviticus 20.10: "If a man commits adultery with the wife of his neighbour, both the adulterer and the adulteress shall be put to death."[68]

6. Why was the woman brought by the Pharisees and scribes to Jesus. We are told that it was 'to try him' or 'to tempt him.' What can this mean? The usual explanation is that this is connected with the Sanhedrin's loss of power to inflict the death penalty.[69] I am not convinced that the Romans had taken from the Sanhedrin the power to impose the penalty of death, but let us take the worst-case scenario for me and assume they had.[70] The argument is, I suppose, that if Jesus said the woman should be stoned, then he would offend the Romans, and be in danger. This approach to the issue I find entirely unconvincing. Why on earth would the Romans be angered if Jesus, a private individual, claimed that an adulteress should be stoned? He would not even be insisting that a verdict of the Sanhedrin should be enforced. There had been none.

Even more to the point, on this approach the Pharisees are putting themselves, not Jesus, at risk with the Romans. It is they who claim that the law of Moses that they follow imposes the penalty of death by stoning. They even said "Moses commanded *us* to stone such women." The supposed scenario and its explanation are entirely implausible.

---

[68] See also Deuteronomy 22.22.

[69] See, e.g. Barrett, *St. John*, pp. 591f.; Perkins, *Jerome*, p. 965; Morris, *John*, p. 782.

[70] Alan Watson, *The Trial of Jesus* (Athens, GA, 1995), pp. 100ff.; with slight modification, *Jesus: A Profile* (Athens, GA. 1998), p. 85. Still, I would accept that at least later the Romans claimed sole authority to try secular capital crimes, and they might include adultery among these: Origen (in the translation by Rufinus) on Romans 6.7. But it should be noted that Jesus' invitation, "Let the one among you that is without sin be the first to throw a stone." implies that in fact an adulteress was liable to be stoned by the Jews. Moreover, the very clear implication of Origen's Letter 14 is that still in the third century Jews were putting criminals to death in accordance with the law, although without Roman authority: see, e.g., David Daube, *The New Testament and Rabbinic Judaism* (London, 1956), pp. 306f.; Watson, *Trial*, pp. 110f.

7. The outcome, when Jesus says "Let anyone who is among you without sin be the first to throw a stone at her" (v.7), is psychologically unreal. The normal reaction would be for everyone to grab a rock, not to disappear (v.9). To some at least the words would seem to be a challenge. Actually, this translation of *The New Revised Standard Version* is not quite accurate. More accurate would be "Let the one who is among you without sin . . ."

8. Why is the person without sin singular, not plural, and what sin is he free from? And, in the rabbinic tradition, it is the witnesses who have to throw stones first.[71]

9. What is the purpose of Jesus writing on the ground? Why is the act of writing stressed – we are twice told of it, at v.6 and again at v.8 – when we are not told, and cannot discover, what he wrote?[72]

10. Why was this an issue on which to test Jesus? What had it to do with him?

With all these problems the representation in the pericope cannot have historical accuracy. Reasonably, Duncan Derrett claims that parts of the text "cannot be understood as they stand." Are we to follow Derrett in thinking the woman was caught in a trap set by her husband who thus was at fault for not preventing a crime? Or should we, like Ulrich Becker, strip away texts of the pericope as secondary.[73]

For my explanation of the episode I wish to make two assumptions that I hope will not be judged unreasonable. My first assumption is that the episode as it was originally had a point. My second assumption is that the troubling elements of the episode should illuminate that point. They are survivals. A satisfactory explanation of the original tradition should cause

---

[71] Deuteronomy 17.6f.; Mishnah Sanhedrin 6.4; cf. Daube, *New Testament*, pp. 304f.; 308ff.; *Collected Works 1 Talmudic Law* (Berkeley, 1992), pp. 167ff.

[72] For one ingenious attempt to discover what he wrote see Derrett, *Law*, pp. 176ff.; see also Brown, *Gospel*, pp. 333ff., and the works he cites.

[73] Derrett, *Law*, pp. 158, 161ff.; Becker, *Jesus*, pp. 165ff.

these elements to be less troubling. The main troubling points are again that proof of adultery is declared, the woman has not been tried, no one condemns the woman, the adulterer does not appear, the supposed witnesses have no role, Jesus is asked his stance vis-à-vis the Mosaic law, his response is ambiguous, "Let the one who is without sin throw the first stone." Above all perhaps, we are expressly told that the Pharisees and scribes were out to trap Jesus.

I would put the episode in a specific historical context. Jesus had declared that a woman whose husband had divorced her and who remarried committed adultery (Matthew 5.31 f.; 19.3ff.; Mark 10.2ff.) The woman brought to Jesus was, I suggest, a remarried divorcée. By Jesus' own claim she was thus an adulteress, but not for the Pharisees. Moses allowed divorce, Jesus forbade it. The trap of the Pharisees for Jesus was this: the law of Moses demanded death by stoning for an adulteress; Jesus claimed remarried divorcées were adulteresses though Moses did not, and neither did the Pharisees. Would Jesus follow his argument to its logical conclusion and impose death on a remarried divorcée? The scribes and Pharisees brought the woman to Jesus very precisely to test him.

We can see now why there was no trial before the Sanhedrin. For the Pharisees there had been no crime. The problem of evidence of adultery and of the difficulties of proof disappears. For Jesus, the remarriage of the divorcée was itself adultery. Besides, we are no longer concerned with a trial and its practical problems. We are confronted rather with a theoretical issue: namely, would Jesus make a divorcée who remarried liable to suffer the Mosaic penalty for adultery?

Jesus wrote on the ground but we are not told what he wrote. The purpose of the writing was to give time for reflection, to put distance between the charge and Jesus' response. What Jesus wrote is thus of no consequence, with no need to record it. The time for reflection was for both Jesus and the Pharisees.

Jesus' "The one among you who is without sin, let him cast the first stone at her" (v.7), is typical of him. Jesus is on the attack against the

Pharisees. "The one without sin" is ironic. This does not mean 'anyone.' He is singling out an individual. The person he means is the ex-husband: for the Pharisees the husband had not sinned in divorcing his wife, for Jesus he had. For the Pharisaic position we have Mishnah Gittin 9.10:

> A. The House of Shammai say, "A man should divorce his wife only because he has found grounds for it in unchastity,
> B. "since it is said, *Because he has found in her indecency in anything* (Dt. 24:1)."
> C. And the House of Hillel say, "Even if she spoiled his dish,
> D. "since it is said, *Because he found in her indecency in anything.*"
> E. R. Aqiba says, "Even if he found someone else prettier than she,
> F. "since it is said, *And it shall be if she find not favor in his eyes* (Dt. 24:1)."[74]

Thus, at least for the supporters of the school of Hillel (of around 70 B.C. to A.D. 10) and Rabbi Akiba (of around 45-135), the divorcing husband needed no excuse for his act, hence was without sin. It would be unreasonable to suppose that their position was not also held even earlier. Much early evidence is lost.[75] Jesus' attitude is different, expressed most notably at Matthew 5.31f.

> "It was also said, 'Whoever divorces his wife, let him give her a certificate of divorce.' But I say to you that anyone who divorces his wife, except on the ground of unchastity, causes her to commit adultery; and whoever marries a divorced woman commits adultery.

---

[74] The translation is that of Jacob Neusner, *The Mishnah: A New Translation* (New Haven, 1988), p. 487.

[75] See, e.g., Daube, *New Testament*, pp. 166ff.; Calum Carmichael, *The Story of Creation* (Ithaca, 1996), p. 39 n. 16.

A husband who divorces his wife, except for unchastity, causes her in the eyes of Jesus to commit adultery, i.e. when she remarries.

We can go further. We know from Matthew 19.3ff. that this was an issue of contention between Pharisees and Jesus:

> Some Pharisees came to him, and to test him they asked, "Is it lawful for a man to divorce his wife for any cause?: 4. He answered, "Have you not read that the one who made them at the beginning 'made them male and female,' 5. and said, 'For this reason a man shall leave his father and mother and be joined to his wife, and the two shall become one flesh?' 6. So they are no longer two, but one flesh. Therefore what God has joined together, let no one separate." 7. They said to him, "Why then did Moses command us to give a certificate of dismissal and to divorce her?" 8. He said to them, "It was because you were so hard-hearted that Moses allowed you to divorce your wives, but from the beginning it was not so. 9. And I say to you, whoever divorces his wife, except for unchastity, and marries another commits adultery."

The very language is the same. The Pharisees put the question of the lawfulness of divorce in the context of testing Jesus. In fact, the Greek πειράζοντες (tempting) is the same in Matthew 19.3, Mark 10.2, and John 8.6.'[76] Also, in all three passages the issue is framed in terms of a supposed disagreement between the law of Moses and the stance of Jesus. This is precisely a tricky issue to bring to Jesus.

C.K. Barrett cites with approval a then unpublished paper of David Daube in which Daube suggests that: "in its original context, the slogan 'He that is without sin among you, let him be the first to cast a stone at her' is directed specifically against the unfair treatment of women by men and their laws; and that it is representative of a strong movement in Tannaitic

---

[76] Cf. Barrett, *St. John*, pp. 591.

Judaism."[77] If this view of Daube is plausible, as it is to me, it would even be strengthened if in the pericope the one without sin who had to cast the first stone was the divorcing husband.

Not only that, but if Jesus' challenge to cast the first stone was not to the crowd in general but to the ex-husband we can understand why there was no response but the crowd melted away. Moreover, for the husband too, his ex-wife would not have committed adultery: he could not cast the first stone.

John v.6, indeed, is very specific. The scribes and Pharisees were 'tempting' Jesus so "that they may have [reason] to accuse him." What was to be the ground of this intended accusation? It cannot have been, I have already claimed, an accusation to the Romans that he was seeking to have the Sanhedrin put the woman to death, a power that the Romans had supposedly taken from the Jews. Rather, the accusation would be before the Jews themselves, that Jesus was seeking to alter the law of Moses. Such an accusation could be seen as plausible. Indeed, one part of the double-headed charge against Stephen--and which led to his lynching after an abortive trial before the Sanhedrin--was precisely that Jesus was speaking "blasphemous words" against Moses (Acts 7.11) and the law (Acts 7.13), and changing the customs which Moses delivered to the Jews (Acts 7.14). The innocent-seeming question, but meant as a trap, to Jesus about the adulteress was full of danger to him.

Jesus' response discomfited the scribes and Pharisees: "They, having heard, and convicted by conscience, went out one by one, beginning from the older to the very last" (John 8.9). Jesus, as elsewhere when faced with a legal issue, sidesteps the question.[78] In this instance his adversaries are defeated because Jesus, not responding directly to the question or giving a legal opinion, transfers the possible crime of the adulteress to the sin of her sinless husband who divorced her. It should be remembered that in Jewish law

---

[77] Ibid., p. 590, referring to David Daube, "Biblical Landmarks in the Struggle for Women's Rights," *23 Juridical Review* (1978): pp. 177 ff.

[78] See, e.g., Mark 2.23ff. And 7.6ff., and the discussions in Alan Watson, *Jesus and the Law* (Athens, Ga., 1996), pp. 37ff., 55ff.

divorce proceeds from the husband.

It has long been recognized that there is a relationship of some kind -- connected with an attempt to make the law apply less unequally to women -- between our passage and rabbinic interpretation of the ancient ordeal of a wife whom a husband suspected of adultery which he could not prove.[79] Numbers 5.11ff. prescribed that the priest make a mixture of water and dust from the floor of the tabernacle, and have the woman drink it and swear an oath, and if she were unfaithful she would suffer a gruesome fate. The rabbis interpreted this to mean that only if the husband were guiltless would she suffer the fate from the curse.[80] Since Johanan ben Zaccai did away with the institution and this must have been before the destruction of the Temple in A.D. 70 (or Johanan's action would have been pointless), then the rabbinic debate and interpretation must have been earlier still.

This modification of the import of the curse will have been present to the minds of the onlookers who put Jesus to the test. The woman was to suffer only if the husband was guiltless. Jesus' reply was thus very much directed towards the sinfulness (in his view) of the husband who divorced. Jesus could only confute the Pharisees and scribes by the use of Scripture. He relied on the new rabbinic interpretation of Numbers 5.30f.: "And if the man is clear of sin, then the woman shall bear her sin."[81] On this view, if the man was not clear of sin, the woman would not bear her sin.

I have left aside to this point the answer to the basic question, "Where is the adulterer?" My reason is that his absence from the scene is the strongest evidence that the pericope as it stands is unrealistic. If she were

---

[79] See Daube, "Biblical Landmarks," pp. 187ff., and the works he cites. An abridged and revised version is in David Daube, *Appeasement or Resistance* (Berkeley, 1987), pp. 29ff.

[80] Siphre on Number 5.31; Jerusalem Talmud Sotah 24a; Babylonian Talmud Sotah 74b. For details of the argument see Daube, "Biblical Landmarks," pp. 189f.

caught in the act then so would he have been, and the penalty for both was the same. He, too, should have been brought before Jesus. His absence must be explained. My answer is that for the Pharisees there was no adultery, no catching in the act, and no adulterer. Their only interest was to test Jesus: would he say the woman was an adulteress to be stoned? Of course, no doubt, they could also have claimed the new husband was an adulterer. But why should they? There was no need for that for the purposes of the test.[82]

The trap set for Jesus by the question did contain a very particular danger. King Herod had married Herodias who was a divorcée, having been married to Herod's half-brother. Jesus' response to the adulteress would be interpreted as his response to Herodias. John the Baptist preached repentance for the remission of sin. The account in Mark 6.17ff. is instructive. Herod, we are told, imprisoned John "for Herodias' sake." John then specifically told Herod that it was not lawful for him to have his brother's wife, and Herodias hated John as a result. Consequently she had him beheaded. Jesus, who had been baptized by John would be seen as his follower, and would arouse the same suspicions in Herodias. Indeed, it appears from Mark 3.6 that the supporters of Herod were deeply hostile to Jesus even before the Pharisees were.[83]

We now see a further reason for the crowd melting away. No one would throw the first stone when the adulteress represented Herodias.[84]

One issue remains. For my thesis to have plausibility I must explain why the pericope never states that the adulteress, caught in the act, is in fact a remarried divorcée. The most plausible explanation is also the simplest. In

---

[81] See Daube, *Appeasement or Resistance*, p. 30.

[82] There is, of course, a strong element of sexual discrimination: it is the woman, not the man, who is humiliated before Jesus. If we leave specifics out, then to produce the woman, not the man, is more dramatic. Adultery by a woman has always been regarded as more serious than adultery by a man.

[83] For the argument see Watson, *Jesus: A Profile*, pp. 23ff.

[84] We do not know where the episode took place. If it was supposed to occur outside the lands of Herod, the first stone-thrower would still be at risk.

the early traditions about Jesus there was recorded this episode. It presented problems that would be blurred in oral repetition. First, Jesus would appear more loving and forgiving if the context were generalized. Second, Jesus would not appear to be faced with an insoluble moral and legal dilemma of his own making if the context were generalized. Such a blurring may appear in Eusebius *Historia Ecclesiae* 3.39.17 when he cites Papias (who was bishop of Hierapolis in the first half of the second century) as having "expounded another story about a woman who was accused before the Lord of many sins, which the Gospel according to the Hebrews contains." We have no other account of a woman being accused before Jesus so probably the episodes are the same. If so, John's version of an accusation of adultery is blurred into an accusation of many sins.[85] The original version may well have been specific. The scribes and Pharisees may have brought the woman to Jesus and said, "Teacher, this woman was divorced and remarried, and so is caught in the very act of adultery . . ."

My approach also helps with a well-known difficulty. The episode is regarded as having existed in the early tradition and as giving the authentic voice of Jesus, even if the episode is not historically accurate. Quite so. The original version must indeed be early because the penalty for adultery was changed to strangulation in the early second century.[86] But then there is a problem with the fact that the pericope is not in the early manuscripts, and its location in John varies with the manuscripts that do contain it, and it even appears in Luke. This would suggest some discomfort with the episode, an unwillingness to ignore it yet a reluctance to accept it. But if my 'Sitz in Leben' of the pericope is acceptable the difficulty disappears. The pericope shows Jesus as having great magnanimity of spirit. He also won the debate with the Pharisees. He does in every debate. But here there is a difference from his other confrontations. His victory here was only in the short term. Even those who were not Pharisees would realize with a little reflection that Jesus was caught in a trap he himself had made. The law of Moses was quite

[85] See, e.g., Morris, *John*, p. 779 n. 5.
[86] Daube, "Biblical Landmarks," p. 188; Becker, *Jesus*, p. 166f.

explicit on the penalty for adultery. Jesus had widened the scope of adultery. He could not deny the death penalty for adultery – he does not – unless he renounced the Mosaic punishment or disclaimed his own stance on divorce or adopted the rabbinic interpretation of the ordeal in Numbers 5.11ff. His supporters sought to control the matter by removing the specifics of the case – a remarried divorced woman – to make him generally merciful: but they still felt discomfort, and were unsure of how to deal with the situation. The problem for the early Christians, separated now from Judaism, was the greater in view of their hostility to divorce, and their strict attitude to sex outside of marriage.

I wrote above that Jesus' victory here was only "in the short term." But I need to be more specific. The problem for his response would appear only when early Christianity began to split from Judaism. Jesus' response was very correct and subtle according to the Pharisaic tradition. I have claimed elsewhere that though Jesus was contemptuous of Pharisaic teaching he could also at times use sophisticated legal argument.[87] Here, I believe, we have another example.

---

[87] Watson, *Jesus and the Law*, pp. 103ff.

Chapter 4

Artificiality, Reality and Roman Contract Law*

This chapter has a different structure than the others in this book. It originated in a lecture I gave in celebration of my teacher, David Daube. Out of piety I have kept the arrangement. The subject matter is very much part of the theme of this book.

Shortly after his eightieth birthday, I sent David Daube a version of this paper. He wrote: "It is powerful, wide-ranging. If I were not so reduced in energy I would make a few suggestions. For instance, in the first paragraph. . . ." David remains my master. The next day, a second letter arrived suggesting that I had treated the quotation from Deuteronomy as giving legal rules, not simply moral prescriptions, because of sympathy for him. He reminded me of his long struggle with Christian theologians who improperly contrast Old Testament *legal* rules with New Testament *moral* precepts, to the apparent ethical disadvantage of the former. Moral precepts often demand a higher standard of good behaviour than do legal rules. When I reread my paper I was surprised to find substance in his claim. I had treated Deuteronomy as having to do with law, though I had avoided saying so. Yet I really knew the passage was setting out moral precepts, and was not concerned with law. With regard to David, the emphasis for me must be on both parts of the word *Doktorvater).*

No teacher could have been more solicitous of his student than David was of me. His generous spirit embraced my scholarship, my career, even my entertainment and, indeed, my happiness. When I handed in a chapter of my thesis, he would arrange for me to have lunch with him, always within a week. Then, he would go over the chapter line by line with me until dinner (with a short break for tea *à l'anglaise).* Though always encouraging, he was not sparing in his criticism. It is just possible (though unlikely) that he was unaware how terrified I was that I would fail to meet his standards. If I had, I would not have been allowed to take up more of his time.

David was my external examiner at the University of Glasgow when I was completing my LL.B., and his first question to me was, "Would you like a job at Oxford?" Thus, I began my career as a law lecturer at Wadham College. So far as I know, no one else who did not have research or teaching experience or an Oxbridge degree was ever given a first post at Oxford, and this fact tells one a great deal about David Daube. Indeed it is remarkable in one who spent so much of his career teaching in Cambridge and Oxford that his pupils were so often overtly non-Establishment.

David has been and is the greatest intellectual influence on my life, first as a teacher then even more as example. It is my boast that the present paper could have been written only by one of his pupils. More modestly, I certainly could never have written it. Yet such a claim, without further claims, suggests an undervaluation. David has enhanced my whole life.

In presenting me a Yarnton Manor on 19 March 1989, Reuven Yaron declared that I was the most Daubeian of Daube's pupils.[88] I can think of no

---

* This chapter appeared in *The Legal History Review*, 57 (1989), 147-56.

[88] Professor Yaron requested that his introductory remarks on the occasion be cited: "We are meeting here today to mark the 80th birthday of our teacher, our colleague, our friend David Daube, but it is not my primary task to present him to you. My topic is the speaker, Daube's pupil Alan Watson. Of all those who were privileged to study under Daube's guidance, he is probably the closest to the master – in erudition and method, in the character of his writings and their scope. Were I to go into the details of his scholarly work, too much of your time would be taken up; let it suffice to mention his Oxford series of books relating to the law of the later Roman republic. To speak about Daube's contribution to Roman law, no one is better qualified than Alan (though Peter Stein, whom we shall hear later in the day, might equal the feat).

Daube came to this country as a refugee, but has become completely absorbed, fully accepted in the community of British scholars and in British society generally. That this was by no means easy he has himself divulged in a delightful little paper which he published recently, entitled "What Price Equality?" Alan Watson is probably the most British of Daube's pupils, with no outsiders amongst his honour so great, and have need of none other.

David, thank you, for everything.

1. When you see a fellow-countryman's sheep or ox straying, do not ignore it but take it back to him. 2. If the owner is not a near neighbour and you do not know who he is, take the animal into your house and keep it with you until he claims it, and then give it back to him. 3. Do the same with his ass or his cloak or anything else that your fellow-countryman has lost, if you find it. You may not ignore it. 4. When you see your fellow-countryman's ass or ox lying on the road, do not ignore it; you must help him to lift it to its feet again (Deut 22:1-4).

In dem times dy wan'n't no town, an' not much money. What folks dey wuz, hatter git 'long by swappin' an' traffickin.' How dey done it, I'll never tell you, but do it dey did, an' it seem like dey wuz in about ez happy ez folks is deze deys.

Well, dish you Mr. Man what I'm a-tellin' you 'bout, he had a truck patch, an' a roas' in-year patch, an' a goober patch. He grow'd wheat an' barley, an' likewise rye, an' kiss de gals an' make um cray. An' on top er dat, he had a whole yard full er chickens ....

ancestors to boast of or conceal. It is in this fact that a psychologist would, perhaps, find the explanation for Alan's evident desire to be different. In a way, one could describe Alan – who went on to become a professor at Glasgow, Edinburgh and currently at the University of Pennsylvania (Philadelphia) – as a "Germanic" scholar. He does not shrink from stating his views clearly, calls a spade a spade – and is not always loved for it, especially by those at whom his criticism is directed. Recently, he blew the whistle when some far-reaching theses were published, which he believed to be mistaken. It is human, yet regrettable, that some paid more attention to form than to substance. I, who have not taken part in that controversy, would like to state my belief, that by speaking out Alan rendered a service to scholarship. Had he, and some others, not done so, some less acutely critical scholars might, for some time, have been led up the garden path."

(From 'Brother Rabbit and the Chickens' in Joel Chandler Harris, *Told by Uncle Remus, New Stories of the Old Plantation* [New York, 1905].)

The first quotation set above is to remind us that though Deuteronomy imposes a positive obligation to assist another when occasion arises without his requesting aid, such an obligation to protect another's property did not exist in Roman law, nor does it exist in modern civil law or common law systems. Roman law did give an action, the *actio negotiorum gestorum*, where someone, reasonably, performed another's business without authority. For instance, the *gestor* who thereby suffered loss could claim for it up to the amount he benefited the other at the time of his acting. Such an action (except for the doctrine of *quantum meruit*) is still unknown to English law. Uncle Remus reminds us of the social importance of barter in societies where money is scarce. But Roman law never really developed a full contract of barter. *Permutatio*, which emerged four centuries at the earliest after the contract of sale, *emptio venditio*, significantly is classified with the innominate contracts. It does not rate a discussion in the elementary student textbooks, the *Institutes* of Gaius or of Justinian.

Law is very much an artificial creation in the sense that its divisions into contract or tort, property or obligation, sale and hire, and so on, are the invention of legislators, jurists or judges, rather than belonging to the nature of things. A legal institution is a social institution surrounded by legal rules and looked at from a legal point of view. But which social institutions are provided with legal rules and the nature of these rules are matters which are determined by the legal élite. This paper will examine the fabric from which law is made to demonstrate the artificiality of law, and the distorted mirror effect it gives to social relationships. For specificity, one branch of law, contracts, will be chosen and one system, Roman law. But, I dare to hope, this one example illuminates others.

I.

To set the scene, to show the issues which may arise in life, I wish to work from a concrete instance in a small, isolated community where money exists but is scarce, where many people are generalists (in the sense that in their work they may undertake many different tasks), though others are specialists. The example is real, accurate in its details, set in the rather remote parish of Kilfinan, in Highland Argyll in Scotland in 1987. I am not suggesting contemporary Argyll is like ancient Rome – only that, *mutatis mutandis*, human situations in the one today can help us envisage situations in the other in the past.

The example: Benny is a typical generalist. He runs a few sheep, collects and sells firewood, does house repairs, has a small garden, and is employed at lambing and calving time by bigger farmers. A rather wealthy farmer, X, who is expanding, buys a farmhouse, removes from it a new door which cost £680, and builds in a porch. Benny sees the door lying in a barn, asks X what he wants for it and is told £500. Benny replies that is ridiculous, he will never again release X's sheep caught in fences, and so on. X says: 'Don't be like that. £50.' Benny agrees. Benny is not buying the door without a purpose. He takes it to a friend's house and together they install it. The friend, Dougie (not his real name), gives Benny the £50. No more money is offered or expected. Dougie is rather better off than Benny. He has more than enough land, and allows Benny to run his sheep there along with his own. He lambs and shears them along with his own and even takes them to market. This represents work for Dougie, but, in the context, not so very much more. In return, Benny works for Dougie on the sheep when four hands are better than two, and, when needed, will work for a whole day or more with Dougie even on things other than sheep.

II.

The question to be answered is, can law, and, in particular, Roman law, do justice to such a state of affairs? The answer is that law operates only in a way that gives a distorted image of what's going on. And yet, the factual situation has nothing out of the usual, nothing extraordinary, in it.

III.

What, in terms of law, is going on between Benny and X? There is no obvious valuation to be placed on the door. The population is not huge, the number of people who might want it is small. But X puts a money price on it. His immediate reduction of £500 to £50 does not imply that £50 is the right money valuation for him. He is taking into account Benny's future services plus, probably, his past services. But how are these services to be estimated in money? Probably not in terms of Benny's hourly or daily rates since Benny's services for X are usually special, even emergency. But it is equally implausible to suggest they should be just a little below the value of the sheep. No clear answer emerges. Benny, too, thinks £50 is well below the monetary value, and he is binding himself, morally, for the future.

Is there a contract of sale, *emptio venditio*, between X and Benny? The price would be, say 10% of the door's monetary value plus services. But there is no Roman text on whether there can be sale when the price is money plus obligation, where the money price is a small part of the value,[89] far less when some of the services are past services, far less when the services are so unspecific. Indeed when the services, the *quid pro quo*, are left so vague it is doubtful whether in later classical law an *actio praescriptis verbis* would lie under Paul's celebrated *do ut facias* (D. 19.5.5pr.), even amended to *do ut des et facias*. It is technically possible for X to take a *stipulatio* from Benny for future performances which would then have to be specified. (And in English law, presumably, there could be an agreement under seal.) But in practice this is unthinkable. The very mention of the idea, though, highlights that it is the formality, not the form, of *stipulatio* which makes it actionable. Benny and X are probably not thinking in terms of law at all: but in some other circumstances that would not rule out the possibility of a legally binding contract.

Benny rescues a sheep of X but he tears his clothes. If this happened after the deal with X, it is not clear what legal rights Benny would have. If it happened before or without the deal, Benny would have an *actio negotiorum gestorum* for his loss up to the amount his act was beneficial to X when it was

---

[89] For the proposition that some jurists would give an action on sale when the price was money plus obligation see *D*. 18.1.79.

performed. But his action would be restricted to the benefit he conferred on X on this occasion. Yet there is a pattern of behaviour in Benny's acting to rescue X's sheep whenever he can. It distorts the relationship for the law to take into account only the one act in isolation, in which Benny's clothes were ruined. Interestingly, the issue is never raised in any Roman text. But the example indicates one might have reciprocal patterns of people engaging in acts of unauthorized administration. I rescue your sheep whenever I see them in trouble, and you do the same for me. Members of the society, may, in general, perform such services, unasked, for one another. In fact, this very notion of generalised willingness to help on both sides makes the whole concept of *negotiorum gestio* more comprehensible, both as a matter of fact and of law. Yet the notion does not emerge in any of the Roman sources.

The relationship between Benny and X, it must be stressed, is not necessarily between friends or social and economic equals. It is enough that they know each other and have some degree of reliance on the good faith of the other. Nor should it be seen as rural only: all that it requires, even in the widest case, is a group of people who know one another. Merchants constitute an obvious example.

IV.

At this stage one might list some of the issues which come into prominence when we look at the transaction between Benny and X, but which would cause problems in Roman classical law.

(a) There is no Roman contract for delivery of a thing in return for services.

(b) The Roman contract of sale does not take into account the surrounding circumstances which may have an impact on the price.

(c) Neither the *emptio venditio* nor any other Roman contract regulates delivery of a thing in return for a small sum of money plus a greater obligation.

(d) *Emptio venditio* demands for its creation, and therefore actionability, very great precision of the main terms: the price must be certain, there must be a thing.

(e) The *actio negotiorum gestorum* available to either party does not take into account the possibility that any particular act by one party may be only one event in a chain of reciprocal acts.

(g) A series of acts of *negotiorum gestio* may receive recompense not in money – as here in a much reduced price for the door – but this fact cannot be taken into account.

The precision of the Roman system of contracts and of quasi-contracts thus distorts the social realities. Moreover, the points just made indicate that even in the *bonae fidei* contracts the recognition allowed by law to good faith was severely restricted. And the unacknowledged realities of *negotiorum gestio* show that the boundary line between contract and non-contract on the basis of agreement can be slim and virtually meaningless. Most interestingly perhaps, no Roman legal text actually casts any light on any of the seven issues; not, for instance, why there is no contract of services in return for a thing, not why the price in sale must be certain, not why *negotiorum gestio* is (needlessly) seen always as a single act.

V.

The foregoing discussion, it is suggested, can help us to understand some aspects of the development of Roman law.

First, the nature of *stipulatio*, as Rome's oldest contract, appears more clearly. *Stipulatio* was a formal, oral, unilateral contract in which the promisee asked 'Do you promise . . . ?' and the promisor immediately, 'I promise,' necessarily using the same verb. Originally only one verb, *spondere*, could be used. No witnesses were required for validity. *Stipulatio* is thus a contract created by formalities, not by form, the difference being that a contract created by formalities involves an unnecessary step, one not inherent in its factual creation, whereas a contract created by form such as *depositum*, deposit, is created when a step – in this case, delivery – inherent in the nature of the transaction is undertaken. This nature of *stipulatio* is exactly appropriate. Its essence is that it is intended to be precise and legally binding, in contrast to the many arrangements where legal enforcement is not given importance.[90] *Stipulatio* is in fact the paradigm example of a formal contract. The formalities serve no other purpose: they do not provide evidence for outsiders in the event of a dispute of the existence of the contract or of the terms of the contract: they show only the parties themselves that they intended to make a *contract*.

It is entirely in keeping with the view of *stipulatio* as a contract, contrasted in early times with other arrangements with vaguer terms as non-contracts, that the promisor is bound by the actual verbal terms of his promise. It is this precision that is the hallmark of the *stipulatio*. The law wants to enforce the wording, not to take into account all the circumstances of the promise. But the real point is to give effect to the intention of the parties. It is absolutely right that the *stipulatio* can be used to make any kind of lawful promise into a contract. There is no reason for it to be restricted in subject matter. Likewise, the very demand for simplicity and clarity in the contract entailed that the *stipulatio* would be unilateral. It could be matched by a counter-*stipulatio*, but that was up to the parties. Indeed it often would be matched by a second *stipulatio*, and the ignoring of this in the legal sources seriously distorts the understanding of the contract.

A second early Roman contract is *mutuum*, loan for consumption, i.e. the loan of a fungible such as money or grain which is consumed by use, with the obligation to return the exact equivalent, not the very thing that was lent. I have argued elsewhere that once *stipulatio* was in existence, lawyers' thinking about law dictated that every other contract – with the sole exception of *societas*, partnership, which had its origin in the law of succession – came into existence in a situation where for practical or moral reasons the *stipulatio* was impossible or inappropriate.[91] *Mutuum*, loan for consumption, is a case in point and it became actionable for money loans of a definite amount by the

---

[90] Proof is not possible, but this explanation lends credence to the idea that originally *stipulatio* or *sponsio* was regarded as creating a sacred, only later, a legal obligation.

[91] *The Evolution of Law* (Baltimore, 1985), p. 44 ff.

lex Silia and for loans of other things later by the *lex Calpurnia*. It was of necessity gratuitous. The action was for the return of the exact equivalent. If interest was wanted, it had to be provided for by a *stipulatio* external to the loan. (In these circumstances in practice the *stipulatio* would be for the return of the property plus interest, and there would be no *mutuum*.) It was thus a contract between friends, relatives and neighbours or, at least, persons who knew one another: a farmer lends to a neighbour who has run short of seed corn to be returned after the harvest. What concerns us here, though, is a different issue. The available action was called a *condictio* which was a general action which did not set out the ground of the complaint but claimed that the defendant had something which he ought to give the plaintiff. There had to be a preceding *datio*, 'a giving' to the defendant. The main case of the *condictio* was always loan, but the *condictio* was also available in non-contractual situations such as where someone paid a debt which either did not exist or was not due, the so-called *condictio indebiti*, and even on a theft, the *condictio furtiva*. Thus, in its inception and conception, *mutuum* was not separated from non-contractual situations, and agreement was not a central issue in the arrangement. Indeed agreement need not be spelled out or even be clear. This corresponds to the social realities where in practice the dividing line between agreement and non-agreement can be very thin. But the Roman jurists remove *mutuum* from its background. There is not even a sign in the texts that the gratuitous nature of *mutuum* restricted its use to relatives and friends. But there is, incidentally, an indication that originally its contractual nature was not stressed. Thus, although the jurist Gaius discusses *mutuum* as a contract created *re* (G.3.90) he deals with *indebiti solutio* (payment of a debt not owed) in exactly the same context but he does not deal there with the other real contracts of *depositum*, *commodatum* and *pignus*. This treatment is explicable only on the supposition that *mutuum* and *indebiti solutio* were at one stage more conceptually linked in the minds of jurists (because of the *condictio*) than were *mutuum* and the other real contracts.[92]

---

[92] Against notions of the sort that Gaius' treatment of the other real contracts have been lost, see already the argument in Alan Watson, *Law-Making in the Later*

What is noteworthy, though, is that there never developed a specific Roman contract for return of a fungible plus interest or, more likely, a service. 'Yes,' says the neighbour, 'Here is the seed you ask for, but I hope you will help me for a day or two to bring in the harvest.' The explanation lies in the dominating role of the *stipulatio* in juristic thinking.

Another trait of juristic thinking, removing contract from its social background, and which is illumined by the Benny example, relates to *commodatum*, loan for use. This, too, was always gratuitous. If there was a reward for the use, the contract would not be *commodatum*, but hire, *locatio conductio*. So this contract, too, was socially restricted to friends, neighbours and relatives or at least to those who knew one another. But what if the object lent is returned damaged? Who bears the loss? The Roman answer is basically that party who is to benefit from the loan. Ulpian says that this is usually only the borrower, hence he approves of the view of the Republican Quintus Mucius that the borrower is liable for negligence.[93] But when it is only in the interest of the lender, then the borrower is, Ulpian holds, liable only for fraud.[94] The distinctions have subtlety but, as the Benny example indicates, they concentrate only on the one transaction to the detriment of social reality. A farmer lends an ox to a neighbour to help with his spring ploughing. In Ulpian's analysis this is solely for the benefit of the borrower who will be liable for negligence. But the loan is not an isolated happening. There will be surrounding transactions of various types. The small borrower may give his services free to bring in his large neighbour's harvest. The bulk of the benefit may be with the owner of the ox. Rightly or wrongly, this wider context of *commodatum* is excluded for issues of liability by the jurists, who always discuss one act of the *commodatum* in isolation.

VI.

I have used the Benny example because of its immediacy. But the

---

Roman Republic (Oxford, 1974), p. 146.

[93] *D.* 13.6.5.3 (Ulpian, 28 *ad ed.*).

[94] *D.* 13.6.5.10. An example is a praetor who is putting on a spectacle lending garments to the actors.

economic circumstances of ancient Rome provide an equivalent background for continuing, complex social interactions. I have a country estate where I spend some time each year. In my absence it is worked by my slaves. You are a friendly farm neighbour who keeps an eye open to check that my overseer is doing his job and not disturbing the domestic harmony of my other slaves by copulating with the "wife" of one of them. Your slaves return any animals of mine that stray and which they come across. At a particularly busy time for you, you may borrow the services of some of my slaves. Or you and I are grain merchants in Rome. I received an urgent request from a customer for 50 tons of wheat of a specific type and quality. I am temporarily out and ask you to be a good chap and lend me some until my shipload arrives next week. The wheels of commerce are oiled by mutual services. In a money economy there is a reaching out beyond money for the needs of commerce. At times this may even establish a special relationship which does not otherwise exist.

This background is obscured by the discussion in the Roman juristic texts and leads to much misapprehension. For instance, Barry Nicholas writes:

> *Relative unimportance of the real contracts.* These contracts are less important than their prominence in the Institutional classification suggest. *Commodatum* and *depositum*, being gratuitous, could be of no commercial significance, and a loan or deposit among friends will only rarely give rise to litigation.[95]

But, as we have seen, even *mutuum* for instance could be very much of commercial significance provided only that there was a relationship between the parties, and in such relationship the parties need not be friends or even of a similar economic or social status. A breach, indeed, could have serious consequences. My failure to restore the wheat to my fellow merchant when I said I would, could lead to a greater disturbance of our commercial relations

---

[95] *Introduction to Roman Law* (Oxford, 1962), p. 169.

than if I bought wheat and failed to pay on time. There is a greater breach of faith. A standard commercial use of *commodatum* would occur where an established customer wished to buy a particular quality of mule from a dealer for a specific purpose. The dealer is temporarily out of stock but says, 'Here, borrow this one of mine and return it next week.' The dealer's act serves to strengthen the relationship. But the dealer will be outraged if the mule is not returned, is not looked after, or is used for a different purpose and suffers injury.

Indeed, it is easy to overlook the role in modern business played by non-monetary transactions, and where a hoped-for counter-prestation is not detailed. I take my car to a repair shop for substantial repairs. The proprietor lends me a runabout until the repairs are completed. Much insider trading occurs without the supplier of information on the movement of a stock specifiying what he wants in return. The whole 'old-boy network' operates on this basis. When a Harvard College graduate confers a business favour on another, he does not necessarily expect the reciprocal benefit to be returned to him directly by the beneficiary but by other Harvard graduates, in turn, favouring him, nor does he expect the reciprocal benefit to be a precise equivalent or to be a single act.

VII.

Another issue demands clarification. How does it come about that the Roman contracts and *negotiorum gestio* which we have looked at here reflect so little of their social context, why do the jurists treat behaviour which is given legal recognition as consisting of single isolated acts which become individual contracts or acts of *negotiorum gestio*, when a significant element in their legal existence and importance is precisely that often they are part of a continuing course of behaviour which may be reciprocal, and why do the Roman legal texts show nothing of this complex background?

I should like to offer a two-fold answer even though the first part may seem merely to beg the question. The first answer is that all this is simply one example of the Roman jurists' habit of seeing law in terms of 'blocks,' separate from one another.[96] Thus, each type of contract is kept separate from each other – *mutuum, commodatum, depositum, mandatum*– with little sign of influence from one to another, substantive law is sharply separated from procedure, private law from public and so on.

The second part of the answer is that this all results from law developing by jurists. They are men of the world, but they consider legal problems in the abstract, as intellectual issues, and they discuss the law remote from practical facts. They are not examining real life situations in which they are forced to notice all the complexities of a relationship.

But then there is another side to this. In the social set-up described here it is very difficult for a legal system of contracts and *negotiorum gestio* to emerge. The parties often have no desire for legal enforceability. I help you put a roof on your house. What I hope for in return is not specified and, often indeed, I do not know what I want in return. It is enough that I can hope for your help when I need it and you can give it. I do not expect one thing or one service in return for one act. Nor is it even expected that any return will be an equivalent.[97] Yet the Roman law of contracts is notoriously precocious. And England, whose law developed largely independent of Roman law, still has no real equivalent of *negotiorum gestio*. It is, I suggest, precisely the Roman juristic ability to compartmentalize that enabled them to develop contract types with their own characteristics, and also *negotiorum gestio*. They could see a loan for use as one act, standing alone, and make a contract type, *commodatum*, out of it; and then give it rules which are clear, but are appropriate only if it is seen out of context.

As David Daube above all has emphasized, money changes things.[98] For Roman contract law the significance is that either a prestation is met with

---

[96] For discussion of this characteristic see already Alan Watson, *The Making of the Civil Law* (Cambridge, Mass., 1981), pp. 14 ff.

[97] See already Alan Watson, "The Prehistory of Contracts with Especial Reference to Roman Law," *Satura Roberto Feenstra*, eds. J.A. Ankum, J.E. Spruit, F.B.J. Wubbe (Fribourg, 1985), p. 37 ff.

[98] "Money and Justiciability," *Zeitschrift der Savigny-Stiftung*. 96 (1979). P.

a counter-prestation in coined money (as in *emptio venditio* and *locatio conductio*) or there is no counter-prestation whether because the contract is unilateral (as in *mutuum*) or is necessarily gratuitous (as in *mandatum*). What this means for us in the present context is that the jurists were either unwilling or unable to deal with the complexities of contractual relationships with counter-prestations unless, with the use of money, they could be simplified and put in the clear terms of a definite sum of money in return for a definite thing or service. The sole exception is partnership, *societas*, which has a very different history from the other contracts with an origin in the law of succession. In other cases where a clear contract was definitely wanted they insisted on using *stipulatio*: from each party if there were definite outstanding obligations, one only if one party had performed. Where *stipulationes* were inappropriate, a new, subsidiary contract such as *commodatum* was created but then it was treated always as standing alone, completely isolated from its context, and never involving a counter-prestation.

Apart from *emptio venditio* and *locatio conductio*, the Roman contract falsifies by law what would be the factual situation. Only sale and hire may represent a one-off agreement with no further relationship between the parties. All the others have socially a necessary background in another contract or agreement or in a continuing relationship. In law, but only in law, they are gratuitous or unilateral. But then it is noticeable that sale and hire come close to being in the law the simplest bilateral agreement. For one party the obligation is only to pay money, and there is little complexity in that. Thus, it is as if the Romans were unable or unwilling to deal with the more complicated bilateral arrangements. This is one more reason for the failure to appear of a contract of barter, or of a contract of services for goods, or of a contract of goods for goods.

It is here that the Benny example becomes particularly illuminating. The factual situation envisaged in it is not unusual. On the contrary, it is the Roman contracts, with the exception of sale and hire, which make no social sense by and in themselves. A stipulation is a formal unilateral promise to

1 ff.

give or do something. When would *stipulatio* be used? Only when the promisee himself had given or done something in return or also gave a stipulation to do something. But that has no place in the *stipulatio*. A loan for use, *mutuum*, had to be gratuitous. When would one ever make a gratuitous loan? Only if the recipient had done or would do something for us, or if there was some other relationship between us. When would one make a loan for use, *commodatum*, which had to be gratuitous, or when would one accept to perform a mandate which had to be gratuitous? The significance of the Benny example is not that it shows an individual or unusual situation of fact that Roman law cannot fully take into account, but that it shows that the Roman contracts in general do not, without something more, fit the social life.

VIII.

This approach tells us much, moreover, of the role of agreement in the development and practice of Roman contract law.

(1) Roman classical jurists stress that, because of the force given to the actual words used, a *stipulatio* was valid even when the wording did not correspond to the intention of the promisor, and was enforceable according to the wording. But the original intention behind the formality of the *stipulatio* was to make an agreement legally binding only when the intention to be bound and the extent of the promise were absolutely clear.

(2) *Mutuum* was not legally distinguished from some non-contractual situations. It was not the fact of agreement that gave rise to the *condictio*.

(3) In *commodatum* and *mandatum* (and in other contracts, too) there could be a valid binding contract even when the party bound had no thought of making a contract.

(4) A course of behaviour might involve repeated acts of *negotiorum gestio* which were not only acceptable to the beneficiary but were expected by him, yet no contract arose.

IX.

The relationship between Benny and Dougie is also illuminating. Dougie allows Benny to graze his sheep on Dougie's land and looks after them to a considerable extent. If in return Dougie were to receive money, we would have in all probability a case of *locatio conductio*, largely of services, *locatio conductio operis,* but also of *locatio conductio rei*. Benny would be renting grazing. But (unlike instances of *locatio conductio rei* discussed in the Roman texts) the land would still be under Dougie's control who would also be using it. Benny's prestation, though, is not in money, so any 'contract type' that can be deduced is not *locatio conductio*. Let us assume that Benny's prestation was definite, a fixed number of days' labour. If he does not perform, what remedy has Dougie under Roman law? Nothing on contract obviously. But also nothing akin to a *condictio* for non-reciprocation, *condictio causa data causa non secuta*. For the *condictio* lies only if there had been a preceding *datio*, delivery of the subject matter of the claim, and only if the claim was in respect of a fixed sum of money, *certa pecunia* or a definite thing, *certa res*. Once again, there would be no remedy until Paul's formulation "I give to you in order that you give, or I give that you do, or I do that you give, or I do that you do" (D. 19.5.5.1).

Issues arising from the "Benny example" have been used to illuminate the growth of Roman law. But, I believe, the example could be equally useful to clarify the growth of law in systems where the development was left to judges, not jurists.

Chapter 5

Justinian's *Corpus Iuris Civilis*: Oddities of Legal Development; and Human Civilization

For this chapter I wish to discuss grand scale legislation.

The most momentous event in secular legal history is also perhaps the strangest: Justinian's compilation now known as the *Corpus Iuris Civilis*. Unsurprisingly, scholars have avoided stressing how odd the *Corpus Iuris* is. The most likely explanation is that it is so highly regarded that they have not noticed. They accept its high reputation, hence for them high quality is a given. This is a theme to which I frequently return and, no doubt, will continue to return. The *Corpus Iuris* is so central in history for understanding how laws develops, and is so important today.

Justinian became coemperor of the Byzantine Empire with his uncle Justin in 527. Later that year, when his uncle died, he became sole emperor. Probably even while Justin had been sole ruler, Justinian was contemplating a legal codification of some kind. He issued a constitution dated February 13, 528, establishing a commission to prepare a new collection, a *Codex*, of imperial constitutions. The word "constitution" here is a general term to include all kinds of imperial legal rulings. The compilers were given extensive powers to collect the constitutions, to omit any, in whole or in part, that were obsolete or unnecessary, and to remove contradictions and repetitions. They were not given power to make alterations in substance. The constitutions were then to be arranged by subject matter in titles, or named chapters, and within each title the constitutions were to be given in chronological order. The *Code*, which was published on April 7, 529, has not survived, but it was replaced by a second revised *Code*, which came into effect on December 29, 534. The revised *Code*, which has survived and is one of the four constituent elements of what came to be called the *Corpus Iuris Civilis*, is divided into twelve books, subdivided into titles in which the constitutions appear chronologically. The constitutions range in date from Hadrian in the early second century to Justinian himself. A considerable proportion of the texts — 2019 as against 2664 — come from the time after the Empire became Christian; in fact, the bulk of the Christian rescripts is much greater.

On December 15, 530, Justinian ordered the compilation of a collection of juristic texts, the *Digest*, and the work came into force on December 30, 533. This massive work, twice the size of the *Code*, is in fifty books, virtually all of which are subdivided into titles. Each title consists of fragments from the writings of jurists who lived between the first century B.C. and the third century A.D. About one-third of the whole work is taken from the jurist and civil servant Ulpian, who was murdered before the middle of 224; a further one-sixth comes from his contemporary Paul. In the opinion of some modern scholars, one jurist, Hermogenianus, was active in the fourth century,[99] but otherwise no *Digest* text is attributable to any jurist who lived after the third century except for the rather obscure Arcadius Charisius. The texts of the jurists include statements of principles, discussions of rules, commentary on the scope or interpretation of edicts and statutes, qualification of other juristic opinion, and the treatment of problem cases, real or hypothetical.

The compilers were instructed to cut out all that was superfluous or imperfect, all contradictions and repetitions, anything that was obsolete, and anything that was already in the *Code*.[100] Contrary, though, to a frequently expressed view the compilers of the *Digest* were not given power to alter the substance of the law or to bring it up to date.[101] Indeed, any such alteration as

---

[99] On the question of dating see D. Liebs, *Hermogenianus Iuris Epitome* (Göttingen, 1964).

[100] *C. Deo auctore* § 7, 9-10.

[101] A typical exaggeration occurs in H. F. Jolowicz and B. Nicholas,

occurred would have been contrary to the spirit of the instructions.

There was very little juristic writing after, say, 235, and there are very few texts after that period in the *Digest*. Changes in the law after that date were almost entirely the result of imperial constitutions. But these constitutions were collected in the *Code*, and the *Digest* commissioners were expressly instructed not to repeat in the *Digest* what was contained in the *Code*. Significantly, the commissioners were to exclude from the *Digest* what was obsolete, meaning in large measure the rules that had been replaced by imperial constitutions which were now collected in the *Code*.

The third part of the compilation is the *Institutes*, an elementary textbook for first-year students, which was planned from 530 and was published on November 21, 533. It is structured on the *Institutes* of Gaius, a work written about 160 A.D., and appears in four books, though unlike Gaius' *Institutes*, the books are further subdivided into titles. The arrangements of topics — sources of law, persons, property, succession, obligations, law of actions — for which the credit should probably be given to Gaius, was the result of planning, and it differs markedly from the arrangement found in the *Digest*, which seems haphazard and is largely the unplanned result of the gradual growth of topics as they were rather unsystematically set out annually in the Edict by the praetor in the later Roman republic and early empire. The absence of a satisfactory arrangement in the *Digest* has long been a matter for unfavourable comment. Like the other parts of the *Corpus Iuris*, the *Institutes*

Historical Introduction to the Study of Roman Law, 3d. ed. (Cambridge, 1972) p. 481: "Full power was given to cut down and alter the texts, and this extended even to the works of ancient *leges* or constitutions which were quoted by the jurists." But *C. Deo auctore* §7 gives power to change quotations from laws and constitutions only where the compilers find they are *non recte scriptum*, "incorrectly set down." It is only to be expected that the decision of the commissioners on the correct reading was to be treated as final. For the full argument against interpolations of substance see Alan Watson, 'Prolegomena to Establishing Pre-Justinianic Texts,' *Tijdschrift voor Rechtsgeschiedenis*. (1994), pp. 113ff.; J. H. A. Lokin, 'The End of an Epoch: Epilegomena to a Century of Interpolation Criticism,' in *Collatio Iuris Romani*, 1, ed. R. Feenstra *et al.* (Amsterdam, 1995) pp. 261ff.

is statute law.

With the second *Code*, Justinian's work of codifying Roman law was complete. But he continued to legislate, and this subsequent legislation is now known as the *Novels*. No official collection of these constitutions was made, but there is considerable knowledge of three unofficial collections. Most of the constitutions were in Greek, some in both Greek and Latin, but translations of most of them into Latin also appeared. The bulk of the *Novels* relate to public or ecclesiastical affairs, though private law is by no means absent. Thus, *Novels* 118 and 127 reform the whole law of intestate succession, and *Novel* 22 sets out the Christian marriage law.

The first thing to notice is that the compilation of Justinian was not conceived of as a unit. It can be no surprise that the first idea was for a collection of imperial rulings. After all, there were precedents in the *Theodosian Code* of 438 and in the unofficial *codices Gregorianus* and *Hermogenianus*. Moreover, from around 235, as already mentioned, the only new law was created by imperial rulings.

The first surprise is with the *Digest*. At some stage, also as already mentioned, after the publication of the *Code*, Justinian or his advisors believed a collection of imperial rulings was not enough, and had to be supplemented by a compendium of abridged juristic texts. Despite the common view, again as already mentioned, the compilers were not told to modernize the texts and they did not do so, with two minor exceptions. The exceptions were (1) where a constitution altered the law and a qualification was needed: (2) if classical law had two institutions on a subject and one was abolished, texts on it might be used for the other. [102] The common view so obviously wrong, yet so long and so firmly held, can only be explained on the basis of a belief that no one would make a codification of law in a way that is so obviously flawed. Some of the consequences of the bizarre methodology will emerge shortly.

But here we should notice a different bizarrerie. The compilers were

---

[102] For this and what follows see Watson, 'Prolegomena'; Lokin 'Epilegomena'

told not to repeat anything that was set out elsewhere, i.e. in the *Code*. Most of the rulings of the emperors would not innovate but repeat existing law. Hence much that is recorded in the *Code* would result from writings of preceding Roman jurists. The result is that the *Digest* will give a very incomplete picture of classical law. It is thus not Byzantine, and only partially classical Roman law.

Another astonishing consequence of the approach of the compilers of the *Digest* is that fiercely Christian Byzantium appears godless. In the body of the work there is not one single reference to Jesus, apostles, saints, fathers of the Church. In all, there are twelve references to 'god', and in none of these can we tell from the wording whether this is the Christian God or a Roman pagan god. The Roman jurists were all pagans.

Things are no different in the *Institutes*. No references to Jesus etc. God appears only in the last text which deals briefly with criminal law (*J.*4.18.12).

> But we have said this much about criminal actions for you to have touched the subject with the tip of your finger and almost with your forefinger. For the rest, with the help of God a fuller knowledge will come to you from the larger volumes of the *Digest* or *Pandects.*

There is here rhetoric but nothing of particular legal or religious significance.

There is rather more of Christianity in the *Code*. But this is not much of an alleviation of the problem. The *Institutes* first, then the *Digest,* took up the first four years of legal education. The fifth -- optional -- year was devoted to the *Code*. By then the students, who were intent on further education, would have their mind-set fixed.[103] Yet there is here still another oddity. At the outset of the compilation, only the *Code*, the collection of imperial rulings, was envisaged. At the end of the enterprise the position of the *Code* had dropped, to be the subject matter of the final, and optional, year

---

[103]For more detail see Alan Watson, *Law Out of Context* (Athens, Ga, 2000), pp. 40 ff.

of legal education.

Again, it is worth emphasizing that the Roman jurists, with the exception of Pomponius and Gaius, were little interested in legal history. The *Digest* title 1.2, *The Origin of the Law and of all the Magistracies and the Succession of the Jurists*, contains one short text from Gaius and one long one from Pomponius. Both jurists had stopped writing by around 170 A.D. So for Justinian, Roman legal history stopped then. No mention of the subsequent famous jurists, Papinian, Paul, Ulpian. Juristic writings were not brought up to date in the *Digest*.

Better examples that the law was not modernized can scarcely be imagined. For historical reasons, connected with the political strife of the fifth century B.C., the jurists were concerned only with interpretation and, at that, almost entirely only interpretation of private law. As a consequence, there is almost no discussion of public law in the *Digest*. The public law has two dimensions. First public law as it interacts with private law. Here we find another surprise. Astonishingly, only two *Digest* texts mention the market. First, *D.* 1.12.1.11 tells us that the meat trade is under control of the urban prefect so the supervision of the pig market is under his control. Second, *D.* 42.4.7.13 which concerns hiding from one's creditors records that the older jurists believed that a person who conducted business in the market was hiding if he lurked around pillars or stalls.[104] But there are more surprises. In sharp contrast to American slave law, in the U.S.A. or in Latin America, there is almost no public dimension to Roman slave law; manumission is scarcely restricted by the state, restriction of punishment of recalcitrant slaves (in the *Code*) is really not enforceable, education is an issue only for the owners, there are no rules for enforcing slave behaviour, nothing about a system of rewards for returning runaways.[105]

The second dimension of public law is administration. Here is

---

[104] See already Alan Watson, *The Spirit of Roman Law* (Athens, GA., 1995), pp. 49 ff.

[105] See, e.g., Alan Watson, *Roman Slave Law* (Baltimore, 1987); *Slave Law in the Americas* (Athens, GA., 1989).

another surprise. Only one half of one book of the *Digest*, namely book 1, titles 9 to 22, deals with public officials. Subjects treated include obsolete matters and the real elements of government do not appear. Every title (or chapter) is very short. The opening title on public offices, specifically, *D*. 1.9, 'Senators', tells the story. The first text, *D*1.9.1. sets the scene:

> Ulpian, *(Edict, book 62)*: That a man of consular rank always takes precedence over a lady of consular rank is a point no one doubts. But whether a man of prefectorial rank takes precedence over a lady of consular rank remains to be seen. I should think he does, because greater dignity inheres in the male sex. 1. "Consular," of course, is a term we apply to ladies married to men who have been consuls. Saturninus adds also their mothers, but no case of this is reported from anywhere, nor has this ever been the received practice.

The last, *D*. 1.9.12 is a fitting closure:

> Ulpian, *(Census, book 2)*: Women who previously have been married to a man of consular rank generally try to prevail on the emperor to let them, albeit very exceptionally, keep their consular rank despite a subsequent marriage to a man of lower rank. One case of which I know: the Emperor Antoninus gave this indulgence to his cousin Julia Mamaea. 1. By senators we should understand people whose descent from patricians and consuls stretches back to illustrious men, because these and only these men are entitled to deliver speeches in the senate.

Nothing in between tells us what the senate does or why being a senator is a matter of importance to the state. Whether the senate even exists in a meaningful way is not brought into issue.

A further peculiarity of the *Corpus Iuris* is that it is overwhelmingly in Latin, a language not understood by the majority of even the educated in

Justinian's Empire. Latin remained the language of legal education.

Even more bizarre is the fact that the compilers of the *Institutes*, as they worked, seem to have had no research tools in front of them except these classical elementary books. They seem not to have looked at the first *Code* or writings on the *Digest*. When the classical elementary works had nothing à propos, the compilers relied on their memories, sometimes with disastrous results. Thus, *J.* 4.6.7 gives the function of the *interdictum Salvianum*[106] to the *actio Serviana*. Both remedies concern real security, but they are very different. Contrary to the *Digest* (*D.* 9.1.1.9, 11), the main action, *actio de pauperie*, for injury caused by an animal lay in the *Institutes* only when the animal acted *contra naturam*, contrary to nature (*J. 4.9 pr*)."[107] The *Digest* allows the action where two rams fight and the aggressor kills the other: behaviour scarcely contrary to nature. *J.* 3.2 pr., gives a very different account of *arra,* earnest money in sale, from *C.* 4.21.17 of 528 from which it derives. Above all, the very long *J.* 4.6 dealing with actions, is a mixture of classical and Byzantine notions, and is quite incomprehensible. Students could not possibly learn the law of procedure from it. The explanation is that the order to compile the elementary textbook was given only when the *Digest* was completed[108] and both works were to come into force on the same day, 30 December 533. The compilers of the *Institutes* were under enormous time constraints.[109] But law casts long shadows. Since so many much later introductory books often indeed entitled *Institutes*, followed the arrangement of Justinian's *Institutes* and Justinian's account of procedure was incomprehensible, it is not surprising that so many of these later books omit procedure altogether. Indeed, the law of procedure developed along different

---

[106]D.43.33

[107]The interpretation of *contra naturam* gives rise to difficulties. In modern South African law it is taken to mean "contrary to the nature of the species:" *O'Callagan v. Chaplin* 1927 A.D. 310; *Hamse v. Hoffman* 1925 T.P.D. 572; *S.A.R. v. Edwards* 1930 A.D. 3.

[108]*Imperatoriam maiestatem*, 3.

[109]See e.g. Alan Watson, *Legal History and a Common Law for Europe: Mystery, Reality, Imagination* (Stockholm, 2001), pp. 54 ff.

lines.

In all of the peculiarities of the *Corpus Iuris* there is remarkable historical irony. Without them, the work could not have had the impact on civilization that it had. Without the *Institutes*, the Reception of Roman law would have been much more difficult, if it could have occurred at all. Certainly, modern civil codes would be very different.[110] If the compilation had been in Greek instead of Latin it would not have penetrated the West.[111] If the *Digest* had reflected Byzantine conditions, it could never have had almost universal Western appeal. If the Byzantine God had been prominent the codification would have had problems in the Age of Reason, and would not have survived the French Revolution into the *code civil*, the most influential modern codification.

---

[110]See e.g. Alan Watson, *The Making of the Civil Law* (Cambridge, Mass., 1981).

[111] See Reuven Yaron. 'The Competitive Coexistence of Latin and Greek in the Roman Empire,' *Collatio Iuris Romani*, 2, pp. 657 ff.

Chapter 6

Justinian's Natural Law and Its Spanish Legacy.

The conjunction of legal borrowing and the need for authority in law results in legal tradition. The notion of a legal tradition means that, though there will be frequent anomalies, there will be an overall logical progression from point A through point B to point C. Thus, one can talk of a "Western Legal Tradition" with its divisions into civil law systems and common law systems. The startling and upsetting conclusion is that a legal system must be understood very largely in terms of its own legal history, not societal, political and economic history in general[112].

This brings me to chaos by which I mean in this context an absence of a necessary logical connection between legal rules, institutions and structures, and the society in which they operate. This absence of a logical connection entails that the great majority even of lawyers cannot explain the reason for the law. Why was the subordination of women's property rights in the early nineteenth century so much greater in the eastern U.S. than in Mexico? Were American men in the east more chauvinistic? Why is or was there a Rule against Perpetuities in England and the U.S. when there was not and is not a similar rule in Scotland or continental Europe? Why is there no sign of the need for the Rule in the extensive Roman sources? Why is the heading of title four, chapter 2 of the French *code civil* 'of delicts and quasi-delicts' when the terms do not occur again, and when the distinction between them is never explained? Why in the same code are there only five articles on torts but 27 on the relatively unimportant contract of *mandat*, mandate? Why is there such a vague provision in the code (article 371) as "The child, of whatever age, owes honour and respect to his father and mother?" Why was the

---

[112]See, e.g. Alan Watson, *The Making of the Civil Law* (Cambridge, Mass., 1981) pp. ix ff.

abolition of a similar provision in the old Dutch civil code so hotly opposed in the preparation of the recent new code when the article had never been applied? Why is there, especially in civil law countries, such a sharp division between public and private law? Why is religion, so fiercely partisan in early Byzantium, so scarce in the Byzantine Justinian's *Digest* and *Institutes*?

It goes without saying that authority is necessary to law and is, in general, a good thing. In this chapter, I want to call attention to aspects of this need for authority that are usually overlooked but cause law to have an unexpected, perhaps unwanted, configuration. Authority is the core of law, but the search for it often leads to an imbalance between law and the society within which it operates.

In the past I have stressed the extreme extent of legal borrowing, and the significance of this for legal development and of the relationship between law and society. I stick to this opinion. Without an understanding of legal transplants there can be no understanding of law in society. But this borrowing illuminates the ultimate fundamental importance of the search for authority.

When a rule, institution, concept or construct is borrowed it frequently undergoes change. This is particularly so when there are intermediaries between the original and the recipient. Often, indeed, the original may be transformed. Yet even then the original may, because of its authority, have an impact on the shape of the recipient which is otherwise unnecessary, and which serves to confuse and complicate the law. The need for authority needs to be emphasized.

In this chapter I will deal with one striking example of the need for authority for transplanting and for transformation: the treatment of *ius naturale*, 'natural law', *ius gentium* (a term with more than one meaning) and *ius civile*, 'the particular law of a state' at the very beginning of Justinian's *Institutes* and then in Spain and its colonies. But I must insist that the example of Spain is only an example of a common phenomenon. I could choose many systems but one is enough.

The categories may seem abstract and of little practical importance. But that would be inaccurate. They have a profound impact on legal thinking. The distinctions are made at the very beginning of Justinian's *Institutes* of 533 which until very recently was the basic textbook in the first-year curriculum of all western European law faculties. *J.* 1.2 pr, 1 in my translation reads:

> Natural law is that which nature taught all animals. For that law is not particular to human kind, but to all animals that are born in the sky, on the land, in the sea. From it descends that mixing together of male and female that we call marriage, from it the procreation and bringing up of children: for we imagine the other animals also with knowledge of this law. 1. But law, whether civil or *gentium,* is thus divided: all peoples who are ruled by laws and customs use law that is partly their own, partly common to all men: for whatever law each people lays down for itself, that is particular to that state and is called *ius civile* (civil law), as if the particular law of that state: but what natural reason laid down among all men, that is kept among all people and everywhere and is called *ius gentium* as if all people use that law. And so the Roman people uses partly its own law, partly the law common to all men. Which each is we will set out in their proper place.[113]

The texts are grandiose, but are utterly confused, and confusing, and have indeed confused!

But first we should notice what is not there: God. Fanatically Christian Byzantium has natural law without God. Indeed, the body of the *Institutes* has no mention of Jesus, apostles, saints, fathers of the Church. In fact, God or a god is mentioned only in the final text; 4.18.12, *deo propitio,*

---

[113] See already Alan Watson, *Legal History and a Common Law for Europe* (Stockholm, 2001), pp. 21 ff.

("God willing."). Likewise, despite both pagan and Christian authorities, natural law has here no philosophical or moral content.

As to what is in the text. First, in the *principium*, nature "taught," *docuit*, in the past, "Once upon a time". Then natural law taught all the animals *inter alia* the rearing of offspring. But we all know that many animals do not rear their young. Then natural law is treated in the *principium* as law, but §1 separates natural law from law, which is either civil law or *ius gentium*. Next *ius gentium* is described (or defined) as law established among all men through natural reason. But then we have a continuation of *ius gentium* in §2.

> ...From the demands of events and human necessities, human societies established certain laws for themselves: for wars broke out, and captivities followed, and slavery which is contrary to natural law. For by natural law, from the beginning all men were free. From this *ius gentium* (law of nations) also almost all of the contracts were introduced, as sale, hire, partnership, deposit, loan for consumption and innumerable others.

So now *ius gentium* has come in §2 to mean first International Law in the modern sense, secondly that part of Roman private law introduced for foreigners as well as for citizens. Hence, *paene*, "almost" all of the contracts were introduced by the *ius gentium:* the contract of *stipulatio,* originally available only to Romans, is significantly omitted from the list. The meaning given to *ius gentium* in §1 does not reappear.

The confusion in the texts comes largely from the authority of Roman classical law, partly from pressure of time. The classical Roman jurists stopped writing books around 235, and they were all pagans. Hence, no Christianity in the law in the *Institutes*. They were positivists, hence no philosophical notion of natural law. Accordingly, the Roman jurists' treatment of natural law was already remote from that of other educated Romans. They were also not much interested in international law but other

Roman writers such as Cicero and Livy used *ius gentium* in that sense, hence its appearance in §2. Again the distinction between private law available only to citizens and such law available also to foreigners had long disappeared before Justinian, but it is here retained. The compilers of the *Institutes* were in a rush. Instructions for the preparation of the elementary textbook were given only when the *Digest* was completed, but both works were to come into force on the same day, and Justinian would not want the *Digest* delayed.

Here we have a striking example of a legal transplant being a legal transformation. If what we have in the *Institutes* accurately represents views expressed in Roman legal elementary texts, then these texts themselves do not represent much of Roman thinking as seen in philosophers. But now the texts appear in a prominent place right at the beginning of legal education in very different Byzantium. The law, in so far as we can talk here of law, has not changed, but society has, drastically. Any meaning of the texts has now a very different impact.

The frailties of Justinian's account of natural law and *ius gentium* are readily observable, and rapidly -- very rapidly -- gave rise to interpretation. At the basic level, natural law in these subsequent writings is given two meanings: the improper one, we are told, is instinct, the proper one is law common to human beings: then *ius gentium* has two senses, one is natural law common to all humans, the other is international law in the modern sense. A striking feature comes to be that God and philosophy are mentioned in the discussion, and international law is given an important place.

Not surprisingly, the texts on natural law and *ius gentium* have always been mistranslated. To show the mistranslation I will give only one example, but with references to others.

A standard translation, that of J.A.C. Thomas[114] of *J.* 1.2.1, begins: "Civil law and the law of nations, however, are distinguished in this way." Other modern translations are to the same effect.[115]   But this is to mistake

---

[114]*The Institutes of Justinian* (Cape Town, 1975), p.4.

[115]See, for example, Peter Birks & Grant McLeod, *Justinian's Institutes* (Ithaca, N.Y., 1987), p. 37; J.E. Spruit *et al.*, *Corpus Iuris Civilis, Tekst en Vertaling*,

completely the point of *Ius autem civile vel gentium ita dividitur*. The precise positioning of *autem*, "but" is ignored, the disjunctive *uel* is mistranslated as the conjunctive "and", and the singular *dividitur* is replaced by the plural "are distinguished". The purpose in the *Institutes* of this part of §1 after the *principium* is to separate *ius naturale* from law, from *ius civile* and *ius gentium*. "But law, whether civil or of nations, is divided thus." Despite the *principium* with its nod towards philosophy, natural law in Justinian's *Institutes* 1.2.1 is certainly not to be seen as law. Yet the mistranslation or, better, misunderstanding seems to be remarkably early. If the *Theophili Paraphrasis* is properly regarded, as seems to be the case, as an expanded paraphrase of the *Institutes*, then it occurs even there. *Th. Par.* 1.2.1. begins:

> We said above, legal rules are either natural, or of peoples, or of a state. Since therefore there was talk of the definition of natural law and of examples of it, it is necessary that we speak also of the law of peoples... [116]

Here *ius naturale*, as law, is put on the same footing as law as *ius gentium* and *ius civile*. It will be noticed, too, that on this basis, the *Paraphrasis* has the natural progression of laws applying to all animals, law applying to all peoples, law applying to one state. This progression is absent from the *Institutes*.

If, as many believe, the Theophilus of the *Paraphrase* is the same Theophilus as one of the draftsmen of the *Institutes*, then the misunderstanding is almost contemporaneous.

An explanation of the mistranslation must include carelessness, but more important is the confusion in *J.* 1.2 pr. and §1, and the authority for subsequent generations of *ius naturale*. Natural law simply could not fail to be regarded as law, and for scholars of private law Justinian had to be taken

---

1 (Zutphen, 1993), p. 12; Okko Behrends *et al.*, *Corpus Iuris Civilis, Text und Übersetzung, 1, Institutionen* (Heidelberg, 1997), p. 3.

[116]My translation.

into account.

Yet it should be emphasized that if Justinian's text at §1 was so often mistranslated, the *principium* is at times properly understood to be nonsense. A prime example is from Arnaldus Vinnius (1657), in his *Institutionum imperialium Commentarius*, 1.2

It is as certain that brute animals have no understanding of law as it is certain they are άλογα or without understanding of reason. For between those who have law it is necessary that between them is reason, and equity and justice and law and society.

And he cites with approval Aristotle, Cicero, Cato the Elder and quotes with approval Grotius: "He is not properly capable of understanding law unless by nature he is using general principles." And Vinnius continues:

Not one of the philosophers, so far as I know, or of the jurists related that any law accrued to beasts, apart from Ulpian . . .

Vinnius is, of course, correct. The definition of natural law that Justinian gives from Ulpian, in *J.* 1.2 pr. is nonsense, hence law in *J.* 1.2.1 is restricted to *ius civile* and *ius gentium*. Law for Justinian is here *duplex*, not *triplex*.

But the Justinianic position on slavery and natural law is complicated, and in an earlier work I got it partly wrong.[117] Neither the *Institutes* nor the *Digest* texts just quoted declare that slavery is contrary to natural law. *J.* 1.2 *pr.*, claims that natural law is what nature taught all animals, and there is no mention of slavery. Nor is there in *D.* 1.1.1.3. On the other hand there is a continuation of Ulpian *D.* 1.1.1.4:

Ius gentium, the law of nations, is that which human nations use. That it is not coextensive with natural law is easily understood, because the latter is common to all animals, the former only to human

---

[117] *Roman Law and Comparative Law* (Athens, GA 1991), pp. 215 ff.

beings among themselves.

The stress in the text is on manumission. Manumission came from the *ius gentium*. One cannot believe that in Ulpian's first book of Institutes manumission (in *D*. 1.1.4) followed immediately on Ulpian's account of the three *genera* of law (in *D* 1.1.1.2-4). Indeed, in the *Digest* 1.1.1 is followed by a text from Pomponius, and another from Florentinus. I suggest that in Ulpian's *Institutes* what is now *D*. 1.1.1.2-4 led on to a discussion of the law of persons at natural law including the statement that all humans were once free, but slavery was introduced *iure gentium*. This was then followed in Ulpian by what is now *D*.1.1.4 on manumission.

If this approach is correct – or even if is not – the extent and contents of *ius naturale* and *ius gentium* could vary over time. This is already shown by *sed posteaquam iure gentium servitus invasit*. "But afterwards, by the *ius gentium*, slavery came in." This would mean that *libertas* may once have possibly been part of the *ius naturale* applying to animals but was so no longer.

We should also note that in *D*. 1. 5.4.1 (Florentinus, *Institutes*, book 4) slavery is part of the *ius gentium*. There is no sign in the Roman texts that slavery is morally wrong though once all humans were free. Florentinus continues at *D*. 1.5.4.1.

Slaves '*servi*' are so called because generals have the habit of selling their captives and in this way save (*servare*), not kill them.

It is an open question whether this text is indicative of some malaise about the morality of slaves.

From Justinian I want to jump to the celebrated declarations of Spanish law. These are to be found in *Las Siete Partidas*, the enormous compilation promulgated by Alfonso X, the Wise. Its final shape was probably fixed around 1265, and it was to have a great impact on the Spanish

New World. *Las Siete Partidas*, 4.22, at the beginning of the prologue declares: "By nature all the creatures of the world love and covet liberty. How much more do men who have understanding above all the others, and especially those who have a noble heart." And 4.21.1:

> Slavery is a condition and institution which nations made in ancient times, by which men who were naturally free became slaves. They were subjected to the ownership of others contrary to the reason of nature. The slave (*siervo*) took this name from a word that they call in Latin *servare*, which is as much as to say in Spanish, "to save". And this saving was established by the emperors. For in ancient times, as many as they captured, they killed.

The dependence of these texts on the Roman ones is readily apparent. By the time of Alfonso, of course, theologians had substantially developed the notion of natural law, but again it would be methodologically wrong to assume that it is the theological notion that explains the meaning and intention of the legislator rather than his Roman models.

First, consider the texts as they stand. There is no indication that the institution of slavery is morally wrong. Love of liberty is natural, but this is true for all animals as well as for humans, as we are expressly told. It follows that if slavery is morally wrong, then so is the captivity and domestication of animals. The emphasis is on liberty as the original, therefore natural, status. I have suggested that the derivation of the word *servus*, slave, from *servare*, to save, in the Roman texts might indicate some uneasiness over the morality. Even if that is so, the text of the *Partidas* seems to be no more than an explanation of the existence of slavery.

The same approach is needed for the preface to *Las Siete Partidas*, 4.5, which begins:

> "Slavery is the lowest and most depised thing that can exist between men. Because man, who is the most noble and free creature, among

all the other creatures, that God made, is placed by it in the power of another: in such a way that they can do with him whatever they want, as they can with their other property alive or dead."[118]

In this (and in the rest of the preface that has not been quoted) there is no condemnation of slavery as immoral. The legislator is making what is for him a statement of fact: slavery is the most wretched condition of man.

But we must place these texts in the context of the lawmakers' general understanding of natural law. *Las Siete Partidas*, 1.1.2, declares:

> *Ius naturale* in Latin means in Spanish *derecho natural (*natural law), which all men have in them naturally, and even the other animals which have feeling. Following the direction of this law, the male unites with the female, which we call marriage; and on this account, humans care for their children; and so do all animals. Furthermore there is *ius gentium* (in Latin), which means the law common to all nations, and not to the other animals. And this was created with reason and also from necessity, because men could not well live with one another in harmony, and in peace if all did not use this law.

Later in the same law, Alfonso declares that by the *ius gentium* all men are bound to love God, to obey their parents and their native land. Thus, in the main law discussing natural law, no moral content is given to it. That is reserved, if at all, to *ius gentium*.

Those modern scholars who attribute an awareness of the immorality of slavery to the Spanish lawmakers are being anachronistic. But their opinion should not be surprising. From a modern standpoint, after centuries in which the doctrine of natural law has held a central place in theological debate, it is not easy to approach the early legal sources on their own terms. A detail in

---

[118] For a typical misunderstanding of the point of the Spanish texts that slavery is contrary to natural law, see A. Levaggi, "La condición juridica del esclavo en la epoca hispanica," *Revista de Historia del Derecho 1 (1973): 83ff., at p. 149.*

the standard gloss to *Las Siete Partidas* that was written in the sixteenth century by Gregorio López, a member of the Consejo Real de Indias, is revealing for Spanish legal attitudes in his time. In his gloss on the general treatment of natural law in *Las Siete Partidas* at 1.1.1. he says, among other things: "but following the nature which man has in common with angels, that is the power of reasoning, it is thus defined: 'Natural law is a certain reason of nature implanted in the human creature to do good and to avoid the opposite." Thus, in this context for López natural law has a moral quality. And he proceeds to develop this definition following and citing Aquinas. But when he glosses the law on slavery there is no indication that he regards the institution as immoral, even though in his gloss on *Las Siete Partidas*, 4.21.1, he says it is contrary to nature.

Chapter 7

The Failure of Scottish Legal Education in the 17th Century, and the American Civil War.

I

Law requires authority. This need frequently bends law out of shape. Law is wanted, say needed, by a judge. But there is no authority. The judge cannot say: "This is my judgment because I like it!" So the judge borrows from an approved system such as Roman law. But what if there is no law there, or it cannot be discovered? Then the judge is tempted -- or even compelled -- to invent it. A favorite approach throughout history has been to tear texts out of their context and give them a new meaning. Others may object to your choice of texts or your result. But not to your methodology. It is used by everyone! The supreme example, I believe, is the development of a modern law for 19th century Germany from Roman law by the Pandectist school. In law, imagination need have no bounds.

A favourite example of mine is conflict of laws: the study of the law to be applied when more than one jurisdiction is involved. Roman law should have provided little help, whether because the subject did not exist or because the jurists were interested only in *iudicia legitima,* that is, what went on at Rome or its immediate vicinity.

The most famous exponent was the great Bartolus (1314-1357) but our concern is with another great scholar, Ulrich Huber (1635-1694) of Friesland. Oddly, on conflict of law his views had little impact in continental Europe: indeed, none outside of the Dutch Republic.

His theory is elegant and beautifully simple.[119] It is based on three axioms. An axiom is a mathematical term to denote a proposition that is self-evidently true, and needs no proof. Inevitably, and properly, the axioms of

---

[119]Set out in his *Praelectiones juris romani et hodierni,*2.1.3.

Huber are based on Roman law.

Axiom 1. "The laws of each sovereign authority have force within the boundaries of its state, and bind all subject to it, but not beyond." For this axiom, Huber relies on the authority of *D.* 2.1.20:

> One who administers justice beyond the limits of his territory may be disobeyed with impunity. The same applies where he purports to administer justice in a case exceeding the amount established for his jurisdiction.

The *Digest* text is fairly used by the conventions regularly accepted, though obviously it is not quite in point.

Axiom 2. "Those people are held to be subject to a sovereign authority who are found within its boundaries, whether they are there permanently or temporarily." Huber's authority this time is *D.* 48.22.7.10:

> The governor can bar someone from the province which he himself rules, but not from another; and the deified brothers wrote in a rescript to this effect. The consequence of this was that a person who has been relegated from the province in which he had his domicile could remain in the place from which he originated. However, our emperor and his deified father have provided for this. For they wrote in a rescript to Maecius Probus, governor of the province of Spain, that a person could also be barred from the province from which he originated by the governor of the province where he had his domicile. It is also proper that persons who, though not residents of a province, commit an offence there, should come under the force of [this] rescript.

This is not quite so good a fit, but is still possible by the accepted standards of the time.

Axiom 3. "The rulers of states so act from comity (*comiter*) that the rights of each people exercised within its own boundaries should retain their force everywhere, insofar as they do not prejudice the power or rights of another state or its citizens."

This is where problems should really begin for Huber. There is no Roman authority, and Huber freely admits this. But Huber has two lines of defence. An axiom as an axiom is self-evidently true. So no proof is needed. Then he claims that this axiom comes from the *ius gentium*, not the *ius civile*. The most common Roman understanding was that the *ius gentium* was that law established everywhere (or, at least, among civilized nations.), *ius civile* was the law found for a particular state. Accordingly, axiom 3 was law found among all peoples, hence is part of Roman law, even if no text said so! (Roman law approached this way, or in any other way, is fun.)

The court must act *comiter*. The judge does not have a choice.[120] Foreign law is binding. Of course, since it is binding only indirectly, whereas the law of the local jurisdiction is binding directly, foreign law would not prevail where it was expressly excluded by the local law, say by statute. This is not stated by Huber, but it is implicit in the distinction he makes between axioms 1 and 2 on the one hand, and axiom 3 on the other.

But axiom 3 admits of exceptions. Foreign legal rules are binding "insofar as they do not prejudice the power or rights of another state or its citizens." Huber sets out his understanding of the exceptions; briefly as is appropriate for axioms. The exceptions are very restricted as is shown in his rather fuller treatment in *Heedendaegse Reschtsgeleertheyd* 1.3.18 ff.

We can now restate Huber's axiom 3, with the exceptions. An act or transaction in one state has no direct legal effect beyond the territory of the state, but a state is bound by the law of nations to act *comiter*, courteously, in order to give effect to foreign law in judging the effects of acts or transactions occurring in another state; subject to the sole exceptions that (1) local law will be applied if there has been a deliberate attempt to evade local jurisdiction by one subject to it, (2) local law will be applied where there is more than one act or transaction, one of which occurred locally, and where superiority of transaction depends on which law is applied. In addition -- not an exception, but vitally important --, an act valid where it was made (or a status valid by

---

[120]For Huber. The view of other Dutch jurists was not always the same: see Watson, *Story*, p. 8ff.

the domicile), but void by the law of nations, is void elsewhere. These, for Huber, are the sole qualifications to his axiom 3. Again I stress that for Huber the courts had no discretion whether to recognize the foreign law or not. A clinching argument for this proposition, if one were needed, is that nowhere in his discussion does Huber indicate a situation where a court might have a choice.

II.

That Huber could be misunderstood is apparent. Indeed, the earliest Dutch use of *comitas* and *comiter* is by Paulus Voet (1619-1667), who has a different stance. Thus, in the section headings of his *De statutis eorumque concursu* he denominates 4.2.17 as "A territorial statute is often observed outside of its territory for comity and equity." Thus, for him there is no obligation to observe such law: it happens often, but it need not happen. The section itself, making the point even clearer, reads: "And so, sometimes, when a neighbouring people wishes to observe the customs of a neighbour out of comity, and lest many matters properly accomplished be thrown into confusion, on account of custom statutes migrate beyond the territory of the law maker, when their effect has been examined." Thus, for Voet, it does not always happen that the relevant foreign law is recognized: when it does, it happens only after an examination of the effect of the foreign statute. There is no legal obligation to put the neighbouring law into effect. For Voet, in contrast to Huber, courts have discretion. Other passages from the same work confirm this interpretation of Paulus Voet's use of *comiter*.

III

From an early date Scots studied law in continental Europe.[121] The

---

[121]See above all, R. Feenstra, 'Scottish-Dutch Legal Relations in the Seventeenth and Eighteenth Centuries,' in *Scotland and Europe*, 1200-1850, ed. T.C. Smout (Edinburgh, 1982), pp. 128ff., and the authorities he cites; Paul Nève, '*Disputationes* of Scots Students Attending University in the Northern Netherlands,' in *Acts of the British Legal History Conference* (1989), ed. W.M. Gordon and T.D. Fergus (London, 1991), pp. 95ff.; J.W. Cairns, 'William Crosse, Regius Professor of

War of Independence at the beginning of the fourteenth century (and subsequent religious differences) closed Oxford and Cambridge to the Scots, and there were no Scottish universities until the fifteenth century. For a time, after its foundation in 1425, the University of Louvain, for instance, was a powerful draw. The Scottish law faculties, once established, languished, and the tradition of going abroad to study continued: mainly to France until the 1570s, and thereafter primarily to the Dutch Republic.   Statistics are difficult: not all law students matriculated, some matriculated at more than one university, some may not have remained long. The best figures now (with his detailed *caveat*) are probably those of Robert Feenstra. For the periods that concern us he estimates Scottish law students at Leiden to be 24 for the period 1626-1650, 89 for 1651-1675, 235 for 1676-1700, 187 for 1701-1725, 115 for 1725-1750, 26 for 1751-1775. At Franeker, where Ulrich Huber was law professor, Feenstra gives 2 students for 1661-1670, 10 for 1671-1680, 10 for 1681-1690, 5 for 1691-1700, 2 for 1701-1720, 3 for 1721-1730. Scottish law students at Groningen and Utrecht were comparable in numbers. Feenstra states that for the period 1661-1750, when the total number of candidates admitted to the Scottish Faculty of Advocates was 663, 275 or about two-fifths, are known to have studied in the Netherlands.

Thus, Dutch jurists exercised great influence on Scottish lawyers and judges in the seventeenth and eighteenth centuries. Equally to the point is the fact that students – even today – buy books that are recommended by their professors and that are inherent in their tradition. Availability of books is important in shaping the course of legal development. Books that are not available cannot be used and cannot be influential. Scottish public libraries, unlike those in London, became rich in continental, particularly Dutch, law books. James Kent stated:

A curious fact is mentioned by Mr. Robertson, in his Treatise on the

Civil Law in the University of Glasgow, 1746-1649; A Failure of Enlightened Patronage,' in *Acts of the British Legal History Conference* (1991), ed. P. Birks (London, 1992).

Law of Personal Succession. He says that of the ninety-one
continental writers on the subject of the Conflict of Laws, quoted or
referred to by the American jurists, Livermore and Story, a large
proportion of them was not to be found in the public law libraries in
London, but all of them, except six, were to be met with in that
admirable repertory of books of law, the library of the faculty of
advocates in Edinburgh. Mr. Livermore, while a practicing lawyer in
New Orleans, had collected from continental Europe most of those
rare works as part of his valuable law library, and which library he
bequeathed by will to Harvard University, in Massachusetts.[122]

The extent of the holdings in the Faculty of Advocates library, great
though it is , is rather misleading, since such libraries refuse or dispose of
many duplicate copies. Much more to the point is the frequency with which
one comes across seventeenth-century Dutch legal works in Scottish private
libraries. As an indication of a Scottish connection with Huber and his work I
should mention that my own copy of the fourth edition of his *Positiones juris*
(Franeker, 1685) (which was formerly in the Minto library) is inscribed
Franequerae 23 Octob: 1685. *Empt. fl. 36 viz g b li 16 stirl. Ex mandato
Authoris professoris miei* (Franeker 23 October 1685. Bought for 36 florins,
i.e. 16 pounds sterling, on the instructions of the author, my professor); and
below, *Incepi Relegere in feriis 22 Jun. 1686* (I began to reread in the
vacation, 22 June 1686). The provenance of the volume plus the translation
of the price from Dutch florins into pounds sterling make it very likely that
the purchaser was a Scottish student of Huber at Franeker. In contrast, even
at the present time the British Library does not seem to have a copy of
Positiones juris. Again, my edition of Huber's *Praelectiones juris romani et
hodierni*, which was also formerly in the Minto library is dated 1698: the
earliest edition in the British Library is dated 1707.[123]

---

[122] *Commentaries on American Law*, vol 2, 12th ed. (1873), p. 455, note b.

[123] The National Library of Scotland has part 3 of Huber's *Praelectiones*,
published at Franeker, 1690; and the whole work, Leipzig, 1707, and Louvain, 1766.

In this field of conflict of laws, Huber was always likely to dominate in a distant, foreign, country where there was a tradition of relying upon Dutch authority. To begin with, in contrast to Paulus Voet, Huber placed his treatment of the subject in an elementary textbook, lectures on the *Digest*; and in a prominent place, at that. This is precisely the kind of book students would buy, take home, and use when needed. Paulus Voet's treatment was in a specialist book on its own, *De statutis eorumque concursu,* and consequently rarely brought back to Scotland. I have found no reference to Paulus Voet in the Scottish cases of the time. Indeed, in the preface to the second edition (1870) of his translation of Savigny's *Conflict of Laws,* William Guthrie claimed this was among the rarest of books on jurisprudence. Then, in contrast to Johannes Voet, Huber's treatment was explicitly on the theme of conflict of laws and was fully developed in one place. Johannes Voet's views have to be gleaned from his discussion of individual substantive topics, such as marriage.

Specifically on conflict of laws Huber does appear prominently in the Scottish cases, as do Johannes Voet and, to a lesser extent, Rodenburgh.[124] On comity Huber is cited with approval as early as 1713 in *Goddart v. Sir John Swynton.*[125] The case of *Nicholas Junquet La Pine v. Creditors of Lord Semple* also suggests that by 1721 Huber's doctrine of comity had won some acceptance in Scotland: "This he did in the only way it was possible, by

---

Of this work, Edinburgh University Library has editions of 1735 (Leipzig) and 1749 (Frankfurt). Of the *Positiones,* the National Library has the Leipzig edition of 1685, Edinburgh University Library has the Franeker edition of 1710.

[124]J. Voet: *Simon Lord Lovat v. James Lord Forbes,* M. 452 (1742); *Kerr v. Alexander Earl of Home, M.* 4522 (1771); *Edwards v. Prescot,* M. 4535 (1720); *Sinclair and Sutherland v. Frazer,* M. 4542 (1768); *Morison and Others v. Earl of Sutherland,* M. 4595 (1746) (and the same case, M. 4571); *Morison and Others v. Earl of Sutherland,* M. 4595 (1749) (and the same case M. 4598), *Brunsdone v. Wallace* M 4784 (1789); *Dodds v. Westcomb,* M. 4793 (1745); Rodenburgh: *Christie v. Stratton* M. 4569 (and the same case, M. 4571); *Morison and Others v. Earl of Sutherland* M. 4595 (1749), (and the same case M. 4598).

[125]M. 4533

making out a bond in the form of the country where it was granted; which as it was *ex vi legis* directly effectual there, so *ex comitate* in every other civilized country."[126] Though the wording is not that of Huber, the argument that it is binding everywhere because of comity is to that of Huber, and not Paulus Voet's. The court held that a bond that was null in Scotland (because of its form), but valid in England where it was made, was actionable in Scotland. Huber was also expressly cited with approval on conflict of laws in *Simon Lord Lovat v. James Lord Forbes* (17423), *Randal and Elliot v. Innes* (1768), *Sinclair and Sutherland v. Frazer* (1768) and *Kerr v. Alexander Earl of Home* (1771).[127]

More generally, Huber's overall reputation in the seventeenth century was immense. For example, he is cited with great approval by Sir George Mackenzie in his inaugural address in opening the library of the Faculty of Advocates.[128]

IV

The main architect of early English conflicts law was Lord Mansfield, who was a Scot.[129] Although he left Scotland when he was fourteen, never to return, he retained his Scottish connections. England was remarkably bereft of legal scholars in general until the nineteenth century. Moreover, conflict of

---

[126]M. 4451. But *Kinlock v. Fullerton*, M. 4456 (1739), indicates that this approach to *comitas* was not universal. *Comitas* in *Norris v. Wood*, M. 4466 (1743), and *Laycock v. Clark*, M. 4554 (1767), is to the same effect whether on the view of Huber or of the other Dutch jurists.

[127]Respectively, M. 4512, M. 4520, M. 4542, M. 4522.

[128]*Oratio Inauguralis in Aperienda Jurisconsultorum Bibliotheca* (1689); see the edition of Edinburgh, 1989. p. 67, with nn. 29 and 32, by J.W. Cairns.

[129]For the impact of Lord Mansfield on the development of English conflict of laws, see, e.g., Cheshire and North's *Private International Law*, 11th edd., P.M. North and J.J. Fawcett (London, 1987), pp. 24 ff.; A.E. Anton, "The Introduction into English Practice of Continental Theories on the Conflict of Laws," 5 *International and Comparative Law Quarterly* (1956), pp. 534ff., at pp. 538ff.; C.P. Rodgers, "Continental Literature and the Development of the Common Law by the King's Bench: c. 1750-1800," in *Courts and the Development of Common Law*, ed. V. Piergiovanni (Berlin, 1987), pp. 161ff., at pp. 182ff.

laws was not really discussed in common-law courts until the time of Lords Hardwicke and Mansfield in the eighteenth century, primarily as a result of issues of jurisdiction. Unless a cause of action arose within a particular jurisdiction it was not actionable there.

It is worthy of remark that the first reference to Huber in the English reports is by Lord Mansfield in 1760 in *Robinson v. Bland*[130]. Yet, it is plausible to suggest that Huber was cited in the English courts before this. He had been cited in Scottish cases with approval on comity from as early as *Goddart v. Sir John Swynton* in 1713, six years after the union with England.[131] That case then came before the House of Lords in 1715 on appeal, and though the report does not say so, it seems likely that Huber (and à Sande) were prominent in the written pleadings. Moreover, between 1736 and 1756 there were five reported cases from Scotland involving points of conflicts law before the House of Lords, and Mansfield (who became Lord Chief Justice in the latter year) appeared as counsel in every one of them.[132] Mansfield's predilection for Huber in this area is one of the themes of this chapter.

The authority of Huber also in the U.S. is impressive. It is not just that special prominence was given to him when in 1797 – ten years after the Constitution – Alexander James Dallas, the reporter of the U.S. Supreme Court, paid Huber the honour, never repeated for other scholars of the subject, of translating the relevant chapter, and inserting it into the reports of the Supreme Court.[133] The translation, he said, was made "for, and read in this cause; and I am persuaded, that its insertion here will be approved by the profession." Remarkably and significantly, Dallas's translation was reprinted in 1831 in the first (and only) volume of the *Carolina Law Journal*.[134] Even more to the point, as early as 1760 Lord Mansfield was citing Huber – and

---

[130]1 Bl. W. 234 at p. 257; 2 Burr. 1077.
[131]M. 4533 (1713).
[132]See Anton, 'Introduction to Law,' at pp. 538f.
[133]*Emory v. Greenough*, 3 Dallas 369 (U.S., 1797).
[134]Pp. 449ff.

Huber alone among European scholars – with approval on comity; and it is comity which is, indeed, our main concern.[135]

Strikingly, given the trauma of the Boston Tea Party of 1773, is a statement in 1775 in *Holman v. Johnson*.[136] Mansfield cited Huber and followed his proposition of law. He said, "I entirely agree with him." The relevant passage in Huber is from his *Praelectiones* 2.1.3.5, which reads:

> What we have said about wills also applies to *inter vivos* acts. Provided contracts are made in accordance with the law of the place in which they are entered into, they will be upheld everywhere, in court and out of court, even where, made in that way, they would not be valid. For example: in a certain place particular kinds of merchandise are prohibited. If they are sold there, the contract is void. But if the same merchandise is sold elsewhere where it is not forbidden, and an action is brought on that contract where the prohibition is in force, the purchaser will be condemned: because the contract there was valid from the beginning. But if the merchandise sold were to be delivered in another place where they were prohibited, the purchaser would not be condemned; because it would be contrary to the law and convenience of the state which prohibited the merchandise, in accordance with the limitation of the third axiom. On the other hand, if the merchandise were secretly sold in a place where they were prohibited, the sale would be void from the beginning, nor would it give rise to an action, in whatever place it was initiated, to compel delivery: for if, having got delivery, the buyer refused to pay the price he would be bound, not by the contract but by the fact of delivery insofar as he would be enriched by the loss of another.

At the root of *Holman v. Johnson* was the fact that in England the sale of tea

---

[135]*Robinson v. Bland*, 1 Bl. W. 234 at p. 257; 2 Burr. 1077
[136]1 Cowp. R. 341.

on which duty was not paid was prohibited. Mansfield quoted Huber's general case in his *Praelectiones* 2.1.3.5 and gave as a translation adapted to the particular case:

> In England, tea which has not paid duty, is prohibited; and if sold there the contract is null and void. But if sold and delivered at a place where it is not prohibited, as at Dunkirk, and an action is brought for the price of it in England, the buyer shall be condemned to pay the price; because the original contact was good and valid. . . . But if the goods were to be delivered in England, where they are prohibited; the contract is void, and the buyer shall not be liable in an action for the price, because it would be an inconvenience and prejudice to the State if such an action could be maintained.

And he held it be irrelevant that the point of the transaction was that the tea was to be smuggled into England. The case is decided very much in accordance with Huber's axiom 3 and its exception.

The last point must be stressed. Huber said with regard to his exception: "If the rulers of another people would thereby suffer a serious inconvenience they would not be bound to give effect to such acts and transactions."[137] This was, as we know, interpreted by him very strictly. And so it was by Mansfield. The rulers of England would suffer "a serious inconvenience," one might think, if duty was not paid on tea. And deliberate avoidance of paying duty on tea was at the root of the transaction. But for Huber, as also for Mansfield, the contract was valid. Nothing could better illustrate Mansfield's complete adoption of Huber on comity.[138] Again,

---

[137]Sec. 3

[138]See C.P. Rodgers, "Continental Literature and the Development of the Common Law by the King's Bench, c. 1750-1800," in *Comparative Studies in Continental and Anglo-American Legal History*, vol. 2: *Courts and the Development of Common Law,* ed. V. Piergiovanni (Berlin, 1987), pp. 161ff., at pp. 182ff.

Mansfield's reasoning is in conflict with the passages quoted from Story.[139]

Mansfield's prestige did, of course, play a role in promoting the authority of Huber. This emerges no more clearly than in the 1808 Pennsylvania case of *Denesbats v. Berquier*, a conflicts case on the law relevant to personal property under a will.[140] It was argued by the plaintiff that Huber, whose authority was against him, "is spoken of with little respect in 1. Collec. Jurid. 116."[141] Of course, then in contrast, for the defendant, Huber was the strongest authority – and Dallas's translation was cited – though Vattel was also brought in. Counsel for the defendant claimed, really talking about Huber, "The precise question has perhaps never been litigated in England; but the opinions of learned men whose writings are respected by all the world, and are received as authority on this subject as a branch of the laws of nations, are conclusive of the point."[142] One judge, Jasper Yeates, then expressly approved Emer de Vattel and Huber: "It has been said that Sir James Marriott has spoken lightly of the *praelections* of Huber; but it is well known that Lord Mansfield has cited his work with approbation."[143]

Huber's preeminence in conflicts of laws in Anglo-American jurisprudence was already established. In a learned English case of 1792, *Hog v. Lashley,* in which Johannes Voet, Vattel, Grotius, and Pufendorf were also cited, counsel argued: "This, which is fairly to be inferred from the opinions of Voet, is distinctly laid down by Huber, an eminent Dutch lawyer. . . . It might also be supposed, that this opinion was given upon this very case, and will decide it, as far at least as the opinions of foreign lawyers can have any weight."[144]

For the United States one might single out for special attention the

---

[139]But Story approved of the reasoning in this case and he cites Huber in connection with it (*Conflict*, pp. 208f.).

[140]1 Binn. 336.

[141]The reference is to *The Ship Columbus*, See Watson *Story*, pp. 90ff.

[142]P. 342.

[143]Presumably the reference to Marriott is in *The Ship Columbus*; the reference to Mansfield is in p. 348.

[144]6 Brown 577, at p. 596.

note of the reporter of *Andrews v. Herriot* in 1828.[145] On the issue of *lex loci* or *lex fori* he said: "This subject in itself deserves a treatise, but I can do nothing more here than to arrange and refer to the authorities, giving the substance of some of them. Huberus, in his title *De Conflictu Legum*, has broken the ground most effectually, I believe, of all the European writers; but even yet, it must be considered as but little more than broken for the use of the American student."[146] He also observed that Huber was much appreciated by Lord Mansfield and Mr. Hargrave (a counsel in *Somerset's* case). Indeed, in an earlier New York case of 1817, it was even claimed in argument that Huber had invented the distinction between the *lex fori* and the *lex loci contractus*.[147]

V

In 1834, when he was Dane Professor of Law at Harvard, Joseph Story published at Boston his *Commentaries on the Conflict of Laws*.[148] In the second chapter, entitled General Maxims of International Jurisprudence, he adverts "to a few general maxims or axioms, which constitute the basis, upon which all reasonings on the subject must necessarily rest."[149] After some discussion of these he comes to Huber:

> Huberus has laid down three axioms, which he deems sufficient to solve all the intricacies of the subject. The first is, that the laws of every empire have force only within the limits of its own government, and bind all, who are subject to it, but not beyond those limits. The

---

[145]4 Cowen 508 (New York)

[146]P. 510

[147]*Decouche v. Savetier*, 3 Johns. Ch. 190, at p. 202. See also the later English case of *Birtwhistle v. Vardell*, 7 CP & F. 895 (1839-40), at p. 915, per Lord Brougham.

[148]For Story's knowledge and use of Roman and civil law see M.H. Hoeflich, 'John Austin and Joseph Story: Two Nineteenth Century Perspectives on the Utility of the Civil Law for the Common Lawyer,' 29 *American Journal of Legal History* (1985), pp. 36ff., at pp. 56ff.

[149]P. 19.

second is, that all persons, who are found within the limits of a government, whether their residence is permanent or temporary, are to be deemed subjects thereof. The third is, that the rulers of every empire from comity admit, that the laws of every people in force within its own limits, ought to have the same force everywhere, so far as they do not prejudice the power or rights of other governments, or of their citizens. "From this," he adds, "it appears, that this matter is to be determined, not simply by the civil laws, but by the convenience and tacit consent of different people, for since the laws of one people cannot have any direct force among another people, so nothing could be more inconvenient in the commerce and general intercourse of nations, than that what is valid by the laws of one place should become without effect by the diversity of laws of another; and that this is the true reason of the last axiom, of which no one hitherto seems to have entertained any doubt."[150]

Story accepted the authority of Huber, against critics such as Hertius and, more particularly, against Livermore, soon to be noticed.[151] He claimed for Huber that he "has at least this satisfactory foundation for his most important rule, that he is mainly guided in it by the practice of nations; and he thus aimed, as Grotius had done before him, to avail himself of the practice of nations, as a solid proof of the acknowledged laws of nations."[152] He continued:

Some attempts have been made, but without success, to undervalue the authority of Huberus. It is certainly true, that he is not often spoken of, except by jurists belonging to the Dutch School.

---

[150] P. 30.

[151] See, e.g. *Conflict*, pp. 31ff.

[152] *Conflict*, p. 32. Actually, there is no sign in Huber that he is following the practice of nations. Huber does cite Grotius, *De iure belli ac pacis* (On the law of war and peace). 2.11.5, but not for anything relevant to Story's proposition.

Boulenois, however, has quoted his third and last axiom with manifest approbation. But it will require very little aid of authority to countenance his merits, if his maxims are well founded; and if they are not, no approbation, founded on foreign recognitions, can disguise their defects. It is not, however, a slight recommendation of his works, that hitherto he has possessed an undisputed preference on this subject over other continental jurists, as well in England as in America. Indeed, his two first maxims will in the present day scarcely be disputed by any one; and the last seems irresistibly to flow from the right and duty of every nation to protect its own subjects against injuries resulting from the unjust and prejudicial influence of foreign laws; and to refuse its aid to carry into effect any foreign laws, which are repugnant to its own interests and polity.[153]

Story's commendation is self-evident. And that Story followed Huber for the basic principles of conflict of laws is believed by all subsequent scholars.[154] But there can also be no doubt that Story misunderstood or misrepresented Huber. The best evidence comes from the end of the passage just quoted and his own very next paragraphs:

It is difficult to conceive, upon what ground a claim can be rested, to give to any municipal laws an extra-territorial effect, when those laws are prejudicial to the rights of other nations or their subjects. It would at once annihilate the sovereignty and equality of the nations, which should be called upon to recognize and enforce them; or compel them to desert their own proper interest and duty in favor of strangers, who were regardless of both. A claim, so naked of principle and authority to support it, is wholly inadmissible.

It has been thought by some jurists, that the term, "comity," is not sufficiently expressive of the obligation of nations to give effect to foreign laws, when they are not prejudicial to their own rights and

---

[153]*Conflict* p. 32.

[154]See the references in Watson, *Story*, p. 107 n.7.

interests. And it has been suggested, that the doctrine rests on a deeper foundation; that it is not so much a matter of comity, or courtesy, as of paramount moral duty. Now, assuming, that such a moral duty does exist, it is clearly one of imperfect obligation, like that of beneficence, humanity, and charity. Every nation must be the final judge for itself, not only of the nature and extent of the duty, but of the occasions, on which its exercise may be justly demanded. And, certainly, there can be no pretense to say, that any foreign nation has a right to require the full recognition and execution of its own laws in other territories, when those laws are deemed oppressive or injurious to the rights or interests of the inhabitants of the latter or where their moral character is questionable, or their provisions impolitic. Even in other cases, it is difficult to perceive a clear foundation in morals, or in natural law, for declaring, that any nation has a right (all others being equal in sovereignty) to insist, that its own possible laws shall be of superior obligation in a foreign realm to the domestic laws of the latter, of an equally positive character. What intrinsic right has one nation to declare, that no contract shall be binding, which is made by any of its subjects in a foreign country, unless they are twenty-five years of age, more than another nation, where the contract is made, to declare, that such contract shall be binding, if made by any persons of twenty-one years of age? One should suppose, that if there be any thing clearly within the scope of national sovereignty, it is the right to fix, what shall be the rule to govern contracts made within its own territories.

That a nation ought not to make its own jurisprudence an instrument of injustice for other nations, or their subjects, may be admitted. But in a vast variety of cases, which may be put, the rejection of the laws of a foreign nation may work less injustice, than the enforcement of them will remedy. And, here again, every nation must judge for itself, what is its true duty in the administration of justice. It is not to be taken for granted, that the rule of the foreign nation is right, and that its own is wrong.

The true foundation, on which the administration of international law must rest, is, that the rules, which are to govern, are those, which arise from mutual interest and utility, from a sense of the inconveniences, which would result from a contrary doctrine, and from a sort of moral necessity to do justice, in order that justice may be done to us in return.[155]

The passage is so clear in itself as almost to require no comment. But perhaps the beginning of the second paragraph should be specially noted. It has been claimed, Story says, that comity is not sufficiently suggestive of the obligation to give effect to the foreign law and that there is a paramount moral duty to do so. Here he is, of course, referring to Livermore. But if there is such a moral duty, then, urges Story, it is one of imperfect obligation, "like that of beneficence, humanity, and charity." Now the distinction between perfect obligation and imperfect obligation was well known, not only to philosophers, but also to continental jurists, such as Robert Pothier.[156] A perfect obligation is owed to a specific person or body, whether it can be enforced in court or not. The obligation remains perfect, even if it can be enforced only in the forum of conscience. An imperfect obligation is definitely an obligation, but one not due to any person or body specifically, except to God. There is an obligation to be charitable, but not to donate to any particular charity. The obligation is imperfect, and is not owed to any specific person or body. If, however, when in deep distress one was succoured by A, and subsequently A became indigent, one would have a perfect obligation toward A, even when this was not actionable in court. But for Story, if it were accepted that there was an obligation above the notion of comity to enforce foreign law, then it would be only an imperfect obligation, not owed to any person or body.

---

[155]*Conflict*, pp. 33f.

[156]See, e.g., *Traité des obligations,* preliminary article, §1. For a slightly different version of this notion of perfect and imperfect obligations, see, E. de Vattel, *Le droit des gens* (1708), préliminaires, § 17.

Nothing could better illustrate Story's distance from Huber: comity (lesser than this supposed imperfect moral obligation) does not for Story impose a duty to give effect to the law of any particular foreign nation or state. For Huber comity itself gives rise to a perfect obligation; and this is a binding obligation that should be enforced in court, not just in the forum of conscience.

Story says further:

> But of the nature, and extent, and utility of this recognition of foreign laws, respecting the state and condition of persons, every nation must judge for itself, and certainly is not bound to recognize them, when they would be prejudicial to its own interests. The very terms, in which the doctrine is commonly enunciated, carry along with them this necessary qualification and limitation of it. Mutual utility presupposes, that the interest of all nations is consulted, and not that of one only. Now, this demonstrates, that the doctrine owes its origin and authority to the voluntary adoption and consent of nations. It is, therefore, in the strictest sense a matter of the comity of nations, and not of absolute paramount obligation, superseding all discretion on the subject.[157]

Thus, Story has taken away from Huber the idea – the one idea that was particularly his – that a state is under an obligation to follow the law of another state where the act or transaction in question occurred, and he has replaced it with the notion that each state should be the judge for itself in deciding when and to what extent foreign law should be recognized, but should so recognize such foreign law from a sense of mutual interest and utility and should do it justice in order that justice be done in return. The first passage quoted from Story shows that, when he says "this matter is to be determined, not simply by the civil laws, but by the convenience and tacit consent of different people," he had misunderstood Huber on the nature of the

---

[157]*Conflict* pp. 35f.

obligation of comity. For Story, the obligation is not imposed by law ("by the civil laws," as he puts it); for Huber, the obligation is a legal obligation deriving from Roman law, not indeed the Roman *ius civile*, particular to the Romans, but the *ius gentium*, binding on all people.

VI

This – Story's – notion of comity is lacking in precision. Indeed, a modern scholar of the subject, Paul Finkelman, writes of "the unenforceable and unpredictable legal theories of the international law of comity."[158]

But Story was not the first to misstate Huber in the United States. Certainly in England and in common law U.S. the cases show that Huber was properly understood.[159] But a change came with the Louisiana case of *Saul v. His Creditors*[160] in 1827. Judge Porter, who did not mention Huber, took the notion of comity to mean that a state could apply its own law whenever the other law would be disadvantageous to people in the state.

The very restricted exceptions to Huber's axiom 3 were ignored. Samuel Livermore, an attorney on the losing side of the case published an angry book in 1828, *Dissertations on the Questions Which Arise from the Contrariety of the Positive Laws of Different States and Nations.* He condemns the notion of comity which he assumes to be that set out by Porter in *Saul*, and presents his own view on conflict of laws which is actually remarkably like that of Ulrich Huber. Chancellor Kent in the second edition of his *Commentaries on American Law* (1832) accepted fully the doctrine of comity as it was set out in *Saul*[161] And he was then followed by his friend Joseph Story who indeed dedicated his *Commentary* to him. Story, of course, thought he was following Huber.

The above applies, of course, only if the situation in issue did not fall foul of one of Huber's exceptions. But it did not in *Saul*. The situation did not "prejudice the power of another state" because that exception applied only

---

[158]*Imperfect Union*, p. 21.
[159]See Watson, *Story* pp. 50 ff.
[160]See Watson, *Story,* pp. 28ff.
[161]See Watson, *Story*, pp. 27f.

where a party had moved out of a territory deliberately to avoid that territory's jurisdiction over the issue in question. Nor did it "prejudice the rights of the citizens of another state" because that exception applied only where what was in issue was the legal priority of two or more transactions.

VII

At this point we should stop to ask the obvious question. What practical difference did it make that Story's theory of comity, supposedly based on Huber, was not that propounded by the Frisian? The most obvious answer is that on Huber's theory, the *Dred Scott* case could never have arisen, far less have come before the Supreme Court in 1856! And *Dred Scott v. Sandford* was perhaps the Supreme Court decision that attracted most public attention, debate, and uproar until *Roe v. Wade.*[162]

There were three main issues in the *Dred Scott* case. First, could free blacks be citizens and thus be entitled to sue in the Supreme Court? Second, did the congressional power to govern the territories extend to the exclusion of slaves from them? Third, did *Dred Scott's* residence in the free state of Illinois so affect his status that, as Chief Justice Roger Taney put it, "he was not again reduced to a state of slavery by being brought back to Missouri"?[163]

We are here concerned with the third issue. The basic facts were as follows: Scott had been born a slave in Virginia in 1795 and came to Missouri with his owner in 1827. The owner died in 1831 and Scott became the property of the owner's daughter, who sold him in Missouri to an army surgeon, John Emerson. Emerson was transferred by the War Department to Illinois in 1834, subsequently to the Wisconsin Territory, and he returned to Missouri in 1838. Scott went with him and returned to Missouri with him. At this state of our discussion we should ignore English and U.S. precedents and

---

[162]*Dred Scott*: 19 Howard 393 (U.S.). An important precursor was *Strader v. Graham,* 10 Howard 82 (U.S.), heard in 1851. The case appeared twice before the Kentucky Court of Chancery; *Graham v. Strader*, 5 Ben Monroe 173 (1846); *Strader v Graham*, 7 Ben Monroe 633 (1847): cf. D.E. Fehrenbacher, *The Dred Scott Case* (New York, 1978), pp. 260ff. *Roe v. Wade:* 410 U.S. 113 (1973). See, e.g. L.M. Friedman, *History of American Law*, 2d ed. (New York, 1985), p. 671.

consider the issue only from the perspective of Huber's theory.

Under the Constitution of Illinois, slaves who entered the State, with the owner's permission and established residence, automatically became free.[164] Dred Scott returned (or was returned) to Missouri. The issue then arises as to whether he was reenslaved. Under Huber's doctrine, the Missouri court would have to apply the law of Illinois to decide the question. And then, on this basis, Dred Scott would be free. Such in fact was the holding in a number of Missouri cases, before and also shortly after the publication of Story's *Commentaries*.[165] If Huber's doctrine had remained in place, the law would have been so settled to the effect that Dred Scott was free, that no such case could ever have come before the Supreme Court.

But could it be argued that on Huber's view as expressed at 2.1.3.8 the law of Missouri could be disallowed on the ground that it was "too revolting? Again the answer must be in the negative. Huber's axiom 3 rests on the *ius gentium*. Law valid in its own territory is valid everywhere according to his section 8 unless it is so revolting that it is contrary to the law of nations; which means, it is not accepted elsewhere. Slavery was certainly not such a case, since in the United States alone it was accepted in thirteen States. Despite the growing body of opinion in the Western world that slavery should be outlawed, there were still too many slave States in the

---

[163]P. 452.

[164]The Northwest Ordinance of 1787 was also relevant.

[165]*Winny v. Whitesides*, 1 Mo. 472 (1824), in which Huber in Dallas's translation is cited; *Merry v. Tiffin and Menard*, 1 Mo. 725 (1827); *Milly (a woman of color) v. Smith*, 2 Mo. 36 (1828); *Vincent (a man of color) v. Duncan*, 2 Mo. 24 (1830); *Ralph (a man of color) v. Duncan*, 3 Mo. 194 (1833); *Julia (a woman of color) v. McKinney*, 3 Mo. 270 (1833); *Nat (a man of color) v. Ruddle*, 3 Mo. 400 (1834); cf. *La Grange v. Chouteau*, 2 Mo. 19 (1828). From 1836, just after the publication of Story's *Conflict*, comes the leading Missouri precedent to the same effect: *Rachael (a woman of color) v. Walker*, 4 Mo. 350; see also *Wilson (a colored man) v. Melvin*, 4 Mo. 592 (1837). The Northwest Ordinance of 1787 was also a relevant factor in the decisions. For an early, very sophisticated, case recognizing the importance of foreign jurisdictions, but accepting the priority of an overriding statute, see *Mahoney v. Ashton*, 4 Harris and McHenry 295 (Md. 1799).

United States to make possible the argument that, following Huber on the subject of too revolting an example, slavery was contrary to the *ius gentium*. Moreover, the United States itself had recognized and protected the institution of slavery in the Constitution and Fugitive Slave laws. Huber, moreover, as we have seen, argues that the principles of conflict of laws had to be sought in Roman law, and according to Roman law, slavery was emphatically part of the *ius gentium*. Slavery might be, as Justinian's *Institutes* 1.3.2 states, contrary to nature, but as the same passage claims, it is part of the law of nations. Huber also stresses, it will be recalled, that it can scarcely ever be the case that law valid in one place will be contrary to the law of nations.[166]

VIII

It is widely accepted by historians that one of the consequences of the *Dred Scott* case and the public furor that followed it was that the Illinois senatorial race of 1858 between Stephen A. Douglas and Abraham Lincoln centered solely on slavery, above all on the issues of slavery raised by the decision in *Dred Scott* and the Kansas-Nebraska Act of 1854.[167] It is also widely accepted that Lecompton[168] and *Dred Scott* accounted for much of the Republican gain in the election, even though that party was not victorious. It has recently been authoritatively claimed: "For Lincoln the election was a victory in defeat. He had battled the famous Douglas on at least even terms, clarified the issues between Republicans and northern Democrats more sharply than ever, and emerged as a Republican spokesman of national

---

[166]One might also add that for Huber slavery was not contrary to natural law: *Praelectiones juris civilis* on the *Institutes* 1.3: see Alan Watson, *Slave Law in the Americas* (Athens, GA. 1989). P. 94.

[167]See, above all, H. Jaffa, *Crisis of the House Divided* (Chicago, 1959); also e.g. C.B. Swisher, *History of the Supreme Court of the United States*, vol. 5; *The Taney Period,* 1836-1864 (New York: 1974), pp. 631ff.; D.E. Fehrenbacher, *The Dred Scott Case* (New York, 1978), pp. 449ff.; J.M. McPherson, *Battle Cry of Freedom:* The Civil War Era (New York, 1988), pp. 177ff.

[168]The Kansas proslavery Constitution of 1858, printed in D.W. Wilder, *The Annals of Kansas* (Topeka, 1875), pp. 134ff.; see esp. pp. 140, 146.

stature."[169]

Of course, the *Dred Scott* case itself was a consequence of the crisis as well as a cause for increasing it. Douglas was the author of the popular-sovereignty doctrine in the Senate that had led to the Kansas-Nebraska Act, and he would have been challenged by the Republicans over slavery precisely on that score. But what matters here is that the *Dred Scott* case gave the issue a popular immediacy that it would not have otherwise had.

On this basis, it would seem very possible that, without *Dred Scott* (which was more immediate than the Kansas-Nebraska Act), Abraham Lincoln would not have been elected President in 1860.[170] The secession of the southern States would seem to be the direct consequence of Lincoln's election.[171] Secession was the immediate cause of the Civil War, whether one believes the war was fought over State sovereignty or for or against slavery. Probably one should not separate the issues.[172]

One need take only one element, Story's theory of comity, out of the causation equation and replace it with Huber's theory to realize that we do not know what the course of American history would otherwise have been. Tensions would, of course, have existed between slave States and free States, and they would have had to be resolved in some way at some time; almost certainly with violence. Let us even suppose that, given all the other circumstances, a civil war would have been inevitable. For the South to have won, it need only not have lost. Its victory did not require the conquest of the North. But the conquest of the South was a mammoth task, and some northern generals showed a corresponding reluctance to undertake it, especially in the early days of the war. Without Lincoln's astonishing fervour to preserve the union no matter the cost in American lives, the South might

---

[169]McPherson, *Battle Cry*, p. 188.

[170]On the election campaign see, e.g., McPherson, *Battle Cry,* pp. 223ff.

[171]See the history of events in McPherson, *Battle Cry,* pp. 234ff.

[172]On the issues see, e.g., W.M. Wiececk, *The Sources of Antislavery Constitutionalism in America*, 1760-1848 (Ithaca, 1977); H.M. Hyman and W.M. Wiececk, *Equal Justice under Law: Constitutional Development* (New York, 1982).

well have won. A northern triumph perhaps required the presidency of Abraham Lincoln.[173]

IX

The theme of this chapter, as of all gathered here, is the extreme importance of the need for authority in law, and how this need deforms law and its connection with society.

So far as we know, conflict of laws was unknown to the Romans: but our sources are defective. With the growth of medieval Italian city states, French customary law, and the seven provinces of the Dutch Republic, conflict of laws became a subject of engrossing interest. The tradition was to find Roman legal authority. None existed. But irrelevant texts were forced into service. Theories abounded. But we are concerned only with that of the Frisian Ulrich Huber. His theory was his own invention, not accepted to any extent in continental Europe. But Scottish legal education in the 17th century was pitiful, so Scottish students migrated to the equally Calvinist Dutch Republic. As students will, they bought the books recommended by their professors. Huber's published lecture notes became one of the commonest law books in late 17th century Scotland. His treatment of conflict of laws was prominent in his book and became the fundamental basis of Scottish case law. Societal input is not apparent. But Scots law on the subject was important, given the flight of English heiresses to Scotland for a marriage where the law was different.

---

[173]A further counterfactual hypothesis may be envisioned. Story, let us assume, followed Huber correctly and this approach to comity was generally accepted. Nonetheless, somehow the *Dred Scott* case came before the U.S. Supreme Court, and, let us assume, Taney accepted that Scott was a free man. Lincoln and Douglas had their debates (but in a different form), Lincoln was elected president, secession and the Civil War followed. The main outlines of history would be preserved, but the writing of history would be different. *Dred Scott* would not have been among the causes of the war. I pose this hypothesis because in discussion with historians I find a reluctance on their part to accept that the doctrine of comity, which was adopted by accident, could have a profound impact on outcomes in the society. Yet historians stress *Dred Scott* among the causes of the Civil War.

For local jurisdictional reasons, England had no system of conflict of laws. But because the House of Lords had jurisdiction and heard appeals from both Scotland and England, the issue of conflict of laws became important. Lord Mansfield was the main architect of the subject .

Mansfield was a Scot. He made his reputation at the English bar with these Scottish appeal cases. Huber then became the authority on the subject in England. Again, there is no sign of any societal influence.

From England Huber's theories migrated to the U.S. Again, there is no sign of any imput from the society. But authority was needed, and it was found in English law.

In 1834 Joseph Story wrote a celebrated commentary on conflict of laws based, as he supposed, on the theory of Huber. Again, authority was found to be needed; again there is no evidence of an input from the conditions of society.

But Story misstated Huber. The famous *Dred Scott* case was a consequence, and Dred Scott was declared a slave. On Huber's theory, the case could never have arisen because Dred Scott would have been obviously free.

The *Dred Scott* case played an important role in the election of Abraham Lincoln as U.S. President. Without Lincoln, the American civil war would have occurred at a different time and in different circumstances with possibly a different outcome.

Chapter 8

Lord Mansfield: Judicial Integrity or its Lack; *Somerset's Case*

Probably the most famous decision in English law is that of Lord Mansfield in *Somerset v. Stewart*[174] in 1772. It is very short and very dramatic. Indeed, it is so rhetorical that much of what is vital is overlooked. As it was meant to be.

Somerset was a slave of Stewart in Virginia and was brought to England by his owner. Somerset traveled extensively in the service of his master; to Bristol and Edinburgh, for example. But two years after they left America, Somerset left Stewart. Stewart was incensed by Somerset's ingratitude and advertised for his return. Somerset was captured by slave-catchers and on Stewart's orders was put on the *Ann and Mary* bound for Jamaica. Virtually a death sentence for Somerset. On request from Somerset's friends, Long Mansfield issued a writ of *habeas corpus* to the ship's captain, and Somerset was removed from the ship and placed under the authority of the Court of King's Bench. The case of *Somerset v. Stewart* was heard in the Court of King's Bench before Mansfield on 14 May, 1772.[175]

Mansfield opens his judgment: "The question is, if the owner has a right to detain the slave, for the sending him over to be sold in Jamaica." The issue as so expressed is a very narrow one. On the face of it, the issue is not whether Somerset is free or not. Even less is it a declaration that there can be no slaves in England. As Wise puts it: "*Somerset* was Mansfields' minimum antislavery position." His decision against Stewart was understood as meaning that in his view there could be no slaves in England. But in subsequent correspondence Mansfield wrote: "[N]othing more was then

---

[174] 1 *Lofft*, p. 499 ff. at p. 509

[175] See most recently, S.M. Wise, *Though the Heavens May Fall: The Landmark Trial that Led to the End of Human Slavery*, (Cambridge, Mass. 2005)

determined, than that there was no right in the master forcibly to take the slave and carry him abroad." Again he insisted that he had gone "no further than to determine the Master had no right to compel the slave to go into a foreign country."[176] What seems to follow from Mansfield's opening sentence in the case and these quotations is that he thought Somerset was a slave.

I believe that the correspondence -- obfuscating as it is -- gives his true position on the case. Mansfield is "hiding the ball." As he should! The opening statement of the action at the beginning of the case reads:

> On return to an habeas corpus, requiring Captain Knowles to shew cause for the seizure and detainure of the complainant Somerset, a negro – the case appeared to be this --

The second sentence of Mansfield's judgment reads: "In five or six cases of this nature, I have known it to be accommodated by agreement between the parties: on its first coming before me, I strongly recommended it here." Indeed he had. In this case also he ordered five separate hearings and he frequently urged Stewart to render the issue moot by freeing Somerset.[177]

But why? Mansfield continues: "But if the parties will have it decided, we must give our opinion. Compassion will not, on the one hand, nor inconvenience on the other, be to decide; but the law: in which the difficulty will be principally from the inconvenience on both sides." If Mansfield declared Somerset free, the main inconvenience would be the financial loss to the slave owners. "The setting 14,000 or 15,000 men at once free loose by a solemn opinion, is much disagreeable in the effect it threatens." The figures of the number of slaves in England may not be wholly

---

[176] For sources see Wise, *Though the Heavens May Fall*, p. 209.

[177] See, e.g. W.M. Wiececk, '*Somerset*: Lord Mansfield and the Legitimacy of Slavery in the Anglo-American World,' 42 *University of Chicago Law Review* (1976), pp. 86 ff. at p. 102.

accurate, but they are Mansfield's figures, and that is what matters here. He reckons that £50 per slave would not be a high price, and so the owners' loss would be above £700,000. And this, he adds, does not include further loss to the owners by actions for slave wages or on slight coercion by the master. He continues: "Mr. Stewart may end the question, by discharging or giving freedom to the negro." If not, as Mansfield had said just before: "If the parties will have judgment, fiat justitia, ruat coelum,"[178] let justice be done whatever the consequences.

Mansfield does not want to decide the case, he is most reluctant to do so, but he will have to unless Stewart acts; and the consequence will be – though that is not what he is deciding – that all the slaves in England will be free. As Mansfield said earlier in his brief judgment: "The difficulty of adopting the relation, without adopting it in all its consequences, is indeed extreme; and yet, many of those consequences are absolutely contrary to the municipal law of England."

Mansfield's arguments for his own position convinced people then and scholars since. He would have to find for Somerset on the narrow issue thus framed but the consequence, he knew, would be the end of slavery with resulting financial catastrophe for many in England. And, as has frequently been pointed out, many of those who would lose financially were Mansfield's friends.

The problem for Mansfield is not quite as it seems. His superb rhetorical skill – and it is outstanding – conceals what is going on in his head. Yet, paradoxically, at the same time it reveals that all is not as it seems. Mansfield regrets that the economic consequences of his decision will be ruinous. But he trumpets them: "Let the heavens fall!" The case, of course, attracted much public attention, but it is Mansfield who spells out consequences that might – I say only might – have otherwise largely passed unnoticed. And, as we have just seen, he later removes himself from the consequences. His decision, as he says, was a narrow one. Mansfield, in fact, was in a quandary.

---

[178] "Let justice be done, though the sky fall."

But then there is another immediate problem in Mansfield's judgment. He cites no legal precedent, statute or principle for his decision.[179] On what legal argument can the owner be barred from removing Somerset from England? I know of none. This absence of any known basis for Mansfield's judgment is remarkable and demands an explanation.

For Mansfield's own approach to law, Somerset is, and should remain, a slave. For this there can be no doubt. The issue, never stated but obvious, is one of conflict of laws. This was a subject on which Mansfield had wide experience.

The basic question in conflict of laws is what is to be done when a legal question involves the law of more than one state – in this issue Virginia and England -- and the answer depends on the law of which state is to be recognized. Roman law had nothing on the issue, but for subsequent scholars when an answer had to be found then, in the absence of legislation, it was to be found in Roman law. And Roman law, to be useful, had to be fabricated. One theory, generally disregarded but vital here, was that of the Frisian, Ulrich Huber (1634-1694).

The factual position in the case was that Somerset was acquired as a slave by Stewart in Virginia. Virginia was a slave state and by the law of Virginia Somerset was the property of Stewart. But Somerset was in England, the lawsuit was raised in England. Which law, that of Virginia or that of England, was to apply? There were many approaches to the issue, but which approach was to be chosen? Oddly, fascinatingly, the question was not raised in the case, not even by the attorneys. But it had to be there. And Mansfield had made his career very largely on this question of conflict of laws. And his position on the subject was one hundred percent plain. He knew the issue, and he knew the answer.

Mansfield had adopted the theory of Huber. Huber's views on conflict of laws were not well-known – they represented, after all, only one view among many on the subject. Naturally they were known in the Dutch

---

[179] In Scottish reported cases of the time judges seldom set out the reasons for their decision. But this is not a Scottish case.

Republic, but then so were many others.

But they were accepted in Scotland. Legal education was virtually non-existent in 17th century Scotland, English Universities were closed to the Scots so the ambitious flocked to the Universities, especially of Leiden and Utrecht, of the Dutch Republic, a fellow-Calvinist country. Naturally, students take home the books they bought for their classes, and Scotland – in contrast to England — has a fabulous number of 17th century Dutch law books. Among them is Ulrich Huber, *Praelectiones juris romani et hodierni* (Lectures on Roman and Contemporary Law) in three volumes, which was first published in 1689.[180]

England, for reasons relating to the jurisdiction of the various courts, had no theories of conflict of laws, but in Scotland it was a "hot topic." There were several issues but one appears more obviously than any others – it is still a hot subject – marriage.

In Scotland of the time a woman could marry at the age of twelve, and parental consent was not needed. In England the marriage age for a woman was sixteen and the father's consent was needed until she was twenty-one. The resulting legal scenario is obvious. A rogue makes love to a young English heiress, runs off with her to Scotland and they marry at the first possible point, the blacksmith's shop at Gretna Green. (No religious ceremony was needed for marriage in Scotland). Was the marriage valid in England?

It is now time to set out Huber's approach to conflict of laws which, of course, in the nature of things had to be based on Roman law. There was nothing else that could be thought appropriate. But there was nothing to the point in Roman law, so the Roman sources had to be manipulated, as they so often were in so many contexts by so many jurists. Huber's solution is, as was to be expected, brilliant.[181]

---

[180] See Alan Watson, *Joseph Story and the Comity of Errors* (Athens, GA., 1992), pp. 1 ff. and *passim*.

[181] What follows on Huber is an abridged and slightly modified version of my *Joseph Story and the Comity of Errors*, pp. 3-13.

Huber was very much a Frisian and during his teaching career – he was a judge for three years in Friesland – remained a faithful professor of the University of Franeker, twice rejecting professorships at Leiden. His reputation was enormous and extended well beyond Friesland, attracting many students from other places, especially from Holland, Germany, and Scotland. His main treatment of conflict of laws is in a few pages of the second volume of his *Praelectiones juris romani et hodierni* (Lectures on Roman and Contemporary Law); 2.1.3, which, like the first volume, was presumably written when he was a professor at Franeker. Volume 1 of the *Praelectiones* was devoted to Justinian's *Institutes*, and he turned to the *Digest* in volume 2. So his treatment of conflict of laws in 2.1.3. is right at the beginning of his commentary on the *Digest*. Very prominent and accessible. It would be well-known to students who make use of textbooks.

Huber claims in his section 1 that there is nothing on conflict of laws in Roman law, but that nonetheless the fundamental rules by which this system should be determined must be sought in Roman law, though the issue relates more to the *ius gentium* than the *ius civile*. These two terms had more than one meaning in the Roman legal sources, but Huber is using them in this context in the sense found in Justinian's *Institutes* 1.2.1. *Ius civile* is law which each people has established for itself and is particular to itself. *Ius gentium* is declared at this point in the *Institutes* to be law established by reason among all men and observed equally by all nations. In fact, for an institution to be characterized in this sense as belonging to the *ius gentium* it seems to be enough that it is accepted in Rome and other states. *Ius gentium* in this context is very much part of Roman private law. It should be stressed that Huber here is not using *ius gentium* in the sense of "law established between peoples," that is, international law. Though that was one meaning in Huber's own time, the term *ius gentium* was not so used in Roman law. Huber goes on: "In order to lay bare the subtlety of this particularly intricate question we will set out three axioms which being accepted, as undoubtedly in appears they must be, seem to make straightforward the way to the remaining issues." At the beginning of the first volume of his *Praelectiones*, Huber had explained what he meant by axioms. Budaeus, he declared, had not absurdly said that rules of law were handed down by *axiomata* or by *positiones*, terms that he said were taken from the usage of mathematicians. "For axioms are nothing other than statements that require no proof." Their correctness is thus self-evident.

Accordingly, conflict of laws as a system exists for Huber only if one accepts, as he feels and says we must, his three axioms (which significantly he prints in italics in section 2). As axioms they require no proof. The first two he expressly and reasonably – according to the approach of his time – bases on Roman law, on *Digest* 2.1.20 and *Digest* 48.22.7.10 respectively. The first axiom is, *"The laws of each sovereign authority have force within the boundaries of its state, and bind all subject to it, but not beyond."* The second reads: *"Those people are held to be subject to a sovereign authority who are found within its boundaries, whether they are there permanently or temporarily."* The third axiom is referred to no such authority but is Huber's own contribution. It must, for Huber, be treated like the other two as a binding rule, in order to have a systematic basis for conflict of laws. It reads: *The rulers of states so act from comity* (comiter) *that the rights of each people exercised within its own boundaries should retain their force everywhere, insofar as they do not prejudice the power or rights of another state or its citizens.*

The absence of stated authority for the third axiom does not mean that for Huber there was no authority for it. Indeed, he has already stated that the fundamental rules for the subject have to be sought in Roman law. The position for him is that by Roman law axiom 3 is part of the *ius gentium* – because it is accepted among all peoples – and so it need not be expressly set out in any particular jurisdiction – Rome, for instance – in order to be valid there. In fact, as we shall see, Huber goes on to claim in the same section of his work that no doubt has ever existed as to the validity of the third axiom. This is not true except in a perverted sense, since Huber seems to be the architect of the scope of the axiom. Though axiom 3 is not stated by Huber in a normative way, it is for him a rule of law and is normative. That is the very nature of an axiom.

This course of reasoning is entirely appropriate for Huber. He is attempting to set out the principles on which a particular branch of law, namely conflict of laws, is established. For this he does require authority. Roman law was looked to in all continental European countries to supply legal authority in general. Its status varied from jurisdiction to jurisdiction, though notoriously there had been a greater reception of Roman law in Friesland than elsewhere in the United Provinces. But Huber is not here concerned particularly with the law of Friesland. He is actually attempting to set out the principles which all states are bound to apply in conflicts situations. The only principles that could be binding, not in one territory alone but everywhere, had to be drawn from Roman law. There just was no other appropriate system. For the Romans, *ius gentium*, law that was accepted everywhere, was *ipso facto* part of Roman law. Therefore, if the validity of axiom 3 has not been doubted (as Huber claims), it is part of Roman private law; and it is as Roman law that it is authoritative. Huber is not out of line with other scholars in this approach. In exactly the same way, when Bartolus was earlier attempting to build up a system of conflicts law, he based (or purported to base) his propositions on Roman law.

Huber's axiom 3 was, of course, not found in Roman law. Nor, of course, were axioms 1 and 2 part of a system of conflicts law, but concerned issues of jurisdiction. Huber was well aware of this and did not hide the fact, since he had said in this very same paragraph that to use Roman law to build up new law unknown to the Romans was standard juristic practice. Indeed, in the absence of other authority, it was necessary if law was to grow. It is important to determine the precise meaning of axiom 3 for Huber. It is fully in accordance with this that he proceeds: "From this it is clear that this subject is to be sought not from the uncompounded civil law (*ius civile*) but from the benefits and tacit agreement of peoples: because just as the laws of one people cannot have direct force among another, so nothing could be more inconvenient than that what is valid by the law of a certain place be rendered invalid by a difference in law in another place. This is the reason for the third axiom on which hitherto there has been no doubt."

That Huber regarded the application of foreign law as binding becomes even clearer when we bring into account his earliest treatment of the subject in the second edition of his *De jure civitatis* (On the Law of the State), published in 1684 at 3.10.1: "Among the matters that different peoples reciprocally owe one another is properly included the observance of laws of other states in other realms. To which, even if they are not bound by agreement or the necessity of being subordinate, nonetheless, the rationale of common intercourse between peoples demands mutual indulgence in this area." By *ius gentium* in its other, non-Roman, sense of "international law" – and that sense is also relevant for this passage – one state is bound to observe the law of another, first if it is subject to it, second if there is an agreement to that effect. That was well established. In addition, for Huber, one state is equally bound to observe the law of another on a further rationale which is, namely, comity. Comity is binding.

It is the application of axiom 3 as a binding rule of law that gives private law transnational force. The laws of a state do not directly apply outside the territory of the state, but the rulers of other states must apply them *comiter* even when their own rules are different.

There is admirable skillful sleight-of-hand in all this. Huber's axiom 3 did not exist in Roman law, and this he admits even though he bases his whole system supposedly on Roman law. But then he claims his axiom 3 has never been doubted and is part of the *ius gentium*, accepted everywhere. In an upside-down sense, the first part of his claim is perfectly accurate. Axiom 3 had never been expressed before and hence was never doubted! Other Dutch jurists such as Paulus Voet had a very different notion of *comitas*. Huber provides no evidence that *comitas* in his sense was part of the *ius gentium*, accepted everywhere. And, of course, he cannot provide such evidence because his view is novel. But he is not required to provide any evidence because he sets out his legal proposition in an axiom, and by definition an axiom is a rule that requires no proof because it is self-evident.

Huber's aim was to provide conflict of laws with a legal basis.

Axiom 3 determines when and whether a state can raise an exception to recognizing that the law of another jurisdiction rules. It is not to be up to the individual court to be able to reject the foreign law because it finds it unpalatable or prefers its own rules.

Huber does not allow for free discretion in applying foreign law. At the beginning of the next section, 3, he writes, again with italics:

> This proposition flows from the above: *All transactions and acts both in court and extrajudicial, whether in contemplation of death or inter vivos, properly executed according to the law of a particular place are valid even where a different law prevails, and where if they were performed as they were performed they would have been invalid.*

And, on the other hand, transactions and acts executed in a particular place contrary to the laws of that place, since they are invalid from the beginning, cannot be valid anywhere.

Foreign law is binding. Of course, since it is binding only indirectly, whereas the law of the local jurisdiction is binding directly, foreign law would not prevail where it was expressly excluded by the local law, say by statute. This is not stated by Huber, but it is implicit in the distinction he makes between axioms 1 and 2 on the one hand, and axiom 3 on the other.

This necessary recognition of foreign law is, of course, subject to the exception to axiom 3: transactions and acts elsewhere are recognized "insofar as they do not prejudice the power or rights of another state or its citizens." In keeping with the brevity of axioms, the practical meaning of the exception requires elucidation. Huber glosses it a little further on in section 3: "But it is subject to this exception: if the rulers of another people would thereby suffer a serious inconvenience they would not be bound to give effect to such acts and transactions, according to the limitation of the third axiom." The point deserves to be explained by examples. The examples he gives here and in another work, *Heedensdaegse Rechtsgeleertheyt* (Contemporary Jurisprudence, 1686), best clarify Huber's meaning. The situations mentioned as giving rise to the exception can be fitted into a very small number of distinct classes.

The basic rule for Huber is that the validity and rules of a contract depend upon the place where the contract was made. Likewise, if a marriage is lawful in the state where it was contracted and celebrated, it will be valid everywhere (subject to any exception in axiom 3). But this is dependent, as Huber notes in section 10, on a fiction of Roman law that is set out in *Digest* 44.7.21: "Everyone is considered to have contracted in that place in which he is bound to perform." Hence, for marriage, for instance, the place of a marriage contract is not where the marriage contract was entered into, but where the parties intend to conduct the marriage, which will be the normal residence of the parties. This case, of course, has an important effect on community of property and other property relations of the spouses, but the effect does not follow from the exception to axiom 3.

A first category within the exception is where persons subject to a jurisdiction take themselves out of the territory deliberately in order to avoid the jurisdiction. Most examples would amount to a *fraus legis*. The following instances occur in Huber. Where a Frisian, who is forbidden by law to marry his niece, goes with a niece deliberately to Brabant and marries her, the marriage will not be recognized in Friesland. (On the other hand, when someone from Brabant marries there within the prohibited degrees under a papal dispensation, and the spouses migrate to Friesland, the marriage that was valid in Brabant remains valid). Where young persons under guardianship in West Friesland go to East Friesland to marry, where consent of guardians is not required, and then immediately return to West Friesland, the marriage is void as a subversion of the law. Again, if goods are sold in one place for delivery in another where they are prohibited, the buyer is not bound in the latter place because of the exception.

A second category for the exception is also of limited extent. If two or more contracts are made in different states and the rights of creditors would vary in different states according to the priority or value accorded to each contract, the sovereign need not, and indeed cannot, extend the law of the foreign territory to the prejudice of his own citizens. For instance, some states give validity to the pledge of property without delivery for a valid hypothec. If state A does not demand delivery, and a pledge is made there without delivery, and the issue comes somehow before the court of state B, state B in the ordinary case would recognize the hypothec as valid because it was valid in state A. But if the same hypothec is made in state A, a second hypothec with delivery is made in state B to a citizen of B, and the issue comes before the court of B, the court must decide the issue of priority according to its own law, because in the event of a straight conflict of rights, a court cannot extend the law of a foreign state to the detriment of its citizens. In such a case of conflict it is more reasonable, says Huber, to follow one's own law than a foreign law.

The limited scope of this category should be noticed. It exists only when there are at least two contracts, contracted in different territories with different laws, where these contracts have to be pitted against one another, and where one party is a citizen of the state where the case is heard. It should be stressed that even in this case Huber is not deciding against the validity of the contract made abroad. It is valid, but its ranking is postponed behind the contract made in the home territory. Huber gives another example. A marriage contract in Holland contains the private bargain, valid in Holland, that the wife will not be liable for debts subsequently contracted by the husband alone. Such an agreement if made in Friesland would be effective against subsequent creditors of the husband only if it was made public or if the creditors could be expected to have knowledge of it. If the husband subsequently contracted a debt in Friesland, the wife was sued for one-half of the debt, and she pled her marriage contract as a defence, the defence was disallowed in Friesland. By the same token, if the wife had been sued in Holland, the defence would have prevailed. This category for the exception exists only where they are contracts with different bases – though this time the contracts are at one remove from the basic act, the private bargain in the marriage contract – and superior ranking has to be granted to one.

A final category – which, as we shall see, is in theory not within the exception – has special significance within the context of this work. Not its sole significance for us is that Huber graces it with only a single example, in section 8 "Marriage also belongs to these rules. If it is lawful in the place where it was contracted and celebrated, it is valid and effective everywhere, subject to this exception, that is does not prejudice others; to which one should add, unless it is too revolting an example. For instance, if a marriage in the second degree, incestuous according to the law of nations, happened to be allowed anywhere. This could scarcely ever be the case." We have already considered what was meant by "prejudice to others." Now we must consider the nonrecognition of foreign law on the ground that it is "too revolting". To judge from Huber's words in the example, this is permitted only when the foreign law is contrary to the law of nations. Moreover, according to Huber, this will scarcely ever be the case. Accordingly, only very rarely will a state be legally entitled to fail to give recognition to another's law on the basis that it is too revolting or immoral, and then the rejection will be on the basis that the rule is contrary to the law of nations. Since axiom 3 is part of the law of nations, and binding on that account, an act or transaction valid where it is made, but void by the *ius gentium*, will by the same *ius gentium* be given no recognition in another jurisdiction when it would have been void if made there. But it must be emphasized that the invalidity does not derive from the exception to axiom 3 but from the very legal basis of that axiom. Slavery, it may be observed, is not contrary to the *ius gentium* in Huber's sense here since it was so widely accepted in many jurisdictions.

We must stress the very limited extent of the true exceptions to Huber's axiom 3. The axiom is a rule of law subject to exceptions. But in the axiom itself, the exceptions are stated so widely that they could swallow up the rule. This cannot be Huber's intention because he is adamant that an axiom contains a binding rule. He is also adamant that the scope of his exceptions is to be explained by the examples. Perhaps we should detect in Huber's broadness of language a sensitivity that, as we shall see, his view of the indirect binding nature of the rule of recognition of foreign law was stricter than that of his contemporaries. What should be stressed above all from Huber's examples is that, in comity, courts have no discretion in deciding whether to recognize foreign law or not: that issue is determined by the facts of the case. That the above mentioned categories are the only ones for the exception best appears in the context of the fuller treatment in Huber's *Heedendaegse Rechtsgeleertheyt* 1.3.

To revert now to the marriage in Scotland of an English woman under twenty-one who did not have the consent of her father. The marriage would be valid even in England unless there was *fraus legis* in Huber's sense, i.e. when the couple intended to return and live in England.

Huber's was the position taken by Mansfield. The first reference to Huber in the English reports is by Lord Mansfield in 1750 in *Robinson v. Bland*. Yet it is plausible to suggest that Huber was cited in the English courts before this. He had been cited in Scottish cases with approval on comity from as early as *Goddart v. Sir John Swynton* in 1713, six years after the union with England. That case then came before the House of Lords in 1715 on appeal, and though the report does not say so, it seems likely that Huber (and à Sande) were prominent in the written pleadings. Moreover, between 1736 and 1756 there were five reported cases from Scotland involving points of conflicts law before the House of Lords, and Mansfield (who became lord chief justice in the latter years) appeared as counsel in every one of them.[182] Mansfield's predilection for Huber in this area is one of the themes of this paper.

Somerset's case, as was emphasized by Mansfield, was decided on the narrow issue of the writ of *habeas corpus*, but in his judgment he makes it clear that he believes a consequence will be that all slaves in England will become free, and that this is something he wants to avoid.

Mansfield's dilemma is extreme. If the issue in front of him had been whether Somerset was free or a slave, then he would have had to decide,

---

[182] See A.E. Anton, "The Introduction into English Practice of Continental Theories on the Conflict of Laws," 5 *International and Comparative Law Quarterly* (1956), pp. 534ff., at pp. 538f.

following Huber, that Somerset was a slave. The law to be applied, Mansfield following Huber, was that of Virginia. This emerges, in startling clarity, in an English case, *Holman v. Johnson*,[183] three years later, in 1775. Mansfield's approach in that case is all the more striking since it is given only very shortly after the Boston Tea Party of 1773. Mansfield cited Huber and followed his proposition of law. He said, "I entirely agree with him." The relevant passage in Huber is from his *Praelectiones* 2.1.3.5, which reads:

> What we have said about wills also applies to *inter vivos* acts. Provided contracts are made in accordance with the law of the place in which they are entered into, they will be upheld everywhere, in court and out of court, even where, made in that way, they would not be valid. For example: in a certain place particular kinds of merchandise are prohibited. If they are sold there, the contract is void. But if the same merchandise is sold elsewhere where it is not forbidden, and an action is brought on that contract where the prohibition is in force, the purchaser will be condemned; because it would be contrary to the law and convenience of the state which prohibited the merchandise, in accordance with the limitation of the third axiom. On the other hand, if the merchandise were secretly sold in a place where they were prohibited, the sale would be void from the beginning, nor would it give rise to an action, in whatever place it was initiated, to compel delivery: for if, having got delivery, the buyer refused to pay the price he would be bound, not by the contract but by the fact of delivery insofar as he would be enriched by the loss of another.

At the root of *Holman v. Johnson* was the fact that in England the sale of tea on which duty was not paid was prohibited. Mansfield quote Huber's general case in his *Praelectiones* 2.1.3.5 and gave as a translation adopted to the particular case:

---

[183] 1 Cowp. R. 341

> In England, tea, which has not paid duty, is prohibited; and if sold there the contract is null and void. But if sold and delivered at a place where it is not prohibited, as at Dunkirk, and an action is brought for the price of it in England, the buyer shall be condemned to pay the price; because the original contract was good and valid... .But if the goods were to be delivered in England, where they are prohibited; the contract is void, and the buyer shall not be liable in an action for the price, because it would be an inconvenience and prejudice to the State if such an action could be maintained.

And he held it to be irrelevant that the point of the transaction was that the tea was to be smuggled into England. The case is decided very much in accordance with Huber's axiom 3 and its exception.

This last point must be stressed. Huber said with regard to his exception: "If the rulers of another people would thereby suffer a serious inconvenience they would not be bound to give effect to such acts and transactions." This was, as we know, interpreted by him very strictly. And so it was by Mansfield. The rulers of England would suffer "a serious inconvenience," one might think, if duty was not paid on tea. And deliberate avoidance of paying duty on tea was at the root of the transaction. But for Huber, as for Mansfield, the contract was valid. Nothing could better illustrate Mansfield's complete adoption of Huber on comity. Thus, if Somerset's case had come before the court on the issue of whether Somerset was a slave, Mansfield, to be true to himself, would have to have held that Somerset was a slave.

A final issue must be mentioned. Neither the attorney speaking for the plaintiff nor that for the defence said anything about conflict of laws. Were they aware of this dimension? If the answer is Yes, then we must ask why they were silent. If the answer is No, then we must question further why Mansfield said nothing. Mansfield's strategy was so successful that even the latest commentator on the case, Steven M. Wise, fails to notice Mansfield's dilemma, and his deliberate – it must be -- avoidance of the central question of conflict of laws.

Chapter 9

Foreign Legal Thinking

William Ewald asks the almost fundamental question for legal history and comparative law: "What was it like to try a rat?"[184] His claim is that an understanding of a foreign legal system cannot be obtained simply by heaping up nuggets of information. I agree. The crucial point for him is that one needs to know how the lawyers of that system think. Again, I agree. This leads him to his question. He shows that sophisticated lawyers and thinkers were involved in trials of animals. What did they think they were about? But Ewald seems not to answer his own question. For his purposes he has no need to. Actually, the question so phrased by Ewald is not quite right. The fundamental question should be: "What was it like to try *the rats*?" The difference in the questions is all-important. Even an exceptionally skilled comparatist can make mistakes. And Ewald's apparently minor error is crucial to this chapter, and to the overreaching issue in this book. There is a real difficulty for the formation of law, for instance a new civil code or a *ius commune* for Europe. The problem is not so much differences in technical legal rules, but in attitudes of lawyers. The thought processes inspired in French lawyers by the *code civil* are very different from those aroused in Germans by the *Bürgerliches Gesetzbuch*. And there is the incomprehensible attitude of English lawyers. And there is Scots law with its mixture of European civil law and English common law, and its own indigenous elements. I have chosen in this chapter to highlight the issue by looking at extreme examples for incomprehension of a foreign system. But the problem is similar for modern Europe, though disguised by apparent likenesses. Indeed, the more alike the systems seem, the greater are the problems caused by misconceptions.

---

[184]'Comparative Jurisprudence (1): What Was It Like to Try a Rat?' 143 *U. Pennsylvania Law Review* (1995), pp. 1889ff.

I

It often happens that persons with a law job to do are in a quandary. There is nothing satisfactory that they can do. Often judges do not know what to decide, but they are nowhere permitted to render the judgment "I do not know." At times law allows for concessions in such and similar dilemmas. (And I use the abstraction, "law allows" deliberately to avoid giving precision to the process). It permits use to be made of what I want to call "The Last Best Chance." I use the term because I have found none better. What we have is a dodge but the dodge cannot be admitted—that would destroy the gravity of the law. The court cannot say "To resolve our perplexity, we leave everything to chance. Let us throw the dice." Rather, the dodge, the figurative throwing of the dice, is imbued with particular solemnity. Legal process intervenes when in reality it should probably keep out.

I am, I must insist, not attributing bad faith to the inventors of The Last Best Chance. They are doing the best they can in face of a serious problem. What really reveals a procedure to us as The Last Best Chance is precisely that it is not used always where an outsider might expect it, but precisely where a dodge is needed. It is given only limited scope. Legal historians and comparative lawyers must be on the lookout for The Last Best Chance because it will always appear in its society with enhanced importance, yet its precise significance is not that which appears.

The Last Best Chance, as I conceive it, is a sub-category of what might be called 'The Second Best' in the law. The special character of The Last Best Chance is that the fact that it is a last resort is concealed, and may not even be fully apparent to those involved. To show what I mean I select an example of The Second Best that is not The Last Best Chance, from Deuteronomy 21.1ff.

> If, in the land that the Lord your God is giving you to possess, a body is found lying in open country, and it is not known who struck the person down, 2. then your elders and your judges shall come out to measure the distances to the towns that are near the body. 3. The

elders of the town nearest the body shall take a heifer that has never been worked, one that has not pulled in the yoke; 4. the elders of that town shall bring the heifer down to a wadi with running water, which is neither plowed now sown, and shall break the heifer's neck there in the wadi. 5. Then the priests, the sons of Levi, shall come forward, for the Lord your God has chosen them to minister to Him and to pronounce blessings in the name of the Lord, and by their decision all cases of dispute and assault shall be settled.

We need not follow up the rest of the ritual. The essential element that initiates the procedure is that a man is slain in open country and the murderer cannot be found. Something must be done. A ritual that is both religious and legal is found to expiate guilt. But that the procedure is The Second Best—it is used because the murderer is not known—is not concealed, and is obvious on its face.[185]

II

A first illustration of The Last Best Chance may be taken from the formal or ritual curse, with legal and religious backing. The curse of this type had a long history but it is mainly used in very limited circumstances, namely (1) where the wrongdoer cannot be established; (2) where the wrongdoer is beyond reach either because he cannot be found or is too powerful; (3) less often, where it cannot be proved that the suspected crime actually has occurred. An illuminating example of this last occurs in the Bible, at Numbers 5.11f. In certain circumstances when a husband accused his wife of adultery, an oath would be taken from her, the priest would utter a curse upon her, and if she was unfaithful she would suffer, perhaps have a miscarriage. When was the curse to be used? God was quite specific.

---

[185]The Second Best is not confined to law. Thus, when Odysseus had not returned to Ithaca many years after the Trojan War the goddess Athene advised his son Telemachus that he should search and if he hear that Odysseus is dead he should heap up a mound and pray funeral rites over it: Homer *Odyssey* 1.289ff.

The Lord spoke to Moses, saying: 12. Speak to the Israelites and say to them: If any man's wife goes astray and is unfaithful to him, 13. if a man has had intercourse with her but it is hidden from her husband, so that she is undetected though she has defiled herself, and there is no witness against her since she was not caught in the act; 14. if a spirit of jealousy comes on him, and he is jealous of his wife who had defiled herself; or if a spirit of jealousy comes on him, and he is jealous of his wife, though she has not defiled herself; 15. then the man shall bring his wife to the priest. And he shall bring the offering required for her, one-tenth of an ephah of barley flour. He shall pour no oil on it and put no frankincense on it, for it is a grain offering of jealousy, a grain offering of remembrance, bringing iniquity to remembrance.

16. Then the priest shall bring her near, and set her before the Lord; 17. the priest shall take holy water in an earthen vessel, and take some of the dust that is on the floor of the tabernacle and put it into the water. 18. The priest shall set the woman before the Lord, dishevel the woman's hair, and place in her hands the grain offering of remembrance, which is the grain offering of jealousy. In his own hand the priest shall have the water of bitterness that brings the curse. 19. Then the priest shall make her take an oath, saying, ☐If no man has lain with you, if you have not turned aside to uncleanness while under your husband's authority, be immune to this water of bitterness the curse. 20. But if you have gone astray while under your husband's authority, if you have defiled yourself and some man other than your husband has had intercourse with you," 21.— let the priest make the woman take the oath of the curse and say to the woman— "the Lord make you an execration and an oath among your people, when the Lord makes your uterus drop, your womb discharge; 22. now may this water that brings the curse enter your bowels and make your womb discharge, your uterus drop!" And the woman shall say,

"Amen. Amen."[186]

The curse was to be used only when there was no legally sufficient proof of the adultery. Numbers 5.29 reads: "This is the law in cases of jealousy, when a wife, while under her husband's authority, goes astray and defiles herself, or when a spirit of jealousy comes on a man and he is jealous of his wife." What we do not find in the history of formal curses in Biblical law is their application to the accused after guilt has been established. The curses in Deuteronomy 27.15ff. are not contrary to this position. What is in issue there is not the ritual cursing of a wrongdoer whose guilt has been proved. The curses are formulated as terms of a treaty. Thus, the opening verse:

> "Cursed be anyone who makes an idol or casts an image, anything abhorrent to the Lord, the work of an artisan, and sets it up in secret." All the people shall respond, saying, "Amen!"[187]

In this verse, indeed, the curse is invoked against anyone who in the future casts an idol and sets it up "in secret."[188] The curse applies to anyone who so acts, whether apprehended or not. Moreover, the cursing of such persons is generalized: so far as our information goes there was no formal curse intoned

---

[186]This is the translation of *The New Revised Standard Version* which I regard as inaccurate for vv. 21, 22, but that issue need not detain us here. For the procedure as it came to be established see Mishnah Sotah. For modern scholarship see Hagith Sivan, 'Revealing the Concealed: Rabbinic and Roman Legal Perspectives on Detecting Adultery,' 116 *Zeitschrift der Savigny Stiftung (romanistische Abteilung)* (1999), pp. 112ff.

[187]The verses have long been seen as a composite, but David Daube rightly sees them as a unity, concerning offences □as may easily evade earthly justice:" 'Some Forms of the Old Testament Legislation,' in *Oxford Society of Historical Theology: Abstract of Proceedings for the Academic Year 1944-45*, pp. 36ff. at p. 39. For present purposes it is interesting that Joseph Blenkinsopp, for example, holds that the provisions are not strictly curses: *The New Jerome Biblical Commentary* (Englewood Cliffs, 1990) edit. Raymond E. Brown, *et al.* p. 106.

[188]See already Daube, 'Forms,' p. 39.

over such an individual. No ritual cursing takes place after conviction. The passage seems always to have been so understood. There is nothing in the Mishnah to show that cursing after conviction was ever part of the penalty.

But why was a curse not so applied? It surely seems appropriate that a heinous wrongdoer be condemned by God as well as man. And it would surely add to the solemnity of the punishment. The ancient Israelites had some fancy penalties.[189] Why ever was a convicted wrongdoer not also cursed to increase the horror of the occasion?

The explanation cannot simply be that the curse was not used by the ancient Israelites as a punishment because it was not needed after guilt was established. Unnecessary punishments have always been fashionable. Thus, for the punishment of a parricide in ancient Rome it was not obviously necessary that he was, after a beating, put into a leather sack along with snakes and other animals—ancient authors name variously a cock, dog, ass—and put on a wagon drawn by black oxen to the Tiber, and thrown in.[190] A person convicted in the contemporary U.S.A. of multiple murders may well be sentenced to a term of imprisonment far longer than he can possibly live.[191] The excess penalty demonstrates the people's horror of the crime, if nothing more. But the ancient Israelites did not add cursing to the penalty for even the most abominable wrong. The legal curse is used when the guilty party is beyond the reach of the law. Not otherwise. It is resorted to only as The Last Best Chance. It is the best that can be done in the circumstances when, it is felt, something must be done.

Likewise, one cannot simply say that the use of the curse was restricted because of a reluctance to implore a deity for active help. In other contexts, prayer for example, such active help was and is continually implored. Rather, the use of formal cursing of an accused person in a legal

---

[189]See, e.g., Mishnah Sanhedrin.

[190]See, e.g., Theodor Mommsen, *Römisches Strafrecht* (Leipzig, 1899), p. 922.

[191]This again may be seen as an example of The Second Best that is not The Last Best Chance.

setting is restricted to cases of The Last Best Chance because there is a feeling that it will not be wholly effective. I am not suggesting bad faith. A devout person may pray every day, firmly believing in the efficacy of prayer, but with no expectation that every prayer will be answered. The feeling is not that the deity does not hear. Rather, the notion is that the deity may not want to act. He does not always intervene.[192] So the legal cursing is reserved for situations where no other solution would possibly help, but some action is felt to be required. What an outsider must not do when investigating an alien society is simply to say "Formal cursing is accepted and approved by the society. That means that that group has faith in divine intervention every time." I do not at all agree with Gerhard von Rad that "Ancient people considered such a curse [i.e., coming from God] to be a real destructive power:"[193]

III

My second example of The Last Best Chance is the oath. Formal, legalized use of the oath has more applications than ritualized cursing had among the Israelites, but we find it above all in various societies in certain typical areas: (1) treaties with foreign powers; (2) oaths of office, such as those administered to Presidents or judges; (3) oaths of jurors or witnesses; (4) oaths of personal allegiance by military officers to dictators. What these cases have in common is that an action for breach of contract—and an oath in some senses is contractual though unilateral—would not be a satisfactory remedy. In Rome, part of a treaty was couched in proper legal form using the wording of a particular contract (*sponsio*) that may have originally involved an oath, but as the jurist Gaius writing around 160 A.D. noted, breach of the treaty would not give rise to a contractual remedy, but to the laws of war.[194]

---

[192] I have a friend and colleague who—I am truly grateful—prays for my salvation every day, but I doubt whether she expects a happy outcome.

[193] *Deuteronomy* (Philadelphia, 1966), p. 167.

[194] *G.* 3.94.

An oath is exacted from a President, not because it will make him *semper fidelis*, but because law generally has no sanction sufficiently powerful to be satisfactory. And a dictator, deserted by his troops, will not find an adequate remedy in the courts: like Hitler he takes a personal oath of loyalty from his officers.

But the oath has still wider applications, perhaps relating to past deeds or to a state of fact, and these oaths are even more revealing for The Last Best Chance. For example, in the whole of Roman private law there was only one situation, apart from procedures in court, where an oath was accorded legal recognition. That was the so-called *iusiurandum liberti* (oath of a freedman).

The background was this. When a Roman changed status (*capitis deminutio*), existing obligations such as those under contract were extinguished.[195] Means were eventually devised to avoid this. But there was one particularly difficult case. A master might wish to free a slave, yet want the slave to continue to provide him with some services after manumission. The master could not take a legally binding promise before manumission—there could be no contract between owner and slave. But the slave, once freed, might simply refuse to give the binding promise by the contract of *stipulatio*. The solution was for the slave to give an oath before he was freed, and this put him under a religious obligation to renew the promise usually by another oath though a *stipulatio* was possible. This second oath was then a formal verbal civil law contract, though the oath made while a slave did not constitute a legal obligation.[196] Thus, the freedman's oath creates a private law obligation, and that is its purpose. It is very secular. It is used to circumvent a private law difficulty. It must be remembered that in no other circumstances does an oath create a Roman contract or legally contribute to one. *Iusiurandum liberti* is a good example of The Last Best Chance. As often, The Last Best Chance involves illogicality that is simply ignored. How

---

[195]See, e.g., Buckland, *Textbook*, pp. 134ff.; Kaser, *Privatrecht*, 1, pp. 271f.

[196]See, e.g., *D.* 40.12.44pr.; 46.4.13pr.; cf. Buckland, *Textbook*, p. 458; J.A.C. Thomas, *Textbook of Roman Law* (Amsterdam, 1976), p. 264.

can a sacred oath, at a time when oaths have no secular legal effect, give rise to a secular legal obligation to make a secular contract?[197]

The oath also appears prominently in the archaic form of Roman procedure called *legis actio*, and was the basis of the *legis actio sacramento*, 'action of the law by oath,' which is considered the oldest Roman action. This action could be brought either *in rem* or *in personam*. It will be enough for us to examine the former. Each party to the action claimed the object in dispute and stated that he had claimed properly. One then challenged the other to an oath with a penalty on the basis that he had claimed wrongly, and the other responded in kind. The penalty was fifty or five hundred *asses* depending on the value of the property claimed, and the penalty was deposited with an official. The next stage of the action proceeded on the issue of the veracity of the oaths, and the loser forfeited the penalty.[198] Of course, the main point—the sole point—of the action, which apparently has now slipped into the background, was the determination of ownership of the thing. But whose oath was true could be determined only on the basis of who had secular legal title. Gaius reports: "Procedure by oath was general. One proceeded by oath for those matters for which otherwise no action was provided by statute."[199] Thus is revealed that once again the oath is used as The Last Best Chance. Where no action is provided, but where there ought to be one, the secular issue can be litigated on the basis of the oath. Again, the secular content of the institution has to be stressed. Magic or intervention of a god is not involved. The oath simply enables the trial to continue, with an examination of the facts by men. The problem at issue, ownership, is a secular one. There is no divine sanction for breach of the oath, simply the secular loss of the secular penalty.

But more seems to be going on. There is again an element of illogicality. Except for the exceptional case of *iusiurandum liberti*, an oath

[197]See, e.g., Alan Watson, *The State, Law and Religion: Pagan Rome* (Athens, Ga., 1992), pp. 44ff.

[198]*G.* 4.10-20.

[199]*G.* 4.13.

cannot create a legal obligation, hence cannot validate the initiation of legal proceedings. How then can legal proceedings be begun in general, without any apparent validation, and then have their progress validated by an oath?

In a second use of the oath in procedure, the *iusiurandum in litem*, 'the oath in the law suit,' the oath was used in more limited circumstances. The award, *condemnatio*, in a Roman private law action was always in money. But at times what the plaintiff really wanted, and it was reasonable for him to have, was the object of the dispute. Then, but only for certain types of action, the instructions to the judge might contain the *clausula arbitraria*, authorization to order restitution to his satisfaction, failing which there would be the *condemnatio* in money. Restitution could not be directly enforced. But if it failed to occur, the judge could condemn either in his own estimation or he could proffer the oath, the *iusiurandum in litem*, to the plaintiff to state the value of the object, and this valuation would then be the judge's monetary award. The jurist Paul writes: 'It is not readily allowed to enquire into the perjury of one who swears the *iusiurandum in litem* under the necessity of law.'[200] It remains to add that the *iusiurandum in litem* could only be taken when the defendant was acting maliciously or contumaciously.[201] We can thus exclude the possibility that the oath was used as a shortcut to find the true valuation. It is intended to force the defendant to return the thing, or suffer for it.

Iusiurandum in litem is a fine example of The Last Best Chance. Its purpose is entirely secular, and it is used to achieve indirectly what cannot be achieved directly.[202] But it may easily be misunderstood by modern scholars. Fritz Schulz objects to the classicality of the oath on the ground that Romans would not easily foreswear themselves.[203]

Once again, I am not suggesting bad faith on the part of those who

---

[200]*D.* 12.3.11.

[201]*D.* 5.1.64 *pr.*; 6.1.68; 6.1.71; 12.3.2; 12.3.4.4; 12.3.5.3; 12.3.8.

[202]For other not dissimilar uses of the oath in litigation see Buckland, *Textbook*, p. 633.

[203]*Classical Roman Law* (Oxford, 1951), p. 370.

invented and continued to use the oath in Roman procedure and substantive law.[204] On the contrary, oaths were very prominent in Roman life, and until late in the Republic Romans were regarded and regarded themselves as the most religious of people.[205] Individuals frequently took oaths when making a contract:[206] only, these oaths did not have legal impact. Indeed, unless there was some belief in the efficacy of oaths, they would have had no place in law at all. Only, there are levels of belief. It is their limited and purely secular role in law that enables us to see these legal oaths as The Last Best Chance. It may just be significant—I feel it must be, but have no proof—that whereas a normal Roman oath was proferred to a particular deity we are nowhere told that the oath with legal effect was made to a specific god or goddess.

IV

But the Roman approach to the legal oath is not the only one. Other possibilities that really do involve an appeal to the supernatural can easily be envisaged. Only three need be mentioned here. First, where there is sufficient rational evidence, the oath may be imposed, and tested by supernatural means. Secondly, where there is little or no rational evidence, the oath may be used, and tested by supernatural means. Thirdly, where there is considerable, but not adequate, rational evidence, the oath may be used, and tested by supernatural means. These approaches may in one system appear separately or together. When the first approach is taken, the oath is not The Last Best Chance. Those involved in the process have more faith in the

---

[204]For Roman manipulation of religion for political ends see, e.g., Alan Watson, *The State, Law and Religion: Pagan Rome* (Athens, Ga., 1992), pp. 58ff.

[205]See, e.g., Cicero *De haruspicum responsis* 9.19; *De natura deorum* 2.3.8; Sallust *Bellum Catilinae* 12.3; *Bellum Jugurthinum* 14.19. Valerius Maximus 1.1.8, 9; Tertullian *Apologeticus* 25.2; Polybius 6.56.6ff. Augustine pokes fun at this notion in *De civitate Dei* 4.8; cf., e.g., Georg Wissowa, *Religion und Kultus der Römer*, 2d edit. (Leipzig, 1912) pp. 386ff.; W.H.C. Frend, *Martyrdom and Persecution in the Early Church* (New York, 1967), pp. 77f.

[206]See, e.g., Cato *de agri cultura* 148.

intervention of the deity than in human reason. With the second approach, one cannot tell without more information. If the oath is used because there is considerable bewilderment about what should be done—but something must be done—then the oath is The Last Best Chance. But there may be in a particular society firm belief in the deity's intervention. With the third approach, where it appears in isolation without also the presence of the other two, we have to do with The Last Best Chance. The basic reliance is on using rational evidence. When there is considerable evidence against the accused, but not quite so much as to constitute the proof required by the legal system, then there may be recourse to the oath. Of course, the hope will exist that the threat of the proof of the oath will induce a guilty accused to confess, thus providing what was lacking for proof.

V

Closely similar to the oath is trial by ordeal. Trial by ordeal has not necessarily always the same justification, not even perhaps in a limited geographical area such as Western Europe. My discussion here will be limited to part of the earliest evidence for Western Europe.

Trial by ordeal seems in Europe to have emerged from Frankish custom, and it is first recorded in the *Pactus Legis Salicae* attributed to King Clovis and which was issued between 507 and 511.[207] The ordeal was that of the cauldron.[208] According to Gregory of Tours, the cauldron was set on a fire, a ring was tossed into the bubbling water, and the person undergoing the ordeal had to pluck it out, not an easy task.[209] The most important provisions of the code for us are 132 and 73:[210]

---

[207]See, e.g., Robert Bartlett, *Trial by Fire and Water* (Oxford, 1980), p.4; Katherine Fischer Drew, *The Laws of the Salian Franks* (Philadelphia, 1991), p. 28.

[208]I am ignoring here the ordeal by lot, which was also accepted in Salic Law.

[209]*De gloria martyrum* 80.

[210]The translations are those of Drew, *Salian Franks*, at pp. 156 and 132f.

132. If a man has witnesses who are proved to be false, [each of them] shall sustain a fine (*multa*) of fifteen solidi. He who accused them [the witnesses] of giving false testimony shall put his hand in the cauldron [i.e., submit to the ordeal of hot water], and if he takes his hand out clean (*sana*), they shall sustain that fine noted above. But if his hand sustains a dirty burn (*conburet*), he [who accused the witnesses of a false testimony] shall sustain a fine of fifteen solidi [to each of the witnesses].

This text shows us the nature of the test, but perhaps more significantly indicates that the ordeal was not the only mode of proof: witnesses could be adduced, as here. Other methods of proof were also possible: oaths and oath-helpers. Oath-helpers were not witnesses, but persons who could give evidence of the general character of a party. Rebecca V. Colman has pointed out in fact that in the Salic law, witnesses are mentioned six times more frequently than the ordeal.[211] The question for us is why, if there was faith that God would inevitably intervene to give the right answer in the ordeal, were other methods of proof used? After all, as the text indicates, witnesses could lie:

73. 2. And if the man summoned comes to the place, then he who called him to court, if the case is such a minor one that the composition involved is less than thirty-five solidi, should offer oath (*videredum* or *wedredo*) with six oathhelpers. And afterwards he who had been summoned, if he believes it proper for him to do so in such a case, shall absolve himself with the oaths of twelve oathhelpers.

3. But if it is a more serious case, one where he who is found guilty will be liable to pay thirty-five solidi or more (but less than forty-

respectively.

[211]'Reason and Unreason in Medieval Law,' 4 *Journal of Interdisciplinary History* (1974), pp. 571ff. at p. 577; cf. Bartlett, *Trial*, p. 26.

five), he who summoned him to court shall offer oath (*videredum* or *wedredo*) with nine oathhelpers. And he who was summoned, if he recognizes it as proper for himself to do so, shall absolve himself with oaths given for him by eighteen oathhelpers.

4. If indeed it is such a case that the composition is forty-five solidi or more -- up to the amount of the wergeld (*ad leudem*) -- he who summoned him to court shall offer oath with twelve oathhelpers; and he who was summoned to court, if he knows that it is proper for him to do so, can absolve himself with oaths given by twenty-five oathhelpers.

[4. If indeed it is such a case that the composition is forty-five solidi or more -- up to the amount of the wergeld (*ad leudem*) -- he who summoned [the others] to court shall offer oath with twelve; and he who was summoned, if he knows that he is innocent, shall absolve himself with oaths given by twenty-five.

5. But if a man has summoned someone to court in a suit involving a judgement that is the amount of the wergeld (*leudem*), he who summoned him should offer oath (*vidrido* or *wedredo iurare*) with twelve; and if he [who was summoned] neglects to come to court or does not want to place his hand in the cauldron, he [who summoned] should heat up the cauldron after fourteen days.

What is here at issue is the summoning to court of one member of the king's retinue by another, as appears from 73.1. Reliance for proof is placed above all on oaths and oath-helpers, not upon the ordeal. More than that, the implication of the text is that the ordeal was used only in the most serious cases. Again, the question must be, if the ordeal unfailingly gave the right outcome, why was it used only for the most serious situations? Certainly, a person who was proven innocent by the ordeal would suffer pain, but still...[212]

The answer to my questions is that from the outset there was no total

---

[212]In some circumstances a person sentenced to the ordeal could redeem his hand: *Pactus Legis Salicae* 53.

reliance on divine intervention in the ordeal. We are once again faced with a last resort, The Last Best Chance. A severe social problem exists. It ought to be solved by law, but the law cannot rationally give an answer in a direct manner. Recourse is had *in extremis* to an apparently irrational mode of proof. Once again I am not suggesting bad faith on the part of the users of the ordeal.[213] Unless there was some degree of faith in its efficacy it would have served no purpose. Again I stress that one sign that we are dealing with The Last Best Chance here, as was the case with the Israelite curse and the Roman legal oath, is the solemnity that surrounds the ordeal. The solemnity of the occasion is well brought out in the formula intoned by priests for the ordeal of the hot iron:

> Oh God, the just judge, who are the author of peace and give fair judgement, we humbly pray you to deign to bless and sanctify this fiery iron, which is used in the just examination of doubtful issues. If this man is innocent of the charge from which he seeks to clear himself, he will take this fiery iron in his hand and appear unharmed; if he is guilty, let your most just power declare that truth in him, so that wickedness may not conquer justice but falsehood always be overcome by the truth. Through Christ.[214]

That skepticism about the ordeal existed from an early date is shown by a capitulary of Charlemagne of 809: "Let all believe the ordeal with no doubting."[215] Doubt existed. But I hesitate to accept Bartlett's judgement that

---

[213]But equally I accept that just as Roman religion was manipulated for political purposes so was the ordeal abused: cf. Bartlett, *Trial*, pp. 13ff. Where there is faith, it can always be abused.

[214]*Monumenta Germaniae Historica: Formulae Merowingici et Karolini Aevi*, ed K. Zeumer (Hanover, 1886), pp. 700f. The translation is that of Bartlett, *Trial*, p. 1.

[215]*Monumenta Germaniae Historica: Capitularia Regum Francorum* 1, edit. Alfred Boretius (Hanover, 1883), p. 150 § 20: '*Ut omnes iuditium Dei credant absque dubitatione.*'

the capitulary also "shows us the king's mind on this matter."[216] If doubt existed in the minds of some and Charlemagne wished the ordeal to continue, he had to insist that no one should doubt.

My point should be generalized. From time to time the claim will be made that the ordeal is not a satisfactory means to reach the truth, and should be abolished. The claim will be opposed, and for long the ordeal may continue. The demand for the retention of the ordeal should not then be seen as necessarily proof that its proponents believe it will always give the right result. Other factors may influence their stance though they cannot say so. First, law is in general very resistant to change.[217] Second, there is the problem of deciding how else the dispute will be resolved. Should it simply be allowed to fester? A serious crime has been committed. There is considerable evidence against the accused, but not enough for the legal standards of the time. Should he just walk away, despite the wrath of members of the community? What if there should be retaliation which many might regard as justified? The main point of a legal process is to resolve a dispute with the aim of inhibiting further unregulated conflict.[218] Third, there is the hope, conscious or unconscious, that the threat of the ordeal will persuade the guilty to confess.

I have chosen to look at aspects of the ordeal from our earliest evidence because the suggestion might be made that The Last Best Chance is simply to be explained by survival from a primitive to a rational age. The suggestion might be, for instance, that when Roman law was perhaps as rational as law can be, the legal oath flourished in its limited circumstances as a survival from the time when all believed in the divine force of the oath. I would rather suggest, though proof can never be adduced for remote origins, that the limited scope and use of legal oath and ordeal in the instances examined are not survivals but original. In no sense, however, do I intend to suggest that there are no cases where a procedure continues to survive long

---

[216]*Trial*, p. 12.

[217]See, e.g., Watson, *Society, passim*.

[218]See Alan Watson, *The Nature of Law* (Edinburgh, 1977).

after the reasons for it have been forgotten. An example from Blackstone will soon appear.

I have, as mentioned, chosen to discuss aspects of the ordeal from the earliest time for which we have evidence, but Robert Bartlett has convincingly shown that in the heyday of the ordeal it was used in criminal cases only when there was considerable but not sufficient evidence.[219]

Finally on the ordeal we should return to provision 132 of the *Pactus Legis Salicae*, the ordeal facing one who accused a witness of being false. The normal use of the ordeal was in the trial of a suspected criminal, but it is no surprise to find it here. To give false evidence can have such serious consequences that evidence is typically given under oath. This is one of the situations I have mentioned where legal oaths are typically and frequently found. But it is equally serious to claim that the evidence is false. The whole legal process is now in jeopardy. To put the claimant on his oath would scarcely be satisfactory: it would be one oath against another. There is a dilemma. The solution of the Salian Franks was to subject the claimant to the ordeal (I am, of course, assuming that the ordeal was imposed when the veracity or otherwise of the claim was not self-evident).[220]

With the ordeal, too, modern scholars must be on their guard when investigating an alien system. I believe J.H. Baker was misled in part when he wrote oaths involved an appeal to God to reveal the truth in human disputes."[221] But he does recognize that the plaintiff had to make out a prima facie case.

VI

My claim should be properly understood. I am not arguing that the examples I am adducing for The Last Best Chance are entirely rational. They

---

[219]*Trial.*

[220]I have not dealt with trial by battle which also involves The Last Best Chance, and is close in nature to the ordeal.

[221]*An Introduction to English Legal History* 3d ed. (London, 1990), p. 5.

are not. Only, the procedure is much less irrational than is usually thought. The persons involved have a problem that they feel must be dealt with, but it cannot be solved directly. They do the best they can. It is not a coincidence that my examples to this point all involve religion. There is nothing so reasonable as one's own religion, nothing so irrational-seeming as another's religion. These two opposing perspectives on religion must be stressed for an understanding of The Last Best Chance. Of the examples looked at so far, the most apparently rational instance is that of the Roman legal oath. The explanation for that, I think, is that it is the one least obviously based on religion. More than that, unlike the Israelite curse and the medieval ordeal, it does not call upon a deity to intervene directly in human affairs. I should not be thought to be suggesting that The Last Best Chance in law always involves religion. Purely secular dodges would include the fictions of English common law such as those to found jurisdiction. Another example from medieval England would be common recovery which in effect barred unbarrable entails.[222] But when The Last Best Chance is purely secular in its nature this is readily apparent.

Indeed, there is a crucial difference between The Last Best Chance that is purely secular and The Last Best Chance that has a basis in religion. For the former the fact of The Last Best Chance may be apparent to all and known to all. For The Last Best Chance with a basis in religion some degree of faith is needed on the part of some of those involved even if only as spectators. In fact, when The Last Best Chance is found in secular law it is usually very close to being The Second Best that does not involve The Last Best Chance.

VII

My last example of The Last Best Chance takes us back to the beginning of this chapter; trials of animals. "What was it like to try the

---

[222]See, e.g., A.W.B. Simpson, *A History of the Land Law*, 2d edit. (Oxford, 1986), pp. 129ff.

rats?"[223] Ewald puts the problem: "What needs to be explained is not why one would put down a dangerous cow, but why one would first bring the matter to the Law Faculty of Leipzig."[224] He shows convincingly that none of the explanations previously adduced for trials of animals is plausible. He also demonstrates that those who were involved in such trials or who favoured them are not to be dismissed as primitive.

But not only animals; inanimate objects also might be put on trial. The mental outlook behind such trials may well not be the same everywhere. The most I wish to claim here is that in the three examples I will consider there are pointers to The Last Best Chance.

1. For ancient Athens, Aristotle records a special procedure: "When the king does not know who committed the act he institutes proceedings against 'the guilty man,' and the king and the tribal kings try the case, as also the prosecutions of inanimate objects and animals for homicide."[225] The case is before the Prutaneion, not the ordinary courts that dealt with prosecution for homicide. The first indication that we have The Last Best Chance to deal with here is that where a human is the slayer this procedure is used only when the killer is unknown. A killing must be dealt with by law, it is felt, and the best that can be done is try 'the guilty one' by a *special* procedure.[226] A second indication of The Last Best Chance is that animals and inanimate things are tried only if they killed. No doubt for a lesser injury a dangerous beast would simply be put down. This limitation was because of the seriousness of killing not simply because of questions of jurisdiction and this also is indicated by Plato in his discussion of ideal laws. He lays down a procedure for trying an animal that commits homicide, and another for an

---

[223] The *locus classicus* is E.P. Evans, *The Criminal Prosecution and Capital Punishment of Animals* (London, 1906).

[224]'Comparative Jurisprudence (1),' p. 1905.

[225]*Athenian Constitution* 57.4. We may assume a religious element in the procedure.

[226]If we had more information we might see here an example of The Second Best that did not involve The Last Best Chance.

inanimate object that kills.[227] He establishes no procedure for prosecuting animals that simply wound.

2. In book 1 of his *Commentaries on the Laws of England* William Blackstone treats the forfeiture of animals and inanimate objects that kill.[228] His discussion makes it very clear that he is puzzled by the forfeiture;[229] which probably should be regarded as a survival from a previous age. Distinctions are drawn in true legal fashion. Thus, if an infant under the years of discretion falls from a stationary cart and is killed the thing is not forfeit, but it is if the person killed is an adult. If a man climbing on a wheel falls and is killed, the wheel alone is forfeit, but if a wheel ran over him and killed him the whole cart and its load are forfeit. Whether or not the object was under the control of its owner is irrelevant for its forfeiture. What must again be stressed is that the procedure is reserved for killing, and is not extended to wounding, an indication that the procedure is to be seen as a last resort.

3. Trials of animals were not uncommon in the past in Europe. One particular example will suffice. In 1522 rats were put on trial in Autun before the ecclesiastical court for the felony of eating and wantonly destroying barley crops. A formal complaint was laid before the bishop's vicar who cited "some rats" to appear on a certain day. Barthelmy Chassenée was appointed for the defence. The rats failed to appear. Chassenée successfully argued: (1) that his clients were spread over a wide area and one summons was insufficient; (2) the summons was addressed only to "some rats," but should have been addressed to all. The court ordered that a second summons addressed to all the rats be read from the pulpit of all the local parish churches. The rats again failed to appear, and Chassenée again successfully pleaded that his clients were widely dispersed and needed more time to make preparations for their journey. After a further summons not heeded by the rats, Chassenée once again successfully argued that the rats were entitled to fair treatment under the law: a person summoned to a place where he cannot

---

[227]*Laws* 9:873E.

[228]1.8.15.

[229]Cf. already Ewald 'Comparative Jurisprudence (1),' pp. 1910ff.

appear in safety may lawfully refuse to appear; the rats were very unpopular in the district, would have to face their natural enemies, the cats, who, moreover, belonged to the plaintiffs. The court adjourned *sine die* on the issue of timing, and judgment for the rats was granted by default.[230] The sophistication of the proceedings and the requirement of due process should be emphasized: we are not dealing here with what might be termed a "primitive mentality."

The people of Autun were faced with a crisis. No doubt, all sorts of other measures to deal with it had been tried, in vain. No doubt, during all these legal proceedings the people of Autun were killing as many rats as they could get hold of. Yet the legal proceedings dealt very seriously with issues of due process. The trial, however instituted, was to be seen as a common endeavour. The community as a whole would be involved. Whatever the technicalities of the pleadings, the plaintiff was in effect the community. The injured individuals were united in a single process against the common enemy. Something had to be done. Recourse was had to law as a last resort. We should not see here infinite faith that a conviction of the rats would stop their felonious behaviour. But all due formalities had to be observed, as is typical with The Last Best Chance.

Trials of animals seem to fall into only two types.[231] First, where a particular animal has committed an especially atrocious act, but not a minor offence. Second, where there is an ongoing crisis of epic proportions, not simply normal predations by beetles or rats. For lesser offences no trial was called for, the creatures were simply put down, further proof that the trials are examples of The Last Best Chance. One should not conclude from the trial of the rats of Autun, as Ewald for instance insists, that those involved would concede to all God's creatures a right to share in the fruits of the earth.[232] Such a feeling is entirely absent for the time from the slaughtering of pigs or

---

[230]See, above all, Evans, *Criminal Prosecution*, pp. 18ff.; cf. Ewald, 'Comparative Jurisprudence (1),' pp. 1898ff.

[231]I am relying on the evidence in Evans, *Criminal Prosecutions*.

[232]'Comparative Jurisprudence (1),' pp. 1914f.

cattle for food, or the mindless killing of rats going about their business in a normal year. I would conjecture that we should not be surprised that the rats of Autun won, yet not by an acquittal, but on a technicality. The same was also true of the beetles that infested the vineyards of St. Julien in 1545 and subsequently.[233] I would suggest that in situations of ongoing destruction by small creatures the judges would be chary of pronouncing a sentence on them which in all probability would be to no avail. The majesty of the law is not lightly to be shown to be contemptible.

Trials of animals incidentally present very real problems for legal theorists such as Hans Kelsen who claim that "norms of a legal order regulate human behaviour."[234] They must emphasize that laws govern *human* behaviour because for them law is about regulating conduct, and only humans can regulate their behaviour according to law. Hence they will wrongly claim that the "absurd legal content is the result of animistic ideas, according to which not only men, but also animals and inanimate objects, have a 'soul' and are therefore basically not different from human beings."[235]

VIII

The Last Best Chance is a legal device. It is an official creation, whether of the church or state, not obviously a creation of individuals that is then acquiesced in by the state.[236] The purpose is to resolve by legal process in some indirect way a pressing problem that cannot be coped with directly by law. It always involves an abuse of the law though I hesitate to suggest bad faith in the invention or use of The Last Best Chance. The Last Best Chance involves a deviation from established principle or accepted practice in law: derogation from accepted standards of evidence, such as two eye-witnesses for proof of adultery in biblical law, or breach of the universal standard in Roman private law that a judicial award was always monetary. Typically, but

---

[233]For this see Evans, *Criminal Prosecutions*, pp 37ff.

[234]*The Pure Theory of Law*, 2d edit. Trsl. Max Knight (Berkeley, 1967), pp. 30ff.

[235]p. 31.

[236]As at Rome were manumission *censu* and *vindicta*.

not inevitably, The Last Best Chance appears at an intersection of law and religion. Then religion may also be abused. From the outsider's perspective there is also always some absence of rationality. But what is rational or an abuse is culturally determined. The existence of other abuses in law or religion in the society does not indicate cynicism in the use of The Last Best Chance. For The Last Best Chance to be appropriately used there must both be proper solemnity and *some* degree of faith in its power.

It is important for comparative legal historians to be on the watch for The Last Best Chance otherwise they will make serious mistakes about the faith patterns and credulity of the people whose law they study, and about the relationship between law, religion, and society.

I have emphasized elsewhere that one often comes across a notion that I have termed 'Law keeps out.'[237] Some problems are often not regulated by law. It is, I suggest, very revealing for the postulates of a particular system that it applies legal rules where another system avoids such regulation. 'Law keeps out' is important for understanding The Last Best Chance. The Last Best Chance often occurs in a particular system precisely where other systems avoid resolution by law of the (very real) problem.[238]

IX

I have claimed that The Last Best Chance involves an abuse of law. More importantly, though less obviously, it functions to preserve the integrity of the system. Thus, for the biblical curse more is involved than a husband wishing to be rid of his wife. Divorce for the male was easy.[239] But the husband in this situation wanted and demanded vengeance though he had not sufficient proof of the adultery. The curse was an innovation to avoid tampering with and reducing the strict standards of proof that were insisted

---

[237]*Spirit*, pp. 172ff.

[238]But 'Law keeps out' is wider in scope than The Last Best Chance. For instance, most societies would not regulate the issue of how long a mother should suckle her baby; but it is provided for -- not by a dodge -- in the Prussian *Allgemeines Landrecht für die preussischen Staaten* of 1794: 2.2 67ff.

[239]Deuteronomy 24.1.

upon for all capital -- indeed all criminal -- cases.[240] The Roman *legis actio sacramento* was provided to allow law to develop for situations not covered. Control was exercised because the elected official responsible would not allow the case to proceed to the next stage unless he felt the plaintiff's claim had some merit. The *iusiurandum in litem* preserved the principle that all awards in a private law suit should be money. Trial by ordeal in the medieval West permitted the strict standards of proof to be otherwise maintained. The action in ancient Athens against a human unknown killer, animal or inanimate object, preserved the integrity of the legal system because it was brought in a special separate court.[241] The trial of the rats of Autun[242] preserved the integrity of the system by the insistence on due process, even in a crisis, even against a hated, non-human adversary. The rats, after all won.[243]

X

I observed that Hans Kelsen had great problems in trying to fit trials of animals into his theory of positive law. He is not alone. Though I did not deal with the issue, such trials do not really fit my own rather different minimal definition of law: "Law is the means adopted to institutionalize dispute situations and to validate decisions given in the appropriate process which itself has the specific object of inhibiting further unregulated conflict."[244]

Kelsen, further, also would have problems with the Israelite curse unless one, rather fatuously, wanted to argue that the rules were designed to

---

[240]Deuteronomy 19.15.

[241]I say nothing about the trials discussed by Blackstone because, like him, I am at a loss to know their origins.

[242]Cf. the trial of the beetles in the vineyards.

[243]I am not suggesting that The Last Best Chance is necessarily intentionally used to preserve the integrity of the system. Other typical features of law operate to the same effect. Thus, the prime factor in legal change is borrowing: but, strangely perhaps, one system is usually chosen to be the source more often than a variety of sources. Again, in a particular system there will be accepted parameters of reasoning: some types of argument, but not others, will be acceptable.

[244]*The Nature of Law* (Edinburgh, 1977), p. 22.

regulate the conduct of the priest.

Legal theory (which in not my concern) has to recognize The Last Best Chance for what it is, and somehow or another take account of its nature.[245]

XI

This chapter has serious implications for an understanding of law, and of its function in society. Law and its operation are not always what they may seem. It is easy to misunderstand the problems of those involved with the law, with its respectability, and with political and social reality. And this inevitably is more the case when we look at foreign law. It will surprise many outside of the U.S.A.—and also many inside the U.S.A.—that the trial of O.J. Simpson for murder is actually an instance of the American criminal trial system working as it is supposed to work. Law-makers must be aware of parameters of thinking and of social problems elsewhere.

Still, it will be suggested that the examples of The Last Best Chance are so extreme that they cannot illuminate any issues in the development, for say, of a common law for the European Union. The opposite is the truth. To outsiders (as we all are), the examples I have adduced are so foreign that they thrust themselves forward for explanation. Yet, in general, as will have been noticed, scholars have taken recourse in cheapening their approach: the participants in The Last Best Chance were, the claim is made, naive or even primitive. Few students have made the attempt to try to understand the phenomena in their historical system. The problem of understanding is greater when the differences are less noticeable. How will English lawyers come to grips with the importance French courts actually give to precedent when previous cases cannot be cited in court? When this role is not that found in England? What will they make of the use of the oath, again in French law? How will they understand the impact on French law of the fear of perjury? How will they understand the elaborate apparatus of cases and juristic opinions in the annual editions of Dalloz' *Code Civil* when these cases

---

[245]I need scarcely add that for understanding the nature of law I find comparative legal history much more valuable than abstract legal theory.

and opinions cannot be referred to in judicial decisions? How will continental Europeans ever understand the English fixation with detailed factual exposition in their law reports. The practical difficulties of understanding foreign law is at its greatest when the societies involved are closely related.

To return to the opening of this chapter: William Ewald's observation that to understand a foreign system one must understand its lawyers' thinking. The Last Best Chance is simply the extreme example of this.

Chapter 10

The Culture of Judges

It will by this stage of the book be apparent that in uncovering the parameters of judges' reasoning and judicial decision making, one must take into account the legal tradition within which the judges work. Often too, this also involves taking a long, hard look at even remote legal history and at the law in other countries.

One factor makes this search particularly intriguing; judges are unable to give society what it expects from them. The populace expects from judges the correct legal decision as a result of their applying the law to the facts. How do good judges arrive at their decisions? It is easier to say what makes a bad judge: his reasoning is lacking in logic, or he fails to know or to understand relevant law. But one cannot say that a good judge, at least in most types of appellate civil case, is one who arrives at the correct decision through the use of logic and the application of the legal rules to established facts.[246] Provided that the attorneys for the parties have done their work adequately and prepared their case, there is no answer that is necessarily correct. The case can go either way. The answer that is correct is the one the judges come to, but it is correct only after, and only because, they come to it. As Justice Robert H. Jackson put it: "There is no doubt that if there were a super Supreme Court, a substantial proportion of our reversals of state courts

---

[246] Most types of appellate civil cases, rather than all, because it may be that one party believes so passionately in the morality of his position that despite the clear meaning of the law, he insists on going to court to make a point or in the faint hope of winning the verdict. Such was the situation on the rendition of fugitive slaves after the U.S. Fugitive Slave Act of 1850: see, e.g., R. Cover, *Justice accused* (1975), pp. 119ff. Such cases, where the judge is caught between the demands of his role and the voice of conscience (Cover, *Justice*, at pp. 6ff.), where he may be asked to go beyond the law in the direction of freedom, will not be discussed here, though they raise similar issues.

would also be reversed. We are not final because we are infallible, but we are infallible only because we are final."[247] So, possibly, all judges who are not obviously bad judges ought to be counted good judges? Yet insiders all believe that there are, in addition to bad judges, mediocre and good judges, and that among good judges some are better than others. What are the criteria for insiders? The answer I suggest is that for insiders a good judge is one who reaches the law to be applied to the facts by a mental process that is thought to be the most appropriate by his brother judges and by well-placed attorneys and legal scholars. What the appropriate mental process is will be determined by the legal culture, and, like other aspects of culture, will scarcely be questioned by those participating in it. The outsider sees things differently. He may be impressed by the "foreign" culture, but some aspects strike him as incongruous.

In this chapter I want to look at four approaches to deciding a case in different societies -- contemporary England; uncodified "mixed," law systems (with an example from seventeenth-century Scotland and another from early-twentieth-century South Africa); nineteenth-century France after codification; and fifteenth-century Germany, with a glance at thirteenth-and fourteenth-century Spain -- where the attempt is made each time to reach the correct decision by applying the mental process thought most appropriate. None of the approaches examined here is result oriented, and to outsiders, especially to lawyers brought up in a different legal culture, the mental process seems artificial, even absurd, but not to those involved in the game. The approach in each case is not atypical for the particular legal culture, but I have tried to find striking examples.

I.

Anyone interested in the vagaries of legal evolution, whether as legal historian or law reformer, must be fascinated by the English doctrine of precedent, especially since the Practice Statement of the House of Lords issued in 1966.[248] From 1898 (according to the usual calculation but actually

---

[247] *Brown v. Allen*, 73 S. Ct. 397, 427 (1953).
[248] Practice Statement (Judicial Precedent) (1966) 1 W.L.R. 1234.

earlier)[249] the Law Lords regarded themselves as bound by their own previous decisions, but in the just-mentioned practice statement they announced that while treating their previous decisions as normally binding, they would depart from a previous decision when it appeared right to do so.[250]

One recent House of Lords case, *President of India v. La Pintada Compañía Navigación S.A.*(1984) 3 W.L.R.10,is instructive for its approach. The legal issue involved was whether, when no interest for delay in performance was specified in a contract, and payment was delayed but made before proceedings were begun, the other contracting party could claim interest for nonpayment among his damages. This issue is the "case 1" referred to by the judges.

Lord Fraser of Tullybelton, who delivered his opinion first, was brief: "I have had the advantage of reading in draft the speech of my noble and learned friend, Lord Brandon of Oakbrook. His reasoning seems to me irresistible and I feel myself driven, though with reluctance, to agree that this appeal must be allowed, with the consequences that the arbitrator's alterative award will be upheld."[251] Now, as I have said, in most types of civil cases at the appellate level, if counsel on both sides have done their work, it should not happen that one decision on the law is forced upon the judges.[252] Otherwise the case would not have got so far. All the more is this true where, as with the House of Lords, the court is not bound by its own or any other precedent. If the decision is not inevitable, then reasoning to it cannot be irresistible. Lord Fraser can only mean that by the type of logic or arguments that judges find persuasive, whatever these may be, Lord Brandon's reasoning to the conclusion is convincing. Nonetheless, Lord Fraser expresses regret at the decision he comes to. He accepts, that is to say, that there are principles

---

[249] *London Street Tramways Co. v. London County Council* (1898) A.C. 375; and see, e.g. R.B. Stevens, *Law and Politics* (Chapel Hill, 1978), pp. 88ff.

[250] For their practice see above all A. Paterson, *The Law Lords* (Toronto, 1982), especially at pp. 162 ff.

[251] *President of India v. La Pintada Compañia Navigación,* at *p. 13.*

that determine what is the law even when injustice is the result. Though he does not say so expressly, he accepts that lawness is to be fixed by these principles even when he is technically free to decide that the law is different. In other words, higher than the notion that judges decide what the law is, when they are free to do so, stands the idea that this decision has to be reached by the application of some conception of lawness–of what constitutes law– even when injustice results. That is, even those who can make law accept the standards of law as being different from their notions of justice.

Lord Scarman's opinion reads:

> My Lords, I agree with the speech to be delivered by my noble and learned friend, Lord Brandon of Oakbrook, a draft of which I have had the opportunity of studying. But I wish to associate myself with the comments made by my noble and learned friend, Lord Roskill. I also reach with regret and reluctance the conclusion that the appeal must be allowed. The sooner there is legislation along the lines proposed by the Law Commission (or some other solution achieving the same end) the better.

This takes us further than Lord Fraser. Again, Lord Scarman gives the unjust decision, though by exercising his judicial right of making law he need not have done so. Yet he expresses the desire that the law be changed, but by legislation. There is a hierarchy of lawmakers, and the legislature has greater powers of lawmaking than have judges. Where the law ought to be changed, judges may feel that it is appropriate for the legislature to make the change, and not themselves, even when they can do so. This remains their position (or at least that of Lord Scarman in this case) even when, first, there is no certainty of legislative intervention, and, second, when legislation, if any, will not rectify the present injustice. In furtherance of some notion of appropriateness in lawmaking, judges are prepared to commit an injustice: not an injustice by some theoretical notion of justice but by the judges' own personal ideas of justice and injustice.

Lord Roskill also finds Lord Brandon's reasoning compelling. Then he continues:

> But I freely confess that I have arrived at this conclusion though without doubt nevertheless with both regret and reluctance. It has long been recognized that A.C. 429 left creditors with a legitimate sense of grievance and an obvious injustice without remedy. I think the House in 1893 recognized those consequences of the decision, but then felt compelled for historical reasons to leave that injustice uncorrected.[253] Since 1893 Parliament has intervened twice, first to remedy what my noble and learned friend has called case 3 and secondly to remedy case 2. On the latter occasion Parliament, with the Law Commission's report before it, had the opportunity also to remedy the injustice to creditors to which case 1 (a debt paid late but before proceedings for its recovery have been begun) can so often give rise. But Parliament neither accepted the Law Commission's proffered solution to case 1 nor provided any substitute solution of its own. It must, I think, therefore be accepted that this inaction was deliberate. If so it cannot be right for this House in its judicial capacity by departing from the *London, Chatham and Dover Railway Co.* case to proffer a remedy which if applicable at all must apply to all three cases and not only to case 1 with the consequence that as regards cases 2 and 3 there would be concurrent and inconsistent remedies, one statutory and discretionary, the other at common law and as of right since once a breach of contract and damages caused by the breach are proved a court has no discretion but must

---

[253] *London, Chatham and Dover Railway Co. v. The South Eastern Railway Co.* (1893)

award the damages claimed in full.[254]

The main authority set out for the decision is the case of 1893, ninety-one years before, and Lord Roskill felt -- rightly as we shall see -- that the House of Lords at that time also thought their decision unjust.

Lord Roskill gives more argument for his decision. He accepts Lord Brandon's view that the *London, Chatham and Dover Railway Co.* decision covered three separate cases. Case 3 was remedied first by Parliament. Then, with a Law Commission report in front of them that covered cases 1 and 2, Parliament remedied case 2 but did nothing about case 1. They neither accepted the Law Commission's recommendations nor proffered their own solution. From this Lord Roskill draws the conclusion that Parliament's inactivity was deliberate (and hence presumably that the House of Lords would be acting against the will of Parliament if they changed the law).[255]

This type of reasoning, which is akin to an argument from silence, is always dangerous. It becomes much more fragile when we take into account that British parliamentary drafting is notoriously bad,[256] that the British House of Commons is famous for its lack of interest in legislating on matters with no party political impact,[257] and that many are the factors extraneous to the deliberate intention of the House of Commons that prevent the passing of legislation or the passing of complete and well-rounded legislation.[258]

---

[254] Ibid., at p. 13.

[255] See also the note by P.M.N. in *Lloyd's Maritime Commercial L.Q.* (1984), pp. 305ff. On discovering the intention of the legislature, see, e.g., H. Friendly, "Mr. Justice Frankfurter and the Reading of Statutes," in *Benchmarks* (1967), pp. 196ff., especially at pp. 200,207, 219ff.

[256] See the materials and discussion in Alan Watson, *Sources of Law, Legal Change, and Ambiguity* Edinburgh (1984), pp. 78ff.

[257] See, e.g., the remarks of various politicians during the passage of the Land Registration (Scotland) Act of 1979, quoted in *Journal of the Law Society of Scotland* 24 (1979); 235ff.; Lord Hailsham of Marylebone, "Obstacles to Law Reform," *Current Legal Problems* 34 (1981), pp. 279ff., especially at pp. 286ff.

[258] See Watson, *Sources of Law*, at pp. 80ff.; *Society and Legal Change*

Moreover, Lord Roskill's words "Parliament, with the Law Commission's report before it" sound a trifle exaggerated. Rather, the Law Commission had submitted a report to Parliament. But that is not to say that members of Parliament were conscious of it, had read it and understood it, or had it in contemplation. The reasoning -- from a failure to act, mind you becomes downright absurd when we consider that British courts refuse to consider legislative history. There is arguably a case for seeking for the (fictitious) intention of the legislature only on the wording of a statute,[259] but there can be none for interpreting a statute by seeking the intention of the legislature through the absence of clauses on a rather different issue.

Lord Roskill's argument at the end of that paragraph derives from that of Lord Brandon and is fundamental, and it is appropriate now to quote from Lord Brandon:

> There are three cases in which the absence of any common law remedy for damage or loss caused by the late payment of a debt may arise, cases which I shall in what follows describe for convenience as case 1, case 2 and case 3. Case 1 is where a debt is paid late, before any proceedings for its recovery have been begun. Case 2 is where a debt is paid late, after proceedings for its recovery have been begun, but before they have been concluded. Case 3 is where a debt remains unpaid until, as a result of proceedings for its recovery being brought and prosecuted to a conclusion, a money judgment is given in which the original debt becomes merged.[260]

Now it seems to me that Lord Roskill is correct. A remedy given in case 1

(Edinburgh, 1977), pp. 61ff.

[259] That is, in fact, to interpret a statute only in terms of the words used.

[260] *President of India v. La Pintada Compañia Navigación*, at p. 23. On the question of statutory and common law remedies existing together one might refer to *Illinois v. City of Milwaukee*, 599 F. 2d 151 (1979).

ought also be given in cases 2 and 3. It would be wrong for there to be a greater right to interest in case 1 where no action was brought before payment, than in cases 2 and 3, where the debtor was being or had been sued. But is there really any argument for saying that the creditor's claim should be greater in cases 2 and 3 than in case 1? Is there any justification for holding that a creditor who has started an action is entitled to interest on the debt, but one who has not is not so entitled? Common sense and justice -- which may have little to do with law -- would suggest not.

But much may depend on the nature of this legal right in cases 2 and 3. The Law Reform (Miscellaneous Provisions) Act of 1934, section 3(1) covers case 3 and provides: "In any proceedings tried in any court of record for the recovery of any debt or damages, the court may, if it thinks fit, order that there shall be included in the sum for which judgment is given interest at such rate as it thinks fit on the whole or any part of the debt or damages." The court may, "if it thinks fit," give interest on the debt where there is a judgment. Schedule 1 of the Administration of Justice Act of 1982 covers case 2: "Subject to rules of court, in proceedings (wherever instituted) before the High Court for the recovery of a debt or damages there may be included in any sum for which judgment is given simple interest, at such rate as the court thinks fit or as rules of court may provide, on all or any part of the debt or damages in respect of which judgment is given or payment is made before judgment." The court "may" award interest. Thus, in cases 2 and 3 the court has discretion to award interest.

But what is the nature of this discretion? It is surely not to be exercised arbitrarily but -- like the right of the House of Lords not to follow its own decision -- to be exercised according to sound standards of judging.[261]

---

[261] I am reminded of article 1 of the *Swiss Civil Code*: "The law regulates all matters to which the letter or the spirit of any of its provisions relates. In the absence of an applicable legal provision, the judge pronounces in accordance with customary law and, in the absence of a custom, according to the rules that he would establish if he had to act as legislator. He is guided by the solutions consecrated by juristic opinion and case law.

What are the appropriate principles to be applied? I think we can state that interest is not to be awarded as a penalty; first, because one would expect that if an award could include a penalty, that would be expressly stated in the legislation; second, because an appropriate penalty would not always correspond to an interest sum; third, because the primary purpose of interest is compensation or recompense; and fourth (and above all), because both statutes expressly declare that their provisions do not apply if interest had been fixed by agreement between the parties or otherwise, a rule that is inappropriate if the judges were in fact being given power to award a penalty.

Now if interest may be awarded, but neither arbitrarily nor as penalty, the award must be to take account of loss suffered by the plaintiff: the interest is to be awarded as damages. It is relevant that under both statutes the discretion of the court, "if it thinks fit," extends not only to the award of interest but also to the rate of interest and the period of time for which it runs.

Let us now return to the question whether there is an argument for saying that the creditor's claim should be greater in cases 2 and 3 than in case 1. If the foregoing analysis is correct, and courts should award interest in cases 2 and 3, where part of the plaintiff's loss is precisely loss of interest that he would have obtained if he had received payment of the debt, then they ought also to award interest in case 1. And, on principle, apart even from cases 2 and 3, interest ought to be awarded in case 1. As we have seen Lord Roskill arguing, at common law, "once a breach of contract and damage caused by that breach are proved a court has no discretion but must award the damages claimed in full." On that sound principle, no one would now doubt -- whatever may have been the situation in 1893 and earlier -- that in the usual situation a creditor on receipt of payment will invest it, at least in a bank. Where he is likely not to have done so, and hence not to have sustained further loss, the court should not grant interest as damages.

Thus, on general principle, in the absence of the 1893 decision— which could have been set aside -- and apart from cases 2 and 3, the court could and should award interest as damages in case 1. But Lord Roskill sees a problem: all three cases would be covered by the common law and would give a remedy as of right, but cases 2 and 3 are also covered by statute that gives only a discretionary remedy. The inconsistency is more technical and aesthetic than substantive. By common law, interest would be given as of right, but only where loss is presumed to have followed from nonpayment or late payment of the debt; by statute, the court, if it thinks fit -- and the discretion must not be taken from the judges -- is to include interest in the award, but it must not act arbitrarily or make the award as a penalty, hence only on account of loss, actual or presumed. The remedies have different bases but they ought not to lead to inconsistent results.

Lord Roskill concludes:

> My Lords, it would be idle to affect ignorance of the fact that the present state of the law in relation to case 1 places the small creditor at grave disadvantage vis-à-vis his substantial and influential debtor. The former may fear to offend the latter by instituting legal proceedings either swiftly or indeed at all and it is notorious that some substantial and influential debtors are not slow to take advantage of this tactical strength, especially in times of financial stringency. It has taken two pieces of legislation, one some 50 years after 1893 and the other almost another half-century later, to remedy the injustice in case 2 and 3. I venture to hope that whatever solution be ultimately adopted in case 1, whether the Law Commission's somewhat complicated solution or something simpler, that solution will be found promptly and the remaining injustice in this branch of the law finally removed.[262]

The first part of that paragraph shows clearly the need to give the creditor in case 1 as much protection as creditors in cases 2 and 3. The unlikelihood of legislative activity to remedy case 1 is brought out by the length of time it

---

[262] *President of India v. La Pintada Compañia Navegación*, at p. 14.

took to remedy cases 2 and 3. Neither Lord Roskill nor any of his brother judges are likely to live to see legislative reform of case 1, a reform they themselves refuse to make.

Lord Brandon of Overbrook gives three main reasons for his decision:

> My first main reason is that the greater part of the injustice to creditors which resulted from the *London, Chatham and Dover Railway Co.* case has now been removed, to a large extent by legislative intervention, and to a lesser extent by judicial qualification of the scope of the decision itself. My second main reason is that when Parliament has given effect by legislation to some recommendations of the Law Commission in a particular field, but has taken what appears to be a policy decision not to give effect to a further such recommendation, any decision of your Lordships' House which would have the result of giving effect by another route, to the very recommendation which Parliament appears to have taken that policy decision to reject, could well be regarded as an unjustifiable usurpation by your Lordships' House of the functions which belong properly to Parliament, rather than as a judicial exercise in departing from an earlier decision on the ground that it has become obsolete and could still, in a limited class of cases, continue to cause some degree of injustice. . . .
>
> My third reason is this. Suppose that your Lordships were to depart from the *London, Chatham and Dover Railway Co.* case (1893) A.C. 429 in such a way as to give all creditors, whose debts either remained unpaid or were late, whether before or after action brought a cause of action for interest by way of general damages for breach of contract, what would be the result? The result, as it seems to me, would be that such cause of action would be available to a

creditor not only in case 1, in respect of which he still has no remedy except where he can prove special damages, but also in cases 2 and 3, in respect of both of which, since the coming into force of the Act of 1982, he already has a statutory remedy. What is more, the new cause of action so applicable to cases 2 and 3 would constitute a remedy as of right for a creditor, whereas the statutory remedy would remain discretionary only. There would, accordingly exist, in relation to cases 2 and 3, two parallel remedies, one as of right and the other discretionary; and the likelihood would be that creditors would, because of this difference, come to rely mainly on the former, rather than the latter, right. It is, in my view, plainly to be inferred from the relevant provisions in the Acts of 1934 and 1982, that Parliament has consistently regarded the award of interest on debts as a remedy to which creditors should not be entitled as of right, but only as a matter of discretion. That being the manifest policy of the legislature, I do not consider that your Lordships should create, in relation to cases 2 and 3, a rival system of remedies which, because they would be remedies as of right, would be inconsistent with that manifest policy.[263]

The first main reason is quite unconvincing and has no force. If a legal rule works unjustly in three situations and is corrected in two, that is scarcely an argument for leaving it uncorrected in the remaining situation. For those who find themselves in that unfortunate situation it is scarcely consolation that in related situations, but not in theirs, injustice will not be done.

The third reason we have already seen, and it also weighed with Lord Bridge of Harwich. Even as set out so expertly by Lord Brandon it seems a trifle forced. The common law rule need not be that in all actions on breach of contract for nonpayment of the debt, interest on the debt would necessarily

---

[263] Ibid., at p. 30

be included in the award of damages, but that, where part of the plaintiff's loss was interest on the unpaid debt, the award of damages would include an amount by way of interest.

To estimate the value of the second main reason we have to consider the 1982 act. The beginning of the act sets out its contents.

> An Act to make further provision with respect to the administration of justice and matters connected therewith; to amend the law relating to actions for damages for personal injuries, including injuries resulting in death and to abolish certain actions for loss of services; to amend the law relating to wills; to make further provisions with respect to funds in court statutory deposits and schemes for the common investment of such funds and deposits and certain other funds; to amend the law relating to deductions by employers under attachment of earning orders; to make further provisions with regard to penalties that may be awarded by the Solicitors Act 1974; to make further provision for the appointment of justices of the peace in England and Wales and in relation to temporary vacancies in the membership of the Law Commission; to enable the title register kept by the Chief Land Registrar to be kept otherwise than in documentary from; and to authorize the payment if traveling, subsistence and financial loss allowances for justices of the peace in Northern Ireland. (28th October 1982).

No mention of our topic! That is slipped in as part 3 of the act after a part entitled "Damages for Personal Injuries, Etc. -- Scotland" and before a part on "Wills." Part 3 reads:

> 15. (1) The section set out in Part I of Schedule 1 to this Act shall be inserted after section 35 of the Supreme Court Act 1981.

(2) The section set out in Part II of the Schedule shall be inserted after section 97 of the County Courts Act 1959.

(3) The Crown Proceedings Act 1947 shall accordingly have effect subject to the amendment in Part III of that Schedule, being an amendment consequential on subsections (1) and (2) above.

(4) The provisions mentioned in subsection (5) below (which this section supersedes so far as they apply to the High Court and county courts) shall cease to have effect in relation to those courts.

(5) The provisions are –

(a) section 3 of the Law Reform (Miscellaneous Provisions) Act 1934; and

(b) in the Administration of Justice Act 1969–

(I) section 22; and

(ii) in section 34(3) the words from "and section 22" onwards.

(6) The section set out in Part IV of Schedule 1 to this Act shall be inserted after section 19 of the Arbitration Act 1950.

16. The following subsection shall be added after section 23(5) of the Matrimonial Cause Act 1973 (financial provision in order in connection with divorce proceedings etc.) –

(6) Where the court —

(a) makes an order under this section for the payment of a lump sum; and

(b) directs —

(I) that payment of that sum or any part of it shall be deferred; or

(ii) that that sum or any part of is shall be paid by installments. The court may order that the amount deferred or the installments shall carry interest at such rate as may be specified by the order from such date of the order, as may be so specified, until the date when payment of it is due.

The statute has much of the charm hinted at by many observers of United Kingdom legislation: several subjects are dealt within one statute; the law on one subject is dealt with in several statutes; legislation is by reference to other legislation (thus increasing the obscurity); and there is a flight from the body of the statute to schedules.[264] Above all, the statute does not indicate that Parliament had given full, rounded consideration to the issue of when interest should be awarded for the nonpayment of a contractual debt.

R, H. S. Crossman records that when he was minister of housing and local government he never bothered to read any of the bills he got through the House of Commons, that "he never bothered to understand the actual clauses, nor did many Members, not even the spokesman for the Opposition."[265] Lord Brandon's argument would have us believe that the members of Parliament not only bothered to read and understand section 15 of the Administration of Justice Act of 1982 -- and understanding the section involves reading and understanding the schedule and the six statutes referred to in the section -- but understood what was not covered by the section and had made the deliberate decision not to have the injustice of case 1 corrected; and this deliberate decision involves them knowing the previous law, including case law. I, for one, remain skeptical and therefore find unpersuasive the second main reason for Lord Brandon's decision. Parliament's treatment of the Law Commission's 1978 Report on Interest (Cmnd.7229) and section 15 of the 1982 Administration of Justice Act do not encourage me to expect speedy reform by legislation. Incidentally, there is

---

[264] See, e.g., W. Dale *Legislative Drafting: A New Approach* (London, 1977), pp. 331ff., the publications of the Statute Law Society entitled *Statute Law: The Key to Clarity* (London, 1972), and *Renton and the Need for Reform* (1979), M. Zander, *The Law-Making Process* (London, 1980), pp. 9ff.

[265] *The Diaries of a Cabinet Minister* (London, 1975), pp.628.

something almost inconsistent in Lords Scarman and Roskill accepting Lord Brandon's reasoning as compelling (that Parliament did not want reform of case 1) and their expressed hope for legislative reform. It is worth recalling that if the lords had reformed case 1, they would not have been flouting the expressed wish of Parliament but altering the basis of a decision of their own of 1893.

A consideration of *President of India v. La Pintada Compañía Navigación* S.A. as an example of the judicial approach to lawmaking would be excessively incomplete without a glance at *London, Chatham and Dover Railway Co. V. The South Eastern Railway*, the case of 1893 from which their Lordships decided not to depart. In that case Lord Herschell, L.C., said:

> I confess that I have considered this part of the case with every inclination to come to a conclusion in favour of the appellant, to the extent at all events, if it were possible, of giving them interest from the date of the action; . . .But I have come to the conclusion, upon a consideration of the authorities, agreeing with the Court below, that it is not possible to do so.

And Lord Watson:

> I regret that I am unable to differ from your Lordships.

And Lord Shand:

> I confess that I have looked with very great anxiety to the possibility under the law of England, as I have heard it argued, of giving interest in this case, for I cannot help thinking that a gross injustice is the result of withholding it. It appears to me that it is a defective state of the law.

Thus, a judgment of 1893 that was regarded as unjust by the judges who issued it and was treated as settling the law leads judges who are not bound by it, ninety-one years later, to issue a judgment which they repeatedly expressly condemn as unjust, when there was no intervening legislation on the point in issue. The 1893 judges, of course, were particularly concerned with cases 2 and 3.

The main purpose of this part of the chapter is to discuss the case as a specimen of the House of Lords' approach to lawmaking. I am not suggesting that the approach taken in the case is unique or even unusual -- far from it. Nor is it relevant to inquire whether *sub specie aeternitatis* the decision ought to be regarded as unjust. Rather, the aim is to indicate that law was treated as existing in its own right, that judgment was to be reached by a mental process appropriate to establishing lawness, not by the judges' own feelings of what was just or what the law ought to be. The decision was unjust in the judges' own express opinion. They could have reached what they believed was the just decision by reversing a decision of their own of almost a century earlier, and they had the power to do so. Instead, they felt bound to come to the unjust decision because of a particular process of legal reasoning. First, they held that the law was previously settled. Second, they accepted that there is a hierarchy of lawmakers: legislators rank above judges. From that they reasoned that if legislators had not made a change in the law when they had the chance, then the judges ought not to make the change, since that would be to usurp the role of the legislators. And they deduced from the simple failure of the legislators to act a deliberate intention not to act. The argument is a legalistic one and will be acceptable to many within the tradition on that ground. But the artificiality -- and the legalistic nature -- of the reasoning is revealed both by the accepted refusal to inquire into the state of intention of the legislators and by the expressed hope that the legislators would change the law. One cannot, I believe, escape from this conclusion by postulating that the judges were shedding crocodile tears, that in fact they had reached the conclusion most acceptable to them for social, economic, or political reasons. First, if they had so thought, they need not have stressed that their judgment was unjust nor have expressed a hope for legislation, thus calling attention to the shortcomings of the decision. Second, it is difficult, and for me impossible, to understand what political, economic, or social bias would have motivated their decision. Third, one of them, Lord Scarman, had been chairman of the Law Commission, which recommended reform.

It will usually be outsiders, and especially outsider lawyers, who see the absurdity of legal reasoning in this fashion, who will ask how people can be paid and highly regarded for reasoning in this way. To the insider the form of lawmaking is hallowed by tradition; he cannot explain why it has come to be as it is, and he will be surprised if he is even asked to explain it.

II.

But the approach of the English judges should not be singled out. They are not alone in seeking a route to an answer they can justify not by the quality or suitability of the result but by a notion of lawness; a route that is artificial and seems bizarre to outsiders, and one the judges need not take.

Elsewhere I have already described one striking case of this kind from seventeenth-century Scotland.[266] Striking through it is, it represents a common attitude for the times both in Scotland and in continental Europe. A landowner had caused the pollution of a tributary of the river Tweed, which resulted in the deaths of Tweed salmon, thus causing loss to the Tweed commercial fishers. The fishers brought an action. The main arguments on both sides of the case proceed on the restrictions on the use of rivers in Roman law, and especially on the issue of whether a riparian owner had the right to pollute flowing water.

The societal economic factor at the heart of the case, where Scottish conditions were different from Italian, namely the existence of a large commercial river fishery, was never discussed in order to determine the relevance of Roman law as a guide. Yet Roman law was not part of Scots law and need not have been employed. But it had become common practice to look to Roman law when there was a gap in Scots law. The arguments

---

[266] Haining's Case, to be found in Sir George Mackenzie, *Works* (1716) 1, pp. 24ff., discussed in Watson *Evolution*, pp. 87ff.

proceeded on a view of lawness established by the legal tradition, an approach that owed much to prevailing fashion and was definitely not mandatory. We do not know the outcome of the case. Nor does it matter. What concerns us is that the attorneys on both sides thought the case ought properly to be adjudged on the basis of Roman rules and that the appropriateness of these rules for Scottish conditions was not brought into issue.

Even today in countries where the *Corpus Juris Civilis* and subsequent developments from it are still regarded as being in some sense part of the law of the land, or at least highly persuasive, the same problem of tradition may arise; judges may be so imbued with their legal culture that they approach their decision making through rules that were made to apply elsewhere and in very different circumstances, without always giving sufficient weight to the particulars of the case before them. The Republic of South Africa, now the predominant civil law country (though with an admixture of common law) where the law is unmodified, presents, naturally enough, the most obvious examples. One, from before independence, will suffice. By way of background it is enough to note that on the orthodox view, Roman-Dutch law and in particular the law of the Province of Holland in the seventeenth century, is authoritative in South Africa even without the impress of South African case law.[267] This Roman-Dutch law includes the *Corpus Juris Civilis* so far as received in the Netherlands (or perhaps so far as not abrogated by subsequent statute or a contrary custom), the writing of the Dutch jurists, and the decisions of the Dutch courts.

Mann v. Mann [1918] C.P.D. 89 was a case in which a woman living separate from her husband but without a judicial separation, and where there was no community of property, brought an action against him for assault both on the grounds of financial loss and of pain and suffering. As part of his judgment Searle, J., said:

---

[267] See, e.g., W.J. Hosten, A.B. Edwards, C. Nathan, and F. Bosman, *Introduction to South African Law and Theory* (1977), p. 222; H.R. Hahlo and E. Kahn, *The South African Legal System and Its Background* (1968), p. 581.

With regard to the Roman-Dutch on the subject, the absence of any known civil action ever having been brought in this Court on such grounds as these by a wife against her husband goes far to show that it has been tacitly recognized as not allowed by our law, but of course this is not conclusive. Under Roman-Dutch Law, marriages ordinarily take place in community of property, all the property of husband and wife is joint, though each may be regarded as entitled to half; the husband has the administration of the whole. Consequently, I do not see how there can be civil actions between them involving the payment of money by the one spouse to the other. If the wife sues the husband, the latter is entitled to have the amount of the judgment paid over to him, as long as the marriage subsists and there is no legal "separation"; it would be of no advantage to the wife to get a judgment against her husband for he still would be entitled to the administration of the proceeds.[268]

The statement is clear and reasonable, but not very helpful for the present case, where, as I have mentioned, the issue was precisely an action for assault where the parties were not married in community. Searle then goes on:

There are not many Roman-Dutch authorities which I have been able to find on this point, other than those quoted by the Magistrate. *Voet* (bk. 47, tit. 10, para. 2) shows, moreover, that a husband has marital power over his wife, but if he abuses that power by inflicting upon her any 'real' injury of a more serious kind, there is nothing to prevent her according to a decision reported by *Sande* suing him on account of injury, provided that the action, for the sake of the respect due to the estate of matrimony, be couched in moderate and

---

[268] Ap p. 94.

temperate language." *Voet* explains in paragraph 7 that by "real injury" he means a serious injury, and undoubtedly the assault here charged, if it be proved to have taken place, would be sufficiently serious to be styled "real." The learned author of this Book on Injuries in commenting on the above passage says at p. 42: "It is very questionable, however, whether a wife can sue a husband in a civil action for an injury done to her by him," and he refers to Brouwer *de Jure Connubiorum* (On the Law of Marriage) (2, 29, 12). This author says: "The Jurisconsults deny the *actio iniuriarum*, which is '*famosa*,' to a wife who has been severely and excessively beaten, without reason, but they allow the *actio in factum*, to the effect that the husband pay compensation for the injuries he has brought upon her. The former is correct, but the latter is not, for the law has provided a fixed penalty for this delict, and we ought to be content with the punishments contained in the laws." He then refers to a penalty prescribed in such case by Justinian, namely that the husband should give out of his own goods to the wife the third part of the goods settled by antenuptial contract; and points out that nowadays wife-beaters are handed over into custody for correction and emendation by the authorities, and that Justinian's penalty has never been adopted in practice, i.e. the practice of the Courts of Holland.

The discussion by the Dutch authorities largely concerns points of Roman pleading affected by substantive Roman law. Under Roman law a spouse could not bring an action against the other that would cause the unsuccessful defendant to be *infamis*, to suffer a kind of technical legal disgrace.[269] Such an action was the *actio iniuriarum*, the private action appropriate to assault.

---

[269] On *infamia* in Roman law see, above all, A.H.J. Greenidge, *Infamia: Its Place in Roman Public and Private Law* (Oxford, 1894).

To avoid *infamia* and to give the injured spouse an action for redress, the Romans granted an action on the facts, an *actio in factum:* an action for damages for assault would be allowed, but the unsuccessful defendant would not become *infamis*. The Dutch had not received the notion of *infamia*, nor the technical aspects of Roman pleading. The Romans, it is worth noting, had no system of matrimonial property regimes.

On the face of it, therefore, there should have been no obstacle in Holland to an injured wife, married without community, suing her estranged husband for assault. The opinion of à Sande and Johannes Voet would therefore seem to be vindicated. Hendryk Brouwer, whose opinion is cited without analysis, seems a trifle confused. If Justinian's penalty had not been accepted (in Holland) as he says, then the Roman jurists could not be inaccurate (for Holland) in allowing the *actio in factum* since that action could not have been displaced (in Holland) by the action with penalty.

Searle continues with further Roman-Dutch authority:

> The decision in *Sande* to which *Voet* refers is to be found in *Dec. Fris.* (Bk. 5, tit. 8, def. 9). After referring to an action against the wife as to which there was some difference of opinion among legal experts, he says: "And therefore Castellianus Catta lays down that a wife cruelly beaten by her husband ought to proceed by the *actio injuriarum* but only by the *actio in factum*, in order that the '*fama*' of the husband may still remain." One difference between the *actio injuriarum* in Roman law and the *actio in factum* ("on the case") consisted in the circumstance that the consequence of a defendant being condemned in the former action was that he suffered "*infama*," [*sic*] involving the loss of certain important civil rights (see *Hunter's* Roman Law, p. 546) whereas the *actio in factum* did not entail these consequences.
>
> *Ulrich Huber* in *Heedensdaegse Rechts Geleertheyt* in pt. 2, bk. 3, ch. 10, para. 21, says that the *actio injuriarum* does

not obtain between spouses, because he who is condemned in such an action loses reputation, or at all events has reputation lessened and such a result ought not to obtain as between spouses. As is pointed out by Mr. De Villiers the authorities thus do not seem to agree. *Voet* seems to think that the *actio injuriarum* lies, but quotes *Sande*, who says that it does not, but that an *actio in factum* does. *Huber* simply says that the *actio injuriarum* does not lie, and *Brouwer* says that neither action lies, because a specific punishment has been provided. *Sande* and *Huber* are Frisian authorities, and the Frisian law seems to have followed the Roman law more closely than the law of Holland, of which *Voet* and *Brouwer* are exponents.

Grotius in his *Introduction* (bk. 1 ch. 5, para. 20) says: "A husband may not beat his wife or otherwise illtreat her; and whichever of the spouses forgets himself or herself as against the other, is liable to such fine as is prescribed at each place for such offense, and is occasionally even more severely punished. In case of protracted quarrels, a separation from cohabitation may be granted by the Court.

Perezius on the *Code* (bk. 9, tit. 15, para. 4) after laying down that it is conceded according to prevailing custom that if the husband vents his rage against his wife he may be restrained according to the discretion of the Judge; and that it is always open to the wife on account of the intolerable cruelty of her husband to leave him and to live apart; and that in like manner a son who is badly treated by his father, may compel the father to grant him emancipation.

Groenewegen, De Leg. Abrog., commenting upon *Novel* 117, para. 14, says that if any one vents his rage against his wife without cause, by our customs he does not fall into this legal penalty (referring to divorce, and Justinian's rule as to the third part of the property, above cited) but he is wont to be fined according to the Judge's discretion; and that the husband may be made liable to pay alimony to a wife suing for it, away from her home; but he adds that it is lawful for a husband to chastise an erring or delinquent wife, and quotes a considerable number of authorities to that effect.

The argument of Ulrich Huber would seem to have little relevance because *infamia* did not exist in Holland. That the possibility or otherwise of a private action between spouses for damages for assault is not mentioned by some Roman-Dutch authorities is not surprising, no more than is the absence in South Africa in 1918 of a precedent, because in seventeenth-century Holland, too, marriage usually entailed full community of property. Thus Hugo Grotius, *Inleiding tot de Hollandische Rechtsgeleertheyd*, 2.11:

> 8.Marriage contracted in Holland or West Friesland produces community of goods between the spouses at common law, except in so far as community is found to be excluded or restricted by ante-nuptial contract; except when a young man beneath the age of five and twenty, or a girl beneath the age of twenty, marries without consent of parents, friends, or of the magistrate, as has been said above in treating of marriage; since in the case of such marriages, though the marriage proceed there is no community goods.
>
> Upon dissolution of the marriage the joint estate is divided equally between the spouses or their heirs: and if there are children who during the marriage have received anything from their parents to advance their marriage or trade and commerce, they must bring this advance in to the common estate before any division: and this bringing-in (*collatio bonorum*) enures for the benefit not only of the other children (we shall speak of this below) but of the surviving

spouse as well.[270]

Searle himself immediately continues:

> It certainly would seem to be an intolerable state of things that if a husband grievously assaulted his wife who was earning her own living apart from him in such manner that she was no longer able to earn it -- as for instance if he broke her arm -- she should only be able to prosecute him or bind him over to keep the peace, but should have no remedy of compensation for the loss she had sustained. For it would surely not be sufficient answer that the husband was bound to maintain his wife; he might be in a very poor position whilst she might be able to earn a large income. But probably the most reasonable view to arrive at is that suggested by Mr. Melius De Villiers in his work quoted above. He says (p. 42), "Where a husband and wife have been divorced or judicially separated there can be no reason why an action should not lie on account of injuries committed subsequent to the claim for divorce or separation being granted." It is true that the text writers do not appear to lay down this rule. Of course it goes without saying that when the parties are divorced and the marriage dissolved a civil action of damages for assault would lie; and although after a judicial separation the parties are still husband and wife, and the order is granted in hope of reconciliation I can see no reason why, as long as the order is in force, the relations between them should not be treated as so distinct that an action of compensation for an assault committed after the date of the order should lie.

---

[270] The translations are by R.W. Lee, *Hugo Grotius: The Jurisprudence of Holland* (Oxford, 1953), pp. 121, 123.

It is precisely here that Searle shows himself go be unnecessarily influenced, overinfluenced, in fact, by the cultural tradition of referring to Roman-Dutch law, which in this case was primarily concerned with a different factual situation. Certainly, as he says, "the law cannot provide for every individual case." But it can provide for marked categories such as where the couple were married without community. The opening sentences of the paragraph just quoted, where Searle voices his opinion on a husband assaulting a wife living apart, apply equally well where the spouses are married with community or without, and logically in the latter case whether the separation is judicial or not. Searle, however, expressly adopts the opinion of Melius De Villiers, with its restrictions: "Where husband and wife have been divorced or judicially separated there can be no reason why an action should not lie on account of injuries committed subsequent to the claim for divorce or separation." But he need not have done so, as he immediately goes on to show: "It is true that the text writers do not appear to lay down this rule." In the absence of a rule established by precedent or jurists he could have stated that an action for damages also lies against a spouse where the couple have separated and were not married in community of property. Further along in his opinion Searle says:

> Upon the whole, therefore, and not without some hesitation and some regret I come to the conclusion that there is no sufficient authority to show that this action is allowed by Roman-Dutch Law or that in the Courts of Holland it has been recognized; that it does not appear to have been recognized by our practice in the Supreme Court; that the bringing of such an action is hedged about with such great difficulties that we must hold that the remedy by way of civil compensation for assault should only be allowed to a wife living apart from her husband under an order of Court for judicial separation.[271]

---

[271] At p. 99

He is not entirely happy with the outcome of his judgment. But his decision is primarily culture determined, and not result oriented. His decision, which was not forced on him by the state of the law, is geared to show that he is a good judge concerned to come to the result by the mental process appropriate to establishing "lawness." (Though, writing in 1918, Searle may have been less sensitive to wife abuse than would often be the case today.)

But his approach is artificial in the extreme and takes little account of changed conditions in the law or social behaviour. The starting point is the refusal of the Romans to grant an *actio iniuriarum* between spouses. But the reason for this refusal -- at the action was infaming -- was long gone before seventeenth-century Holland, not to mention early twentieth-century South Africa. With the reason for the restriction gone, the restriction should also have gone. More could also have been made of the Roman ad hoc remedy on the facts. The absence of -- by no means total -- evidence for the action in Roman-Dutch law, in the courts of Holland, and in South Africa is explicable on the basis that the standard marriage was with community of property, whereas the Manns' marriage was without community. The changed factual situation makes the absence of authority of little relevance. The difficulties that hedge about an action between husband and wife in South African law are largely, as the first quotation from Searle shows, the result of community of property: any award to one against the other involves a withdrawal from joint property coupled with the addition of the same sum to the joint property, with no alteration in the allocation of resources.

Before we leave the case we must backtrack a little and return to a paragraph of Searle's slightly before the last quoted:

> *Voet*, in his book on the *Lex Aquilia*, the action allowed under the Roman-Dutch Law to recover compensation in damages for wrongs done (9, 2, 12), says: "These direct and equitable actions lie against those who have occasioned the damage, even against a wife or husband if the action does not bring

about *infamia*." This, as has been stated, would be the consequence if the *actio injuriarum* succeeds. He quotes in support of this the *Digest* (9, 2, 56) which lays down that a wife may be sued if she damages her husband's property. But *Voet* points out (in 47, 10, 13) that cases of assault to the person all fall under the class of *injuriae* proper; so that the fact that an action under Lex Aquilia can be brought between husband and wife does not take this matter much further.[272]

Mrs. Mann's case, though based on assault, was actually for medical expenses and for pain and suffering. Grotius, in the *Inleiding* (3.34.1, 2), says:

> Wrongs against the body are acts whereby someone loses a limb, is maimed, wounded or otherwise hurt. From this arise obligations to compensate for the surgeon's fee, for damage sustained and profit lost during the recovery, and also afterwards if the injury is lasting. Pain and disfigurement of the body, though properly incapable of compensation, are assessed in money, if such be demanded.

And the appropriate action for pain and suffering as well as for medical expenses was accepted by the Roman-Dutch authorities as being provided by the *lex Aquilia*, though the remedy is a post-Roman development.[273] It did lie between husband and wife because it was not infaming. Mrs. Mann should have succeeded. *Mann v. Mann* was effectively overruled by *Rohloff v. Ocean Accident Guarantee Corp., Ltd.* 1960 (2) S.A. 291 (A.D.), and it seems now to be accepted that an action based on the *lex Aquilia* will lie.[274]

---

[272] At p. 98.

[273] See, e.g., Grotius, *Inleiding*, 3.34.2; Voet, *Commentarius ad Pandectas*, 9.2.11: Matthaeus, *De Criminibus*, 47.3.3.4; Groenewegen, *Tractatus de Legibus Abrogatis et Inusitatis in Hollandia Vicinisque Regionibus*, D. 9.3.7.

[274] See, e.g .J.C. Macintosh and C.N. Scoble, *Negligence in Delict*, 5th ed.

The outsider from another legal tradition may find it bizarre to see judges struggling to interpret law put forth by authorities hundreds of years ago;[275] even more when the appropriate action is hard to discover; still more when the old law, when discovered, is not binding. But when judges in such a position fail to take much account of changes in the reason for the law or in societal conditions, then their approach is incomprehensible except in terms of the enormous impact of legal culture.

III.

A third type of approach is occasioned by one effect of the dominating event in most civil law countries, the promulgation of a civil code. In almost all cases the promulgation of a code involves a break with the references to the preceding law.[276] The reason is clear: what is wanted is a new beginning, and one of the main reasons for codification has often has often been a desire for simplicity in the law, and especially in the sources of the law.[277] Reference to the old law obstructs the fulfillment of this desire.[278] Thus, sooner or later, even for the interpretation of the code, judges and jurists will put a distance between the code and the older rules, even when the latter

---

(1970), p. 41. C. Van de Merwe and R. Olivier, *Die Onregmagtige Daad in Die Suid-Afrikaanse Reg.* 4th ed. (1980), accept Rohloff for the proposition that a delictal action lies between husband and wife not married in community but retain Mann for the proposition that an action does not lie when the marriage is in community; at pp. 302, 355.

[275] For a modern extreme and illuminating South African example see *Du Plessis NO v. Strauss,* 1988 (2) SA 105.

[276] There are, of course, exceptions, including the earliest of the modern civil codes, that of Bavaria, the *Codex Maximilaneus Bavaricus Civilis* (1756), which had only subsidiary force.

[277] See, e.g., Watson, *Civil Law,* p. 101; "Legal Change: Sources of Law and Legal Culture,"131 *University of Pennsylvania Law Review* (1983), pp. 1121ff. at p. 1132. J.P. Dawson, Book Review, 49 *University of "Chicago Law Review* (1982), pp. 595ff. at p. 602.

[278] But an early group of interpreters of the French *code civil*, the *école de l'exégèse,* did look at legislative history; and in the early days of the *code* old authorities were frequently cited in court.

formed the basis of the code provisions.

Yet sometimes there ought to be reference to the old law, for instance when a contract was made before the codification. Then there might be an obvious conflict, to be resolved only in terms of legal culture, between the need to recognize that the old law is deeply relevant and the overwhelming desire to restrict its impact. The issue arises in a particularly striking form when, for example, at the heart of a dispute is a continuing contract, such as a lease, made many years before the code but entailing obligations even into the future.

Such a case is that of the French Cour de Cassation, Chambre Civil, 6 March 1876, *De Galliffet v. Commune de Pélissane.* Insofar as it concerns us here, the Civil Court of Aix found on 18 March 1861 that by a contract of 22 June 1567 Adam de Craponne agreed to construct and maintain an irrigation canal and to irrigate the lands of the commune of Pélissane. In addition, it was agreed that for the irrigation of each carteirade, three sols would be paid to Adam de Craponne or his heirs, and the commune was not to levy taxes on the revenues from the canal. Adam de Craponne agreed to maintain the canal and bridges over it in perpetuity. The court further found, in addition to the terms of the contract, that the costs of irrigation and of maintenance of the canal had risen to such an extent that the cost of irrigation was out of all proportion to the payment and that the enterprise would have to be given up unless the payment for irrigation of each carteirade was raised. The court ordered the cost to be raised to sixty centimes (i.e., about fourfold), and justified this on the ground that when a contract involves successive performances over a long period the court may on equitable principles revise the contract in the light of changed circumstances that make the contract unjust.

After some related actions the Court of Appeals of Aix on 31 December 1873 affirmed the decision of the Civil Court, declaring: "It is recognized in law that contracts resting on periodic performance may be modified by the court when a balance no longer exists between the performance of the one party and the obligation of the other." The commune of Pélissane then raised a *pourvoi* before the Cour de Cassation. The ground that concerns us is based on article 1134 of the *code civil*, which states:

> Legally formed agreements take the place of law for those who made them.
> They can be revoked only by their mutual agreement or for reasons that the law authorizes.
> They must be executed in good faith.

The relevant part of the opinion of the Cour de Cassation reads:

> But, on the first ground of the *pourvoi*:—art. 1134 of the *code civil* duly considered. Whereas the provision of that article is only the reproduction of ancient principles followed in the matter of obligations by agreement, the fact that the contracts giving rise to the lawsuit are anterior to the promulgation of the civil code cannot be, in the instant case an obstacle to the application of the said article;—Whereas the rule that it promulgates is general, absolute, and governs the contracts whose performance extends to successive ages just as it does those of a quite different nature; that in no case is it the function of tribunals, no matter how equitable their decisions may appear to them, to take into account time and circumstances to modify the agreements of the parties and substitute new clauses for those freely accepted by the contracting parties; that in deciding to the contrary and in raising the irrigation charge to 30 centimes from 1834 to 1874, then to 60 centimes from 1874, fixed at 3 sols by the agreement of 1560 and 1567 under the pretext that the sum payable was no longer in relationship with the costs of maintenance of the canal by Craponne, the judgment under attack formally violated art. 1134 above considered.

And the court went on to quash the decision of the court of appeal. The court's response should perhaps be amplified for a non-French audience. Inherent in the argumentation, though not made express as self-explanatory, is a principle of French interpretation that "one must not draw a distinction where the law draws none."[279] Hence, since article 1134 draws no distinction between contracts executed by one single performance and continuing contracts, the court must draw none.

The Cour de Cassation seemed to agree that the decision of the lower court could appear equitable but quashed it nonetheless on the ground that it is not for the court to set aside the agreement of the parties. But the decision was not forced on the court, which might have fixed its gaze on the good faith of the parties under article 1134 rather than on the equitable approach of the courts. It could possibly have held that when changed circumstances rendered the balance between one party's performance and the other's obligation to pay so disproportionate that performance would be impossible for any standard commercial enterprise, then it was contrary to good faith for the second party to insist on the continued performance of the contract; or that changed circumstances external to the parties rendered its performance impossible by a *force majeure* that could not be imputed to the successors of Adam de Craponne.

But our interest lies in a different matter. Obviously for the decision, the law as it was in Pélissane in 1567 when the last contract was made cannot be irrelevant; and the court says of article 1134: "Whereas the provision of this article only reproduces ancient principles continually followed in the law of obligations. . . ." It evinces no desire to show any authority for these ancient principles -- how widely held they were, what exceptions there were to them, and above all whether they applied to contracts made in Pélissane in 1567. All the judges want to do is to make article 1134 the main governing law for the contract. They have to make a bow in the direction of the older law, but in reality they are, again for cultural reasons, taking the *code civil* as the starting

---

[279] See, e.g., A. Weill and F. Terré, *Droit Civil: Introduction Générale*, 4th ed. (1979), p. 184.

point of the law. They might get an apparently fairer answer by looking at the older law, but though they need not do so, they adopt an approach to discovering the law that excludes the possibility.

In fact, there were no ancient principles in Pélissane in 1567 corresponding to article 1134. Pélissane lies in the *pays de droit écrit*, and in the absence of a local rule of customary law (which probably could not have been discovered by the court in 1876), recourse would be had to the *Corpus Juris Civilis* and its common interpretation. Roman law knows no such ancient principle as that indicated by the court. On the contrary, although there is no text exactly on the point of a contract extending over centuries, there is ample evidence for the contract of hire (*locatio conductio*) -- admittedly texts relating to hire of a thing -- to show that changed circumstances could change the contractual obligations. Thus, if in the lease of land, exceptional climatic conditions, such as drought, or a force external to the land that could not be avoided, such as a plague of starlings, ruined the crop, then the tenant was excused from paying the rent for that year.[280] Again, if the windows of a leased building were subsequently obscured by a neighbour, the tenant could avoid the lease.[281] Subsequently, instances such as these came to be categorized; for instance, for Robert Pothier (1699–1772) the lessor implicitly guarantees that the window will not be obstructed by a neighbour, if the light is needed by the tenant.[282]

What Roman law did have, however, which is the historical ultimate source of article 1134, is the rule that parties to a contract might by agreement impose standards different from those settled in law. Thus: *Digest of Justinian*, 16.3.1.6: "If it is agreed in a deposit that there will be liability even for negligence, the agreement is ratified: for the contract became law by the agreement."[283] Normally there was liability in deposit only for fraud. The immediate source of article 1134 is in Jean Domat (1625–96), *Les Loix*

---

[280] *D.* 19.2.15.2,3.

[281] *D.* 19.2.25.2

[282] *Traité du Contrat de Louage*, art. 113.

[283] See also along the same lines *D.* 50.17.23.

Civiles dans Leur Ordre Naturel, 1.1.2.7.: "Where the agreements are completed, whatever has been agreed on stands in place of a law to those who made them; and they cannot be revoked except by the mutual consent of the parties, or by the other ways to be explained in the sixth section." Domat refers to the *Digest* text just quoted and to others that are, at the most, to the same effect.[284] There is no indication that Domat was going beyond the Roman law to reach the proposition that judges have no right (as they had in Roman law) equitably to alter the terms of a contract when conditions had drastically altered. Indeed, Domat accepts at 1.4.2.18 that if, as a result of *force majeure*, the lessee is unable to enjoy the object of the lease, he is excused paying rent. French law before the *code civil* did not know these "ancient principles" spoken of by the Cour de Cassation.

The wording of article 1134 follows that of Domat closely, and from that alone one would probably be justified in thinking that the draftsmen of the *code civil* also were not going beyond Domat and the Roman rules. But we have the *travaux préparatoires*, which also contain no indication that the draftsmen considered themselves to be departing from Domat.[285] The Cour de Cassation either misunderstood or deliberately (and without express recognition) extended the scope of article 1134. The decision was a consequence of the legal culture, which put a distance between the *code civil* and earlier French law. Not surprisingly, the decision, which might appear inequitable, was applauded by the French jurists of the time on account of the judges' mode of reasoning.[286]

IV.

Examples even more remote from us in the legal tradition bring home in a particularly clear manner the absurdity of judges unnecessarily adopting a

---

[284] *D.* 50.17.23, 2.14.1, 50.17.34.

[285] See P.A. Fenet, 13 *Recueil Complet des Travaux Préparatoires du Code Civil* (1827, reprinted 1968), p.54. The sole discussion related to the last sentence. Portalis successfully suggested the deletion of "contractées et" before "executées." See also C. Baudry-Lacantinerie and L. Barde, *Traité Théorique et Pratique de Droit Civil: Les Obligations,* 3d ed. (1906), 1, pp. 381ff.

mental process to establish that their decisions are governed by principles of lawness. Thus, it is common in mediaeval Germany for a town to adopt a "mother" town in legal matters to which it looked for legal opinion, even though it was in no political dependency on the mother. The mother might have been chosen for the "daughter" town by the founder when the town was established, or it might have been voluntarily selected. Especially in the latter case could another mother town be subsequently chosen, and mother towns in their turn often selected a mother town for themselves. Magdeburg in Saxony is the prime example of a mother city, and its law prevailed in most of the towns of Ostfalen, Mark Brandenburg, Mark Meissen, Lausitz, Silesia, Lithuania, the Prussian territories of the Teutonic Order, and the kingdom of Poland, in Stettin, and, for some time, in Stargard in Pomerania and in Moravia. In general, moreover, it was the main influence on the law in Bohemia, and Moravia. Many of the towns though, had a very different law of family property, and hence of succession. Magdeburg had the old Saxon arrangement of the administration and use of the wife's property by the husband with direct descent and widow's portion in the event of death, whereas many towns of Thuringia had the Frankish system of common property in all acquisitions or of general community of property.[287] This difference in law did not stop judges of daughter towns from presenting problems on such matters to the Schöffen -- the title given to the nonprofessional judges -- of Magdeburg. The following case gives a fifteenth-century opinion rendered by the Schöffen of Magdeburg to the court of Schleiz in Thuringia.[288]

The honorable Schöffen of Magdeburg: A legal reply made

---

[286] See Baudry-Lacantinerie and Barde, *Traité,* at p. 383 and n. 1.

[287] See, e.g., Schröder, *Geschicte des Ehelichen Güterrechts in Deutschland,* Teil 2, Abt. 3 (1967, original edition 1874), pp. 69ff., at pp. 187ff.

[288] It appears as number 123 of the first book of the collection of Schöffen opinions of the town of Pössneck: 1 *Die Schöffenspruchsammlung der Stadt Pössneck* (Grosch, ed., 1957), pp. 1118ff. See also vol. 3, at p. 7 (Buchda, ed., 1962). The

for the court at Schleiz relating to succession.

Since you sent us writings of two parties, namely the charge and accusation of Hans Krebis and the counter-plea and reply of Hans Helwig as guardian of his wife, and requested us to state the law, etc., and as each of the two parties in their writings allege some privilege [i.e., a particular right of a legal community, and especially of a town] and town custom, which appears to state, express, and be to the effect that "If a man die without heirs of the body, if the same man graces his wife with all his goods, to enjoy them personally after his death until the end of her life" -- of such custom it does not please us to take notice in law. But we, the Schöffen of Magdeburg, give our reply on the matter in accordance with law on the complaint and answer:

If Hans Helwig, defender of this matter as guardian of his wife, demonstrates with the testimony of the court and completely, in so far as is correct, that Hans Krebis in sound body and good mind gave by way of inheritance, delivered and properly left to his wife before the court, in fear of his death, a meadow situated in Ollssenicz [Olsnitz(?) In Saxony, 60 km south of Leipzig], a barn, a garden, and in addition all his movable goods, that she might do with them as she pleases; if he proves that completely, if the same woman [Frau Helwig] has held the gift and possession for a year and a day and longer without the legal objection of anyone, then the same gift must in law remain in effect; and the widow of Hans Krebis, now the wife of Hans Helwig, has a closer title and better right to such aforementioned goods, namely the meadow, barn, garden, and all moveables, than that Hans Krebis, the nephew of her deceased husband can prevent her and claim from her on account of succession.

translation is mine.

The judges of Schleiz did not need to take the case to the Schöffen of Magdeburg, but they did. They also did not need to follow the opinion of the Schöffen. The pleadings sent by the Schleiz court made it plain that the law at Schleiz on that issue was not the same as the law in Magdeburg. The Schöffen of Magdeburg made it equally plain that they were giving their opinion based only on the Saxon law. Nor were the Magdeburg Schöffen here following a course unusual for them: they did not usually decide according to the law of the petitioners.[289] The judges of Schleiz were unlikely to have been unaware of the Magdeburg practice. We do not know if the judges of Schleiz eventually decided according to the ruling from Magdeburg or not. If they did, then they were overturning the established and usually followed local custom when they did not need to do so and for reasons not inevitably connected with the welfare of the populace or the expectations of the parties to the lawsuit. If they did not, then an outsider might wonder at the odd, superfluous behaviour of the Schleiz judges in approaching the Schöffen of Magdeburg. Whether they did or did not follow the opinion of the Magdeburg Schöffen, the judges of Schleiz were, for the insider, establishing that they were following the proper principles for lawness. It was appropriate but not necessary in a difficult case to have the opinion of the Magdeburg Schöffen, and it was appropriate, though not necessary, to accept that opinion. The Schleiz judges were adopting the appropriate course even when the laws of Schleiz and Magdeburg differed and when the Magdeburg Schöffen would base their opinion solely on the law of Magdeburg.

A system similar to that in Germany of applying to the Schöffen of a mother town also existed elsewhere, in Belgium, for instance, from the twelfth century[290] and in parts of Spain between the twelfth and fourteenth

---

[289] Whereas the Schöffen of Leipzig did attempt to judge according to the law of the petitioners.

[290] For what is now modern Belgium, see J. Gilissen, *Introduction Historique au Droit* (1970), pp. 247ff. He observes that there were very many jurisdictions, even in small communities, and that the échevins, who were both

centuries. In Spain, the *fuero* (that is, town charter or town privileges) of one town might be granted to others by the king or some other lord, or the redactors of a *fuero* might take another as a model. A town whose *fuero* was highly regarded by others, whether it had been granted, borrowed, imitated, or simply admired, would be visited by notables from the other towns. For instance Alfonso II of Aragón said in 1187 that people continually came from Castile, Navarre, and other lands to Jaca to learn the good customs and *fueros* and take them home.[291] In fact, such was the reputation of the extensive *fuero* of Jaca (of 1063) and of its lawyers that towns inhabited by *francos*—a term indicating foreigners on whom had been bestowed particular privileges—such as Estella (whose *fuero* of 1164 received part of the law of Jaca elaborated until that date), San Sebastian (in Viscaya, whose *fuero* authorized by King Sancho el Sabio of Navarre [1150-94] derived from that of Estella), Fuenterrabía (in Castile), and Pamplona (which was granted the *fuero* of Jaca by Alfonso I in 1129), not only consulted Jaca on the interpretation of certain rules but in the case of litigation actually sent appeals to the authorities of Jaca as the true interpreters of the law; this although the law in their towns was by no means identical with that of Jaca. But later the *jurados y hombres buenos* of Pamplona wrote to the judges and notables of the city of Jaca that they had many books of *fueros*, supposedly of Jaca, that, however, did not always give the same law, and they asked that their *fueros* be corrected by the master *fuero* held by the judges of Jaca. The reply of 27 August 1342 refused the request, pointing out that the habit of appealing to Jaca was observed also by cities ruled by the king of Navarre and referring to the ancient bond of love

---

administrators and judges, had no legal training. When difficulties arose in a lawsuit, it became habitual to send the issue to the échevins of a larger town or village "which followed approximately the same custom." In the twelfth and thirteenth centuries the law of many towns was granted to other towns: Bruges, for example, was mother town to more than twenty others.

[291] See, e.g. J.M. Lacarra, *Fueros Derivados de Jaca*, vol. I, *Estella-San Sebastián* (1969), p. 21; J.M. Lacarra and A.J.M. Duque, *Fueros Derivados de Jaca*, vol. 2, *Pamplona* (1975), p. 56.

between Jaca and Pamplona.[292] Presumably, the judges of Jaca refused because if the jurists of Pamplona had the correct text, they would not need to send appeals to Jaca.[293]

No doubt the judges of Jaca, like the Schöffen of Magdeburg, deserved their high regard, but it would be stretching human credulity to believe that at times the appeal to them was not also inappropriate.[294] The approach to Jaca seems unnecessary, but again, it was intended to show that the judges of the other towns had a proper attitude to judging.[295]

V.

Thus, contemporary House of Lords judges in England have such regard for the will of the legislature that they interpret absence of legislation as indicating a deliberate intention not to act and therefore they follow, when they need not, their own ancient precedent to a judgment that they declare unjust; in uncodified civil law or "mixed" systems, courts in seventeenth-century Scotland and twentieth-century South Africa rely on Roman or Roman-Dutch law, which is not binding on them, even when circumstances are very different and the reliance is inappropriate; judges in France a half century and more after the promulgation of the *code civil* so wish to keep themselves removed from the law before the code that they do not look for it when it is relevant and come to misinterpret the basis of provisions of the code; judges in fifteenth-century Germany have such regard for the Schöffen

[292] The reply is reprinted by Lacarra and Duque, *Fueros Derivados*, at pp. 235 ff.; but the accurate version of four chapters was sent.

[293] Ibid. p. 57.

[294] Jaca was by no means the only town whose *fuero* spread widely. Estella itself is another notable example. See in general Tomás y Valiente, *Manual de Historia del Derecho Espanol*, 4th ed. (Madrid, 1983), pp. 150ff.

[295] There is no direct evidence that it was the judges of, say, Pamplona, and not the parties to the lawsuit, who appealed to the judges of Jaca, but it is difficult to imagine the decision of Jaca would have any impact otherwise on the enforceability of the decision in Pamplona. Moreover, the reply from Jaca of 27 August 1342 makes little sense if it was not the judges of Pamplona who raised the appeal. No such decisions of the *"jurados y hombres buenos"* of Jaca seem to have been

of a mother town that they consult them, though they have no obligation to do so, even in a case where they know their law is different and can expect an answer based on the mother's law; in thirteenth- and fourteenth-century Spain judges even sent their appeals to the town whose *fuero* was at the root of their own.

The cases discussed in this chapter have been put together not for the purpose of comparing or contrasting the approaches but to bring out a common theme within the Western legal tradition. Judges set out to establish themselves as good judges, to show that they are correctly analyzing the legal implications of the case before them by a particular mental process -- which may differ from system to system. This process shows a high regard for "lawness," for the establishment of the decision on a foundation other than that of the judges' authority or of their right or power to make law. The process has a legitimating function: the judges have the right and power to chose their decision, but they must not exercise their choice arbitrarily. The process involves going beyond the boundaries of the existing law, and it is culturally determined. The mental process, of course, belongs to the culture of the judges and those who practice before them, not specifically to the culture of the population at large or the ruling elite. The influence of the legal culture is so powerful that the mental process is used even when it leads to results that are inappropriate whether because the decision -- which is not inevitable -- is unjust in the eyes of the judges themselves, or societal conditions have altered in a significant regard, or the legal basis for the approach has gone. Of course, it is precisely when the results are inappropriate that the impact of culture on the judges' attitudes is most apparent, but the cases are not otherwise atypical.

One subsidiary, but rather uncomfortable, conclusion follows. It is not possible to read any judgment so as to understand fully a judge's approach without considerable understanding of the legal culture in which he or she operates, which means in effect that a great deal of knowledge of legal history is needed: legal history, in fact, that in many instances involves the history of

published.

other legal systems.

Chapter 11

The Law of Delict and Quasi Delict in the French *Code Civil*

From the eleventh century until the successful modern codification movement in the eighteenth century, European law in the West presents a picture of overwhelming complexity. There were many strands to the law: local custom, feudal law, local legislation, canon law, and Roman law. The same individual in different aspects of his or her life might be subject to various courts: the feudal court of one's lord, the canon law court of the church, the court of the village or town, with possibly an appeal to a court of different outlook such as the Parlement de Paris or the Reichskammergericht. Two systems of law, Roman law and canon law, were regarded as having transnational significance, even though the extent to which Roman law was received in practice varied from territory to territory. Roman law and canon law worked upon each other, with Roman law the dominant partner, to form eventually the *ius commune*, virtually a common learned law for Western Europe. In any state, of course, the impact of the *ius commune* depended on the strength of the other local elements.[296]

The importance of customary law in the mixture is easily underrated, for various reasons. There was a profusion of customary legal systems,

---

[296] See, in general, H. Coing, *Europäisches Privatrecht*, 1500 bis 1800, vol. I (Munich, 1985). On proliferation of courts in Germany, see G. Strauss, *Law, Resistance and the State* (Princeton, 1986), p. 122. In this present book the terms *private law* and *public law* appear frequently. I am fully aware that the distinction is not easy to draw, that many legal rules or statutes partake of both, and that, especially for medieval law (though also at other times), the distinction has little substance. But, as many others have found, the distinction is, in general, a convenient one. My usage of *private law* is, I hope, consistent as well as useful: the term covers all those topics of law that are dealt with in the *Institutes* of Justinian, with the exception of crimes

varying greatly from one another and often having very limited territorial jurisdiction. Customary law was not studied in the universities of medieval or Renaissance Europe. It lacks the charm of sophistication of Roman law and the *ius commune*. Above all, with the rise of the modern world, much of customary law was abandoned, or if it did survive, it was in a very different guise. An inhabitant of today's world, whether from a civil law or a common law country, will feel more at ease reading the *Institutes* of Justinian than the *Coutumes de Normandie* (Customs of Normandy).[297]

Nonetheless, during the eleventh to eighteenth centuries, the two primary intersecting strands in Western legal development were local customary law and Roman law (Often in the form of the *ius commune*), with the latter, gradually or more swiftly depending on the particular territory, acting to fill gaps in, modify, render more sophisticated, or replace the former.[298] The modern civil codes are largely the result of this intertwining. But the specific contribution of each strand is not easily determined.

Thus, to estimate the force of the Roman law strand, one must find the answer to a question that I have never seen raised. That is, what was the impact of Roman rules on the legal rules in modern civil codes when the Roman rules were inappropriate either because of changed societal conditions or attitudes, or because for some reason the Roman rules themselves were underdeveloped? If the Roman rules were not accepted, must one simply deny any input and restrict the Reception of Roman law to instances of direct borrowing? Is nonacceptance rejection? This certainly seems to have been the attitude of some distinguished scholars who have, perhaps, not quite seen the issue. Thus Jean Brissaud regards codification in France as a victory for

---

and actions: precisely the subject matter of modern civil codes.

[297] To see the impact of this underevaluation of local customary law, it is enough to examine Coing, *Priuatrecht*, vol. I, and the volumes produced under the guidance of H. Coing, *Handbuch*.

[298] For an account of the impact of sophisticated law in writing on customary legal systems see Alan Watson, *The Evolution of Law* (Baltimore, 1985), pp. 66 ff.

customary law over Roman law.[299] For Paul Viollet, "Our codes, considered from the historical point of view, are the concentration and unification of the old French law, dispersed, and often divergent, in the royal *ordonnances* and the customs."[300] And Rudolf B. Schlesinger bluntly states:

> On one point, however, there can be no reasonable difference of opinion: The old adage, all-too-frequently repeated, that the civilian codes presently in force are merely a modernized version of Roman law, is simply nonsense. In many respects, the solutions adopted by the codifiers were not traditional, and of the traditional ones, many were not Roman. The late Professor Reginald Parker was probably right when he said: "I seriously believe it would not be difficult to establish, if such a thing could be statistically approached, that the majority of legal institutes, even within the confines of private law, of a given civil law country are not necessarily of Roman origin."[301]

The implication seems to be that when Roman solutions are not adopted, Roman law has no impact. A further implication seems to be that the impact of Roman law on modern law was not as great as has been supposed and may be safely ignored.

The matter, I believe, is not so simple. I intend no paradox, but this chapter will be devoted to an investigation of the Reception of Roman *law* when the Roman *rules* were not received. The issue is, what happens to the law upon codification when the Roman legal rules are obviously inappropriate and hence not accepted? Each situation of fact and law will be different, and I do not intend to build up a general theory. My temperament and training direct me to proceed from detailed analysis, and I wish here to concentrate on the articles that appear in the French *code civil* of 1804 under the heading

---

[299] See *General Survey of Events, Sources, Persons and Movements in Continental Legal History*, by various European authors (Boston, 1912), p. 286.

[300] *Histoire du droit civil français*, 3d ed. (Paris, 1905), p. 220. However, Viollet would not refuse some place to Roman law: see pp. 11ff.

[301] *Comparative Law*, 4th ed. (Mineola, 1980), p. 280.

"Delicts and Quasi Delicts":

1382. Every action of a human which causes injury to another binds the person through whose fault it occurred to make it good.

1383. Everyone is responsible for the injury which he caused not only by his action, but also by his negligence or imprudence.

1384. One is responsible for the injury which one causes by one's own action, but also for that which is caused by the action of persons for whom one is responsible, or of things which one has under one's guard.

The father, and the mother after the death of the husband, are responsible for the injury caused by their minor children living with them;

Masters and employers for the injury caused by their servants and agents in the functions for which they employed them;

Teachers and craftsmen for the injury caused by their pupils and apprentices during the time that they were under their surveillance.

The above responsibility lies, unless the father and the mother, teachers

and craftsmen prove that they could not have prevented the action which gives

rise to the responsibility.

1385. The owner of an animal or the person who makes use of it, while it is subject to his use, is responsible for the injury which the animal has caused, whether the animal was under his guard, whether it had wandered off or escaped.

1386. The owner of a building is responsible for the injury caused by its fall when that occurred as a consequence of a defect in maintenance or by a fault in its construction.[302]

To begin with, we will take these articles at face value on the subject of the basis of liability. The relationship among the five provisions is by no means clear. Articles 1382 and 1383, dealing with responsibility for one's own actions, make liability clearly dependent on fault, including negligence; and though this is not expressly said, the normal burden of proving negligence will lie with the plaintiff. But how can one understand the basis of liability in article 1384 for the behaviour of persons for whom one is responsible or for things under one's guard? With one crucial exception, that of master and servant, nothing is said about the basis of liability. The first issue to which no answer is given directly is whether the person for whom one is responsible must have been at fault for liability to accrue. One might at first say no, since

---

[302] 1382. Tout fait quelconque de l'homme, qui cause à autrui un dommage, oblige celui par la faute duquel il est arrivé, à le réparer.

1383. Chacun est responsable du dommage qu'il a causé par son propre fait, mais encore par sa négligence ou par son imprudence.

1384. On est responsable, non seulement du dommage que l'on cause par son propre fait, mais encore de celui qui est causé par le fait des personnes dont on doit répondre, ou des choses que l'on a sous sa garde.

Le père, et la mère après le décès du mari, sont responsables du dommage causé par leurs enfans mineurs habitant avec eux; Les maîtres et les commettans, du dommage causé par leurs domestiques et préposés dans les functions auxquelles il les ont employés;

Les instituteurs et les artisans, du dommage causé per leurs élèves et apprentis pendant le temps qui'ils sont sous leur surveillance.

La responsabilité ci-dessus a lieu à moins que les père et mère, instituteurs et artisans, ne prouvent qu'ils n'ont pu empêcher le fait qui donne lieu è cette responsabilité.

1385. Le propriétaire d'un animal, ou celui qui s'en sert, pendant qu'il est à son usage, est responsable du dommage que l'animal a causé soit que l'animal fût sous sa garde, soit qu'il fût égaré ou échappé.

1386. Le propriétaire d'un bâtiment est responsable du dommage causé par sa ruine, lorsqu'elle est arrivée par une suite du défaut d'entretien ou par le vice de la construction.

minor children will often be under the age at which any fault could be attributed to them. Nothing is said to divide minor children into categories, and it is a principle of French law that one cannot make a distinction where the law makes none.[303] Nevertheless, in favour of a positive response is the fact that a master is liable for injuries caused by the action of a servant. Is a master liable for his own behaviour only if he is at fault, but to be automatically and strictly liable for the injury caused by a servant who was not at fault? Common sense would suggest not. Thus, article 1384 does not yield a clear answer, negative or positive. Nor is there any indication on the face of the article whether for liability to be caused by a thing, the thing must have been defective.

When we look elsewhere for the basis of liability, in the behaviour of the "superior," we are left in just as great a state of confusion. For injury caused by the behaviour of servants and agents and things, there is no clear indication whether for liability the superior himself had to have been at fault. One might feel that the superior here was always absolutely liable, even if free from fault, since the sole exception to liability – applying expressly to parents, teachers, and craftsmen – is not stated so as to apply to the master of servants and agents or the guardians of things. But it might be rash to draw such a conclusion. And does article 1384 really equate the liability of the superior for the behaviour of persons with his liability for the behaviour of things? We should suppose so, since they are treated without distinction in the same article. But that conclusion seems unpalatable.

The exception, too, causes problems. Parents, teachers, and craftsmen are excused from liability for injury caused by their children, pupils, and apprentices only if they can show that they could not have prevented the behavior. The basis of liability here is not that for one's own actions put forth in articles 1382 and 1383; at the very least, the burden of proof here has been shifted to the defendant.

More than that, it seems that the defendant is not free from liability if

---

[303] See for example A. Weill and F. Terré, *Droit civil: introduction générale*, 4th ed. (Paris, 1979), p. 184.

he proves he was not negligent; he must show that he could not have prevented the behaviour. And we must remember that we cannot tell whether the behaviour in question had to be negligent or worse on the part of the actual doer.

Article 1385, in its turn, does not on its face provide us with an answer to the two relevant questions: first, whether the animal had to be at "fault" for liability to be imposed on the master or operator, and, second, whether for liability the master had to be at fault in allowing the animal to cause injury.

Article 1386 is clearer in its meaning but leaves us no less confused. The owner of a building that collapses and causes injury is liable for the damage in either of two cases: where the collapse was the result of poor maintenance (fault on the part of the owner), and where the collapse was the result of a fault in the construction (a defect in the building). But this second case leaves us with several problems to which the article, on its face, provides no solution. First, why is the owner liable even when he is without fault -- he may have had no part in the construction and may have been unable to check for defects in construction -- when for his own behaviour he is liable only when at fault? Second, why is a distinction made with regard to a building in article 1386 and things under one's guard in article 1384, and what is the nature of that distinction? Third, why does article 1386 speak expressly only of buildings and not of immovables in general? For example, a tree may fall if it has not been properly looked after or if it is defective. In enumerating the problems of the basis of liability under the five articles, we should finally note that the heading refers to both delicts and quasi-delicts, but neither term appears in the text of the articles.[304] The terminology is not elucidated further, nor is any difference in the basis of liability for one or the other.

We are still not yet concerned with the intention of the drafters of the code. But in light of what has just been said, it should be admitted with regard

---

[304] The terms *délit* and *quasi-délit* do appear in article 1370, along with *quasi-contrat*, as types of obligations that arise without agreement, but they are neither defined nor explained.

to the basis of liability both that the articles were poorly drafted and that the drafters either were hopelessly confused or had no consistent policy. What explanation can be found for these facts? I should emphasize here that the issue is not just of theoretical significance. The basis of liability under these five articles is one of the most controversial issues in the interpretation of the *code civil*, as the merest glance at the battery of apparatus, from both "doctrine" and "jurisprudence," laid out in the *Petit Code Dalloz* edition, would show.

First, the short answer. The confusion occurs above all in situations in which Roman solutions, as set out in Justinian's *Corpus Juris Civilis*, were inappropriate and could not be expressly used because of changed social conditions and societal attitudes -- but in which those solutions or texts had a hidden impact.

Thus, in articles 1382 and 1383, the basis of liability for one's own behaviour -- of which rather more must be said later -- is obviously based on fault. This was the position in Roman law, especially under the *lex Aquilia*.[305]. But the first problem that concerns us arises only in article 1384, which covers liability for the actions of persons for whom one was responsible. Under Roman law, the dependent person for whom a superior was responsible would be a son in the power of his father (a *filiusfamilias*) or a slave. A slave had no legal standing in private law and could not be sued directly, and a *filiusfamilias* owned no property and was not worth suing. The *paterfamilias* was logically the only person who could be sued, and liability vested in him -- as did, for example, rights regarding the contracts of sons or slaves -- because he was the head of the family. Roman law gave the victim an action against the owner or father as the *paterfamilias* for the wrongful behaviour, whether malicious or negligent, of a slave or son, but the defendant could avoid condemnation in the money sum by handing over the slave or son to the victim in noxal surrender before judgment was pronounced.[306] The notion was therefore a primitive form of limited liability. The wrongful behaviour of a

---

[305] See, for example, *D*. 9.2.

[306] See, for example, *D*. 9.2.27.3.; *h.t.*44.1; 9.4.2.*pr.*; 1; *h.t.*4.2; *h.t.*6.

dependent could result in a loss to his or her "superior," but only up to the worth of the wrongdoer. Fault on the part of the superior was irrelevant because liability was based solely on his position as head of the family except that it might in some circumstances exclude his right to hand over the actual perpetrator in noxal surrender.[307] Fault on the part of the dependent was necessary, just as fault alone made a person of independent status (*sui juris*) liable for injury caused by his or her behaviour. The absence in France of noxal surrender (and of anything equivalent to the Roman *patria potestas*) meant that this neat and satisfactory solution could not be adopted. This resulted as I will show in the long answer in some confusion of thought both among the drafters of the *code civil* and among the French legal scholars who preceded them. Hence the failure in the *code civil* to make liability in article 1384 depend clearly either on fault on the part of the dependent perpetrator or on fault on the part of his or her superior.

Similarly, the drafters of the *code* could find no obvious, appropriate solution in Roman law regarding liability for damage caused by an inanimate thing -- nor was one much needed before the days of steam boilers, the internal combustion engine, and high explosives -- but liability for movables occurred in two situations, both classed by the Romans as quasi-delicts. In one, an action was given against a householder from whose dwelling some thing was thrown or poured onto a way that was commonly used, resulting in damage.[308] The action lay against the householder simply because he was the householder whether he did or did not do the throwing, knew of it, or could have prevented it.[309] Ownership of the thing thrown or poured was irrelevant;[310] the action was given in effect against the person who had the thing under his guard. And, of course, there can be no question of the injury

---

[307] The rules are complicated and no consequence here, but see, for example, Alan Watson, *The Law of Obligations in the Later Roman Republic* (Oxford, 1965), pp. 274 ff.

[308] See *D.* 9.3.

[309] See, above all, *D.* 9.3.1.4.

[310] *D.* 9.3.1.4.

222

resulting from a defect in the thing. The Roman approach is sensible, especially in view of the difficulty of proof and because the occupier on any approach would be liable not only for his own behaviour but also for that of his sons or slaves; if the occupier had not thrown or poured out the thing, they might have done so.

In the other situation, an action was given against the occupier of a building from or on whose eave or projecting roof something was suspended or placed, above a way commonly used, and whose fall could cause damage.[311] The action did not lie specifically against the person who placed the thing in its dangerous position, and, since no injury had yet occurred, there could be no relevance in the condition of the thing.[312] The approach is reasonable as a preventive device.

These are both special cases. If one generalized from them -- which obviously one ought not to do -- then one would come up with the proposition that a person was liable for things under his guard whether or not his own behaviour was wrongful and irrespective of any defect in the thing. This is the way article *1384* of the *code civil* seems to have been framed, but if this were the intention of the drafters, it would be highly inappropriate for the following reasons. First, it conflicts with the basis of liability for one's own acts, under articles *1382* and *1383;* second, it probably conflicts with article *1384* regarding the acts of persons for whom one was responsible; and, third, it conflicts with article *1386* concerning the collapse of a building. But Roman law provided no general solution that could be borrowed regarding liability for damage caused by a thing. As an aside, I wish to interject that it would be truly amazing, would it not, if the formulation here in the *code civil* resulted from the Roman *actio de effusis vel deiectis* [action for pouring out or

---

[311] See *D.* 9.3.5,6 ff.

[312] I believe that the occupier was liable only if he placed or knew of the placing of the object: "Liability in the *actio de positis ac suspensis*," *Mélanges Philippe Meylan*(Lausanne, 1963), 1:379ff. My view and its accuracy are irrelevant in the present context, where what matters is the traditional view that the occupier was liable even without fault.

throwing down] and *actio de positis ac suspensis* [action for placing or suspending]? Yet that is what I want to show!

Under Roman law, when an animal caused damage and could be said to be at fault, a remedy under the *actio de pauperie* lay to the victim against the owner of the animal for the amount of the harm done -- but, again, the owner could escape further liability if he chose to surrender the animal.[313] The device of an owner's limited liability was again used. Given that fact, and the fact that the victim had, indeed, suffered loss, it is perfectly understandable that for the *actio de pauperie* to be available, the negligence or otherwise of the owner in keeping the animal from causing harm was not an issue.

But noxal surrender did not exist in France, so the total acceptance of the solution of the *actio de pauperie* was not obviously appropriate. Yet article 1385 on its face says nothing about whether the owner or user of an animal is liable without fault for any damage it causes, or whether, as in the case of the owner's or user's own behaviour, he is liable only if he is at fault. Either interpretation is possible. (It should be remembered that at this stage we are concerned not with the intention of the drafters but rather with their formulation in the *code.*) It will, I hope, be admitted that a pattern in the drafting is emerging. The solution of noxal surrender of the Roman *actio de pauperie,* in which the owner's negligence in preventing the animal from causing harm was irrelevant, was not acceptable in nineteenth-century France. But since the Romans did not discuss this issue of the owner's negligence regarding the *actio de pauperie,* then neither did article 1385 clearly set out the basis of the owner's or user's liability.

Two other remedies were available in Roman law for damage caused by animals, and both are relevant here. The *actio de pastu* gave an action when animals fed on the acorns on another's land. This action is not prominent in the Roman sources; the texts are relatively uninformative, and one of two views may be held. On one view (which I favour), the action was available only when a person actually sent his animals to feed on another's

---

[313] See *D.*9.1

land.[314]   On another view, which has textual support in the postclassical *Pauli Sententiae* (Opinions of Paul), the action allowed noxal surrender,[315] in which case fault on the part of the owner would be irrelevant. The second action was given under the Edict of the curule aediles against someone who had kept a fierce animal (presumably often for gladiatorial games) in such a way that it caused damage where people commonly walked. The basis of liability was exposing people to damage, and no other fault was necessary. Hence the action was penal: a fixed sum was payable if a free human being was killed, the judge decided what was fair if a free human being was injured, and in other cases the penalty was double the loss inflicted.[316]   Thus, there were three Roman actions, though the action that was prominent in the Roman sources was the *actio de pauperie*.

The existence of a pattern is confirmed when we look at article 1386. The "setting in life" of the provision, as a glance at Domat[317] and the discussion of the draft code reveals[318] -- and as we shall see in the long answer -- is in the Roman remedies for *damnum infectum,* that is to say, loss that is threatened but has not yet occurred. In general, as has been mentioned, Roman law gave no remedy for damage caused by a thing, and this was so even for the collapse of a building.[319]   But if a neighbour felt threatened by defective elements on another's land, he might approach the praetor, who would command the latter to give security for restitution if the damage occurred -- the so-called *cautio damni infecti*. The *cautio* was given on account of threatened injury, which means that there must have been a defect in the thing. Hence, even if the injury for which the *cautio* was taken occurred but the defect was not the cause of the injury -- for instance, when a storm was so strong that even a sound building might lose its tiles -- the owner of

---

[314] See *D.* 10.4.9.1; *D.* 19.5.14.3.

[315] See *Pauli Sententiae*, 1.15.1; also see Lenel, *Edictum*, p. 198.

[316] *D.* 21.1.40; *h.t.* 41; *h.t.* 42.

[317] *Les Lois Civiles dans Leur Ordre Naturel* (1689/97), 2.7.3.

[318] Fenet, *Travaux préparatoires,* 13:477.

[319] See, for example *D.* 39.2.7.1.2.

the defective property was not liable under the *cautio*.[320]   If the owner of the dangerous property failed to give the *cautio*, the praetor would grant the threatened neighbour *missio in possessionem*, or detention of the property.[321]

Because French law did not adopt either the *cautio damni infecti* or *missio in possessionem*, there was no remedy for future, threatened damage. Nonetheless, the Roman treatment of *damnum infectum* was the focus for subsequent French discussion of damage by immovable property -- there was no other possible part of Roman law to which discussion could be attached, since, in the absence of the *cautio*, there was no general remedy for damage caused by an inanimate thing[322]

It is this setting that enables us to provide answers to the three problems set out earlier in connection with article 1386. First, the owner in France might be liable without fault on his part because liability in Roman law was based on a defect in the property (which might cause damage). For the Romans, of course, since the defect was observable and the injury foreseeable and made known to the owner, the owner would be at fault if he had failed to carry out the necessary repairs. Second, article 1386 deals only with immovables because threatened damage by immovable property alone was covered by the Roman remedies. The third problem -- why article 1386 speaks expressly of buildings and not also of trees -- requires a greater elucidation. The Roman *cautio de damno infecto* was available not only for damage threatened by defective buildings and other human works but also for threatened damage from defective trees?[323]   But whereas the praetor provided model formulae in his Edict for threatened damage from human works, he appears not to have given one for damage resulting from trees. Likewise, the jurists did not discuss threatened damage by trees and other natural objects on

---

[320] See, for example *D.* 39.2.24.4–11; *h.t..* 43 *pr.*

[321] We need not go into details; see for example, Kaser, *Privatrecht.* 1, pp. 408f.

[322] There were a few other special remedies, such as the *actio aquae pluviae arcendae*, the action for warding off rainwater.

[323] *D.* 39.2.24.9

land in their own right but only in passing in connection with human works?[324] Most importantly, perhaps, *missio in possessionem* was never discussed in connection with damage threatened from natural objects but only regarding human works, and especially buildings. Subsequent French discussion, therefore, came to speak only of damage by human works, above all by buildings. If the argument up to this point is correct -- and detailed evidence will be provided in the long answer -- then we have a particular twist in legal development in article 1386. The basis of liability in article 1386 was determined by Roman remedies that were not accepted in France, yet because of the emphasis in the Roman sources the French provision appeared to be restricted to damage caused by human immovable works and not also (as in Roman law) to damage from trees.[325]

At this stage, some preliminary conclusions may be drawn, if only to show where the argument is going. In the field of wrongful damage, although Roman law provided a coherent set of remedies, some of those remedies were inappropriate for the France of a later era, partly because of changed social conditions and partly because certain Roman legal notions, such as surrender of dependent persons and animals or the concept of threatened damage, were rejected. Still, the discussion in France that formed the basis of the articles of the *code civil* proceeded on the basis of Roman law, resulting in the appalling confusion apparent in the articles -- whether the confusion was mainly in the drafting or also in the minds of the codifiers.

It is the corollary to these conclusions that is most important. When Roman law was inappropriate, and even when it was rejected, the drafters were not necessarily freed from its dominance. They did not always find solutions in local custom. They did not always proffer their own coherent solutions.

Now the long answer. To keep it brief I will deal expressly and at

---

[324] See, above all, Lenel, *Edictum,* p. 551.

[325] But French case law has held that article 1386 also applied to damage from defective trees: see Cour d'Appel, Paris, Première Chambre, 20.8.1877; S. 1878 II, 48.

length with only four issues: liability for a thing under one's guard under article 1384; liability regarding persons for whom one was responsible; liability for an animal under article 1385; and liability for the fall of a building under article 1386.

We may find a satisfactory starting point in Jean Domat's *Les Lois Civiles dan Leur Ordre Naturel* (The Civil Laws in their Natural Order), which first appeared between *1689* and *1697*. Domat's grand plan was to set out a scheme of Christian law for France in an easily comprehensible arrangement. Four kinds of law, he said, ruled in France.[326] First, the royal ordinances had universal authority over all France. Second, customs had particular authority in the place where they were observed. Third, Roman law had two uses: first, as custom in some places in several matters, second, over all France and on all matters, "consisting in this that one observes everywhere these rules of justice and equity that are called 'written reason,' because they are written in Roman law. Thus, for this second use, Roman law has the same authority as have justice and equity on our reason." Fourth, canon law also contained many rules accepted in France, though some had been rejected. Domat went on to claim that he drew up the plan of the book and the choice of subject matter because the natural law of equity lay in the Roman law and because the study of Roman law was so difficult[327]

He introduced the discussion of wrongful damage in book 2, title 8:

One can distinguish three sorts of wrongs from which some damage may arise: those wrongs which amount to a crime or an offence; those wrongs of persons who fail in their agreed on obligations such as a seller who does not deliver the thing sold, a tenant who does not make the repairs he is bound to do; and those wrongs which have no relation with agreements and which do not amount to a crime or an offence, as if light-mindedly one throws something out of a window which spoils a suit; if animals not properly guarded do some damage;

---

[326] *Traité des Lois*, 13.9.
[327] See the first paragraph of his preface to *Les Lois Civiles*.

if one carelessly causes a fire, if a building which threatens to collapse, not being repaired, falls on another and there causes damage.

Of these three types of wrong, only those of the last category are the subject of this title; because crimes and offences ought not to be mixed with civil matters, and everything which concerns agreements has been explained in the first book.

The scene is set for the discussion of the topics that interest us: damage caused by things, animals, and buildings. The discussion under this one category seems very lopsided. The headings of the title are: (1) On what is thrown from a house, or can fall from one and cause loss; (2) Of loss caused by animals; (3) Of the loss which may result from the collapse of a building or some new work; (4) Of other kinds of damage caused by fault, without a crime or offence. In his turn, Pothier, in his *Traité des obligations,* gives short shrift to *délits* and *quasi-délits,* dismissing the subject in half a section.[328]

This approach, which was not restricted to these two lawyers, indicates a disregard for the subject that was to have enormous consequences and must be explained. Domat was discussing other kinds of loss caused by fault, "sans crime ni délit." The translation of the word *délit is* by no means immediately obvious. It is not clear whether it is the Roman *delictum* or the *délit* of later French law. Whatever it is, like *crime* it should not, in the eyes of Domat, be mixed with civil matters. The basic idea can be discovered in a roundabout way by looking at what Domat in fact does not treat -- since he is concerned with civil law -- and examining how other writers, even at a later date, approached the issue.

Domat did not deal with the wrongs that the Romans, as in Justinian's *Institutes,* classed as *delicta,* presumably because, as other writers make plain, they partook of crime. Thus, to take a few examples from other jurisdictions, Sir George Mackenzie, in his *Institutions of the Law of Scotland* (first edition,

---

[328] See Pothier, *Traité des Lois,*13.9

1684), did not deal with delicts, but in the final title of the book, "Of Crimes" (4.4), he wrote: "Private crimes, called also *delicta,* in the Civil Law, oblige the Committers to repair the Dammage, and Interest of the private Party." But he says no more about private crimes. And Marino Guarano in his *Praelectiones ad Institutiones justiniani in Usum Regni Neapolitani* (Lectures on Justinian's *Institutes* for the use of the Kingdom of Naples) (1779) claimed (4.1.3): "*Vitiositas actus in veris delictis est dolus, in quasi delictis est culpa*" (The wickedness of the act in true delicts is malice, in quasi-delicts it is negligence). (See also his 4.5.1.). Giambattista de Luca (1614-83), discussing delicts in *Instituta universale di Tutte le Leggi* (Universal institutes of all the laws) (4.2, 3, 4, 5 § I) , said, "oggi in pratica resta più comoda l'azione Criminale" (today in practice the criminal action is more helpful). He even claimed (at § 7) that it was not worthwhile to spend time on the action of the *lex Aquilia,* which was rarely used.

The main Roman delicts were *furtum* (theft), *rapina* (robbery with violence), *damnum iniuria datum* (wrongful damage to property), and *iniuria* (which covered both defamation and physical assault). In later law (if not also in Roman law), all these were covered by criminal law, because with the sole exception of *damnum iniuria datum,* they all required deliberate malicious conduct on the part of the malefactor. For *damnum iniuria datum* the wrongful action had to be either malicious or simply negligent. In Western Europe in the later Middle Ages, specific difficulties hindered the Reception of the Roman law of delict. In France there was no Reception of the Roman law.[329] The tragedy for France was that in excluding *delicta* from discussion as being, above all, crimes, and as being law that was not received, the French writers also deprived themselves of a treatment of the *lex Aquilia,*[330] since that

---

[329] See, for example, C. de Ferrière, *La Jurisprudence du Digeste* (1677), on D. 9.2; cf. A. Dumas, *Histoire des Obligations dans l'Ancien Droit français* (Aix en Provence, 1972), p. 33; Coing, *Privatrecht,* 1, pp. 504ff.t

[330] There were other reasons for neglecting the *lex Aquilia,* because it could well be doubted whether that statute had been "received" into later law. See the discussion of the opinions of Christianus Thomasius (1655-1728) and J.H. Heineccius

is the context in Roman law in which one finds the treatment par excellence of negligence in all its aspects and of negligent injury to things and human beings. (Injury to human beings comes under *damnum iniuria datum* because slaves were a prime kind of property, and to a great extent dependent children could be analogized in law to slaves.) Hence subsequent treatment by the jurists who took this approach is weak regarding the basis of liability for tortious wrongdoing.

Domat discusses liability for things poured or thrown out of windows or dangerously suspended, but there is no other case of liability for injury proceeding from an inanimate movable thing or from a person's wrongful act except in the most general terms and without analysis (as in book 2, title 8, section 4). Pothier says not a word on the basis of liability for damage by a thing, and in the discussions before the Conseil d'Etat concerning the draft of the *code civil,* no time was spent on the meaning of "dommage ... causé per le fait ... des choses que l'on a sous sa garde." Significantly, the draft contained two other specific articles that would have appeared immediately after the existing article 1381:

> Article 16. If, from a house inhabited by several persons, water or something which causes damage is thrown onto a passerby, those who inhabit the apartment from which it was thrown are all liable in solidarity, unless he who did the throwing is known, in which case he alone has the obligation of restoring the loss.
>
> Article 17. Guests who only inhabit in passing the house from which the thing was thrown are not bound to repair the loss, unless it has been proved that it was they who threw; but he who lodges them is bound.

These two draft articles have supreme significance for understanding the drafting of this part of the *code civil.* They both relate only to the circumstances of the Roman *actio de effusis vel deiectis,* and they both

(1681-1741) in Watson, *Transplants*, pp. 79ff.

concern particular situations: where there is more than one principal inhabitant and where the inhabitants are temporary guests. As particular cases they illuminate the main notion and reveal the context of the discussion. Article 16 was at first accepted without discussion in the Conseil d'Etat, but in discussing article 17, Citizen Miot claimed that the enunciation of the principle sufficed and that examples should be cut back.[331] Not a word was said in the Conseil d'Etat regarding liability for damage by things under what is now article 1384. Likewise, when that part of the *code* was presented before the Corps legislatif on *19* February 1804, not a word on the subject was spoken by Treilhard in his presentation or by the tribune Tarrible in its discussion.[332]

Indeed until the importance of the rule showed up in practice, liability for damage caused by things attracted little scholarly attention. For instance, the long-winded commentator on the code, Toullier, who devoted twenty-one articles to a discussion of damage by animals, gave only one to damage caused by inanimate objects -- and that, after a brief mention of article 1384, is devoted to article 1386.[333] Likewise, even as late as 1877, F. Mourlon in his published lectures on the *code civil* dealt under article 1384 only with persons for whom one is responsible, and under the heading of things under one's guard only with articles 1385 and 1386.[334] Indeed, so little was made of

---

[331] *Procès-Verbaux,* 3:311FF. Cf. C.B. M. Toullier, *Le Droit civil Français,* 5th ed. (Paris, 1830), 11 pp.192f.; C. Baudry-Lacantinerie and L.Barde, *Traité Théorique et Pratique de Droit Civil, Les Obligations,* 3d ed. (Paris, 1908), 4, pp. 653f.

[332] See Fenet, *Travaux préparatoires,* 13, pp.464ff.

[333] Toullier, *Le Droit civil,* pp. 433 ff.; cf., e.g., the remarks of A. Tunc, "A Codified Law of Tort – The French Experience," *Louisiana Law Review* 39 (1979): 1051ff.

[334] F. Mourlon, *Répétitions écrites sur le code civil contenant l'exposé des principes généraux* (Paris, 1877), 2, p. 892ff., especially at p. 895. The same silence is observed by V. Marcadé, *Explication théorique et pratique du code Napoléon expliqué article par article* (Paris, 1877), 2, p. 892ff., especially at p. 895. The same silence is observed by V. Marcadé, *Explication théorique et pratique du code Napoléon expliqué article par article* (Paris, n.d.), pp. 588ff.; A. Duranton, *Cours de*

liability concerning things under one's guard in the debates, so little attention was paid to it in practice before the Teffaine case of 1896,[335] and so obscure is the background to the clause, that it can be said to have been the unanimous opinion in France that the drafters' intentions were to establish liability only for animals and collapsing buildings, and that the relevant part of article 1384 simply announced the particular cases in articles 1385 and 1386.[336]

But we cannot leave article 1384 yet. We must still consider some aspects of liability for the acts of persons for whom one is responsible. Domat says in *Les Loix Civiles* (1.2.8.7): "Schoolmasters, craftsmen and others who receive into their homes students, apprentices or other persons to train them in some art, manufacture or commerce are liable for the behaviour of these people." We have here an early statement regarding liability for other persons' behaviour in French law. As it stands, removed from its context, it has no parallel in Roman law. In Roman law one was generally responsible for the conduct of one's slaves and sons-in-power, but not for pupils, apprentices, and others whom one was training. But the context is important for Domat. The text arises out of the discussion of things poured or thrown out of windows (i.e., by students, etc., in their teacher's home) and probably should be

---

droit civil, 4th ed. (Brussels, 1841), 7, p. 508ff. The same is true for the famous work of C.S. Zacchariae, *Cours de droit civil français,* revu et augmenté par C. Aubry et C. Rau (Strasbourg, 1839), 3, p. 202f.; and also A.M. Demante with E. Colmet de Santerre, *Cours analytique de Code civil,* 5, 2d ed. (Paris, 1883), pp. 660ff. The explication of Bosquet is illuminating. On article 1384 he writes: "Things which one has under one's guard are movable or immovable, they are inanimate or animate. The present article can have intended to speak only of those last named. But, with this understanding, is article 1385 not sufficient?" *Explication du code civil* (Avignon, 1805), vol. 3.

[335] S. 1897.1.17 (to be found in English in A.T. von Mehren and J.R. Gordley, *The Civil Law System,* 2d ed. (Boston, 1977), pp. 608ff.

[336] See G. Viney, *Les Obligations, La Responsabilité: Conditions* (Paris, 1982), in *Traité de Droit Civil*, series directed by J. Ghastin, p. 749. In the case of *Jand'heur v. Galéries Belfortaises,* P. Matter claimed that liability for things under one's guard derived from old French customary law, see Dalloz, *Recueil Périodique et Critique* (1930), 1 p.65.

restricted to that (for Domat), though no restriction is expressed. Then there would be absolute liability in Roman law (just as there would be if there was no relationship between the thrower and the occupant), and Domat expresses the liability in absolute terms. Interestingly, Domat cites in support D. 9.3.5.3, which in fact has a rather different effect. What is at issue there is who is to be regarded as a *habitator,* inhabitant, and the text indicates that an action on the facts will be given if one hires a building to have work done there or to teach pupils there (and one does not sleep there) and damage ensues.

The issue is taken up again by Pothier, who asserts that one is also liable for the acts of persons subject to one's power. Fathers, mothers, tutors, and teachers are so liable when the delict or quasi-delict is committed in their presence, and generally when they could have prevented the injury but did not. But if one could not have prevented it, there is no liability. Pothier adds that one is liable for the wrongs caused by servants and employees even when one could not prevent the wrong, provided that the wrong was committed in the exercise of the functions for which the servants or employees were employed.[337] This brings us closer to the rules set out in the *code civil.* For Bertrand de Greuille, addressing the Tribunat on 6 February 1803, teachers and craftsmen were responsible for the acts of their pupils and apprentices because they took the place of the parents -- not at all the Roman position?[338]

The line of historical development from Domat is fairly plain. He stated absolutely the liability for pupils and such others (and this was proper in its context). Pothier generalized this approach, whether he had Domat or an equivalent statement in mind. But in a general context the liability had to be restricted to wrongs that the parent or teacher could not have prevented. And then Pothier added his treatment of liability for servants and employees. But, as I said before, the basis of one's liability for the acts of children, pupils, and apprentices had consequently become stricter in the *code civil* than the basis

---

[337] The idea had already appeared in practice that an employer was liable for loss caused by the fault or clumsiness of mule drivers, carters, or coachmen; see C. De Ferrière, *Jurisprudence,* on *D.* 9.2.

[338] Reported in Locré *Législation*, 13, p.42.

of liability for one's own acts. The main reasons for this lie first in the removal from the French discussion of any treatment of the *lex Aquilia,* where the principle of no liability without fault is laid out, with the consequent blurring in French law of this all-important principle. The second reason lies in Domat's unqualified statement of absolute liability (but in the limited context of the *actio de effusis vel deiectis),* and Pothier's having had before him some discussion such as Domat's to which he added qualifications (untrammeled by too much consideration of the *lex Aquilia).* Third, Pothier's views were adopted by the code commission without much evidence of independent thought.

For article 1385, the *travaux préparatoires* make the best starting point for the long answer, since the codifiers' intent is readily apparent. Treilhard said nothing in the Conseil d'Etat, but Bertrand de Greuille was explicit:

> The draft then considers the cases where an animal, led by someone or escaped from his hands or having simply wandered off, has caused some wrong. In the first two hypotheses, the draft intends that the person who uses the animal, and in the third it orders the person who is its owner, to be held liable for the reparation of the loss, because the loss must be imputed either to a lack of guard and vigilance on the part of the master, or to the rashness, clumsiness or lack of attention. Nothing belonging to someone can injure another with impunity.[339]

Thus, for de Greuille, the liability of the owner or user of the animal was absolute, and he had two basic arguments. The first is one of imputed fault. The second is that liability for animals falls within the general category of liability for things (under article *1384),* and that liability is absolute. Tarrible's remarks are shorter but base liability on negligence that, however, may be very slight.[340]   Thus there seems to be some conflict regarding the

---

[339] Quoted from ibid., p. 43.
[340] *Ibid.*

interpretation of the article, even among the legislators. But Bertrand de Greuille was the more explicit, and his intention was to establish absolute liability for the acts of animals.

This would correspond accurately to the three remedies of Roman law if one assumed that the *actio de pastu* was not limited to the situation in which the owner sent his animals to feed on another's land, and thus that the action would be noxal. Domat certainly takes this broad view of the *actio de pastu,* though he says nothing about noxal surrender. This is in keeping with the approach that he says he is taking with regard to damage by animals; since customs varied so much, he set down only general rules that might be of common use, not what was particular to local customs or what was contained in Roman law but not in those customs (hence he does not deal with noxal surrender).[341] In fact, what he gives is Roman law, with omissions.[342] There is again in this context no recourse by the drafters to local customary law, though customary law was extensive, especially with regard to pasturage.[343] Here, too, the formulation of article 1385 can be said to be the result of Domat's treatment, which was based on Roman law. From this, however, was excised noxal surrender, which had given the Roman rules a different

---

[341] *Les Lois Civiles,* 1.2.7.2.

[342] However, although he bases his idea on Roman law authority, he seems to hold that for the *actio de pauperie,* in some situations at least, liability depends on the owner's knowing about his animal's bad habits and still not taking care; see ibid., 1.2.7.2.6.7, 8.

[343] For a few examples chosen almost at random, see Guy Coquille, *Conférence des Coustumes de France* (Paris, 1642), p. 211; *Coustumes générales de Berry,* title 10, arts. 1-4 (pasturage); *Coutumes générales du bailliage de Troyes,* art. 118 (wandering animals); arts. 121, 165-172 (pasturage); *Coustumes de Melun,* arts. 302-309 (pasturage); M. Petitjean and M.L. Marchand, *Le Coutumier Bourguignon glosé* (Paris: CNRS, 1982),pp. 232 § 273, 239 §300 (delict), pp. 32 §3, 236 § 287, 291 § 402. Interestingly, despite the practical importance of damage by animals, nothing is said on the subject by writers such as A. Loysel, *Institutes Coutumières* (first published in 1607), or G. Argou, *Institution au Droit françois* (first published in 1692). Very different, though, is de Ferrière, *Jurisprudence,* on *D.* 9.1.

impact.[344]

To establish the connection here concerning liability under article *1386* for the collapse of a building and the very different remedies for *damnum infectum* in Roman law, we need do nothing more now than consider the remarks of Bertrand de Greuille in the Conseil d'Etat:[345]

> It is also as a consequence of that incontestable truth that the last article of the draft holds that the owner of a building is responsible for the loss which it caused by its collapse when that occurred through defective maintenance or by a flaw in its construction. This decision is much less rigorous and more equitable than the provision which is found in Roman law. That authorized the individual whose building could be damaged by the fall of another which was in danger of collapse, to put himself in possession of their neighbouring heritage, if the proprietor did not give him guarantees for the loss one had reason to fear. Thus, apprehension of the harm itself gave an opening for the action, and could bring the dispossession into play: the draft, to the contrary, intends above all that the harm be present.

> It is thus the collapse alone which can legitimate the complaint and the demand of the injured party, and determine a condemnation for his benefit. It is after this collapse that he is allowed to examine the injury, to decide its importance; and it is then that the judge gives a decision on its reparation, if it is established that the negligence of the owner in maintaining his building or the ignorance of the workmen

---

[344] This last sentence may perhaps be misleading. If Domat's treatment of responsibility for other persons was the sole *fons et origo*, then Roman noxal surrender may never have been directly relevant for subsequent French law since it had no place in the *actio de effusis vel deiectis*.

[345] Treilhard said nothing à propos, and the words of Tarrible are vague but suggestive of liability only for fault (contrary to the wording of the article), see Locré, *Législation*, 13, p.58

whom he employed in its construction were the cause of the collapse.

Thus Bertrand de Greuille expressly links liability under article 1386 with the very different Roman remedies for *damnum infectum*. Whether the Roman remedies were or were not less equitable need not concern us. What does matter is a feature that was inappropriately carried over, to a different effect, which caused the French liability for wrongful damage to be unbalanced.

The Roman remedy was given for threatened future damage. That means that the future collapse was apparent if nothing were done; for the owner then to do nothing to prevent the collapse would in fact be negligence. This would be so even when the defect arose from a fault in construction. But the French action was for past damage and was given even for a fault in the construction that was unknown to the owner. Thus French liability came to differ from liability in Roman law. More than that, liability under article 1386 differs from liability under articles 1382 and 1383 in not requiring negligence, and from article 1384 in requiring a defect in the thing (in the absence of negligence).

The obduracy of the inappropriate Roman *damnum infectum* clearly appears when we examine the 24 November 1803 discussion in the Conseil d'Etat and notice that Regnaud wanted to excise the offending "par une suite du défaut d'entretien ou par le vice de la construction" (in consequence of defective maintenance or by a flaw in the construction) and substitute "par sa fault" (through his fault). This attempt to make liability depend on fault was rejected.[346]

With these five articles on wrongful damage in the French *code civil*, we are thus face-to-face with a complex and peculiar phenomenon in legal development. These articles do not at all harmonize on the subject of the basis of legal liability. This does not seem to be the result of careful thought on the different situations by the legislators, nor simply the result of poor draftsmanship. Rather, it is the outcome of past legal history and, above all, the consequence of a reliance on a discussion of liability largely in the context

---

[346] Fenet, *Travaux préparatoires*, 13, p. 455.

of inappropriate Roman law, which had been rejected in large measure. There was no recourse to the rules of customary law. One can say that Roman law here was not received, but it nonetheless was the initial factor -- the dominant factor -- in determining the shape of the French rules in the *code civil.*

To avoid misunderstanding, one point ought to be made explicit. I am, of course, not claiming that there is no place for different standards of liability to operate in different situations for wrongful injury. Nor am I claiming that the French rules were individually necessarily grotesque for the French in 1804. But I am claiming that the various bases of liability in the French articles were adopted, without much thought or social purpose, from rejected Roman originals of which traces survived in old French books; and that the drafting, based as it was on preconceptions deriving from the old works, failed to achieve clarity. A glance at the corresponding articles in the German *Bürgerliches Gesetzbuch (BGB),* §§ 823-853 -- themselves much influenced by Roman law -- or, for the United States, at any edition of Prosser *on Torts,* will show that very different rules could just as easily have been accepted.

These rules of the *code civil* illustrate a proposition that I regard as being of the highest importance and that is inherent in this book and my past work. The proposition is that in any country, approaches to lawmaking (whether by legislators, judges, or jurists), the applicability of law to social institutions, the structure of the legal system, and the formulation and scope of legal rules are all in large measure the result of past history and overwhelmingly the result of past legal history, and that the input of other, even contemporary, societal forces is correspondingly slight. Thus, for instance, to understand why a piece of legislation or a judicial decision is as it is, we must know the legal tradition within which the lawmakers operate. And given the prevalence and importance of legal borrowing and the ancient roots of much of law, this means that to a very great extent, attitudes toward lawmaking, the structure of legal systems, the parameters of legal rules, and the outlook of lawyers can be explained only if we examine the law in its historical relation to other law and over a period of centuries.

One final problem should be considered. Article 1382 reads: "Tout fait quelconque de l'homme, qui cause à autrui un dommage, oblige celui par la faute duquel il est arrivé, à le reparer." *Fait* may reasonably be translated as "action" and in itself does not seem to carry a connotation of blame or wrongful action. The wrong that gives rise to an action is denoted by *faute*, fault, a word that does not necessarily imply deliberate wrongdoing. But article 1383 reads: "Chacun est responsable du dommage qu'il a causé, non seulement part son fait, mais encore par sa négligence ou par son imprudence."

If we take "fait" in this article also to mean action and not to connote blameworthiness, then "par sa negligence ou par son imprudence," appearing in contrast with it, should mean that one is also liable for not acting and should denote a liability for nonfeasance even when there was no affirmative duty to act. "Négligence" is not contrasted with "dol." Article 1383 has "fait," not even "faute," which, in a pinch, to give a proper sense to "négligence" one might even want to translate as "deliberate wrong." Yet we know from the *travaux préparatoires*[347] that it was not the intention to give an action for nonfeasance, but rather to make clear that the action for wrongful loss existed both when there was malice and also when there was merely negligence. Thus, article 1383 was poorly drafted. But what, in any event, is the point of having these two articles? Why not simply have one reading: "Tout fait quelconque de l'homme, qui cause à autrui un dommage, oblige celui par le dol ou la négligence ou l'imprudence duquel il est arrivé, à le reparer." The answer lies in a previous French distortion of Roman law. As early as Pothier, a sharp distinction was made: a *délit* was a wrongful act done maliciously; a *quasi-délit* was a wrongful act done negligently.[348] The point -- unexpressed -- of article 1383 was to indicate that a negligent act that causes harm also creates liability.[349]

---

[347] Locré, *Législation*, 13:31, 40, 59f.

[348] *Traité des obligations*, 1.1.2.2.

[349] Already J.J. Bugnet in his notes on Pothier at this point observed that the redactors of the code who followed others seemed to intend to talk of *délits* in article

For the lack of coherence in these articles of the *code* we cannot wholly excuse Domat, who treated all *delicta* as crimes when he need not have done so. Even if he did not wish to discuss the *lex Aquilia,* he could have made use of the Roman discussion of negligence and liability. By failing to include the basic scenarios of damage caused by someone responsible for his or her own behaviour, Domat lost the emphasis on the basic framework of liability only for fault including negligence; the exceptional cases were not fitted into the scheme of things with their rationales and boundaries explained. A considerable failure of the imagination must be attributed to the drafters of the *code civil,* who seem to have been blithely unaware of the inconsistencies in the articles and of the history of the rules they were perpetuating, especially since they stood at the point at which satisfactory law most easily might have been made.

But failures of the legal imagination have consequences: they entail future failures. Law has practical effects, but, as I have argued elsewhere,[350] it has to a very considerable degree a life of its own. Law has functions related to the practical life, but it also operates at the level of culture, especially regarding the culture of the lawmaking elite, which has the power to make changes in the law. And a living culture is not examined by those who live it. Three typical features of law as culture are pertinent to the present failure of legal imagination, though none will be examined here in depth. First, codified legal rules are resistant to removal or replacement. Secondly, society and lawyers on a day-to-day basis can tolerate much inappropriate, even absurd, law. Thirdly, legal rules, when available in an accessible form, can readily be borrowed often without an inquiry into their effectiveness.

With regard to the first feature, four of the five articles remain unchanged in the current French *code civil,* though there has been subsequent relevant legislation. Article 1384 has undergone modification but mainly with regard to liability for persons for whom one is responsible and for things

---

1382 and of *quasi-délits* in article 1383.

[350] See, e.g., "Legal Change," especially from p. 1151; also see *Evolution,* pp. 115ff.

under one's guard, though only in minor respects.

With regard to the second feature, we should perhaps talk more of an excess than a failure of the legal imagination. S. F. C. Milsom has well stated the issue for the history of English common law:

> The life of the common law has been in the abuse of its elementary ideas. If the rules of property give now what seems an unjust answer, try obligation; and equity has proved that from the materials of obligation you can counterfeit the phenomena of property. If the rules of contract give what now seems an unjust answer, try tort. Your counterfeit will look odd to one brought up on categories of Roman origin; but it will work. If the rules of one tort, say deceit, give what now seems an unjust answer, try another, try negligence. And so the legal world goes round.[351]

Much of Milsom's book, however, serves to demonstrate that though the counterfeits (as he calls them) work, they do not work well; and often indeed the counterfeits cannot be created at the right time. In France, articles 1382 and 1383 have always been interpreted as meaning that for one's own act, liability was based on fault that the victim-plaintiff had to prove. At first, liability for animals under article 1385 was based on fault that was presumed, but by the late nineteenth century, liability was strict and the owner or the person using the animal was liable unless he could show *force majeure*, the act of a third party or the fault of the victim. Interpretation of article 1386 has been reasonably stable: if a building collapsed,[352] the owner was not excused from liability just because he established that he was free from fault; for example, if he had charged a competent builder with the maintenance of the building or if it was humanly impossible to uncover the defect. The greatest

---

[351] *Foundations*, p. 6.

[352] And there must be a collapse or fall: see, e.g., M. Planiol and G. Ripert, *Traité pratique de droit civil français,* vol. 6, *Les Obligations*, 2d ed., ed. P. Esmein (Paris, 1952), pp. 849f.

variation in interpretation -- disparate attempts to make some social sense of the provision -- has occurred with regard to liability under article 1384 for things under one's guard. The range of interpretations has been enormous and will not be examined here, but it has swung from liability only if the keeper could be shown to be at fault, through liability if the thing was defective even if this was not known to the keeper, through strict liability that can be rebutted only if the keeper proves *cas fortuit, force majeure,* or a *cause étrangère* that cannot be imputed to him. It has even been held that when a thing in motion (such as an automobile) is under the control of the keeper, the keeper is liable under article 1384 for damage caused by the thing (even when it is not defective) unless he can show *cas fortuit, force majeure,* or *cause étrangère.* Under this interpretation, an automobile driver may be liable without fault under article 1384, ignoring articles 1382 and 1383.[353]

As to the third typical feature of law as culture -- the easy transplanting of rules without an inquiry into their effectiveness -- we can make a random choice of examples. Thus the *code civil* for the lands of the king of Sardinia of 1837 gives the French provisions verbatim.[354] The Dominican Republic took over the *code civil* in 1845 and translated it into Spanish only in 1884; the French provisions remain unaltered to the present day as articles 1382-1386 of the *código civil.* The Italian *codice civile* of 1865 simply translated the French articles as articles 1151-1155 but with the

[353] For the variety of interpretation of this part of article 1384, see, e.g., Tunc, "A Codified Law of Tort," pp. 1065ff., F.H. Lawson and B.S. Markesinis, *Tortious Liability for Unintentional Harm in the Common Law and Civil Law* (Cambridge, 1982), 1, pp. 146f. There is nothing in that work relevant to the argument of this chapter. For an interpretation of liability for persons for whom one is responsible under article 1384, see, e.g., Tunc, "A Codified Law of Tort," pp. 1062ff. See also Tunc, "It is Wise Not to Take the Civil Codes Too Seriously: Traffic Accidents Compensation in France," *Essays in Memory of Professor F.H. Lawson,* ed. P. Wallington and R.M. Merkin (London, 1980) pp. 71ff. Traffic accident law was revised by the Loi de 5 juillet, 1985; cf. Tunc, *Revue Internationale de Droit Comparé* 37 (1985), pp. 1019ff.

[354] Articles 1300-1304. Additional provisions are in articles 1305-1307,

addition of article 1156 fixing liability *in solidum* if several persons were liable for the delict or quasi delict.

I wish to clarify what I am claiming from the example of articles 1382-1386. I am not asserting that the French *code* civil is nothing but a modernized version of Roman law -- the articles themselves show that much was not received -- nor am I claiming that the explanation of each article of the *code* civil is to be found in Roman law. I am claiming that the articles of the *code* -- and I would extend this to all legislation, I think -- can be fully understood with regard both to their form and their substance only if there is an inquiry into the cultural history behind them, and this inquiry must often span centuries and countries. I would also claim that the force of a reception, in this case of Roman law, is not to be judged simply by the acceptance of rules and structures but by the extent of dependence on a foreign system.

these too have Roman law roots.

Chapter 12

Epilogue: Julius Caesar; Descendant of a Slave?

In this final chapter I wish to return to a theme that surfaced in chapter 3. Much law may be found, and only found, in works that are not specifically legal. I first started writing on this chapter many years ago and sent drafts to various friends in classical departments for their comments. The response was unequivocal. My theory was absurd. But I was unconvinced. According to the Roman historian, Suetonius, the dictator Sulla demanded that Caesar divorce his wife. Casesar did not, and Sulla punished him with three penalties, all of which are exceedingly strange. These have to be explained. My explanation is that, to humiliate Casesar, Sulla was claiming Caesar was descended from a slave. No other explanation fits.

Julius Caesar was born in 100 B.C. into the ancient patrician clan or *gens*, Iulia. He proudly traced his lineage from the earliest ancestors of the Roman people. The founder of the clan, Iulius, was in a special sense the son of Jupiter: The name Iulius is thought to derive etymologically from Iupiter.[355] According to legend, Iulius (also known as Ascanius), who founded the Italian capital of Alba Longa, was the son of Aeneas, who himself was worshiped as Jupiter after his death.[356] Aeneas was the son of the mortal Anchises and the goddess Venus,[357] and according to Virgil's epic poem, Aeneas carried the aged Anchises with the Palladium from burning Troy. The *gens* was naturally proud of this ancestry. A Sextus Julius Caesar, who may be the consul of 90 B.C., issued only one known coin type, but it portrays Venus Genetrix crowned by Cupid in a two-horse chariot.[358] Our C.

---

[355] Cf., e.g., A. Ernout and A. Meillet, *Dictionnaire étymologique de la langue latine*, 4th ed. (Paris, 1959), p. 329.

[356] Livy 1.2.6; Servius *in Verg. Aen.* 1.259.

[357] Homer *Iliad* 2.820f.; 5.247f., 312f.; 20.208f.

[358] See, e.g., Edward A. Sydenham, *The Coinage of the Roman Republic*

Julius Caesar himself, circa 48 B.C., coined a denarius with a bust of Venus on the obverse, Aeneas walking left holding the Palladium and bearing Anchises on his shoulder on the reverse.[359] Caesar even built a temple at Rome to Venus Genetrix which was dedicated on 26 September 46.[360] The appellation is significant: "Venus, the Founding Mother of our *Gens*." Caesar insisted on his ancestry.

The introductory chapters of Suetonius *Divus Iulius* are lost. The surviving manuscripts begin:

> In his sixteenth year he lost his father. During the next consulship, when he was appointed Priest of Jupiter [*flamen Dialis*] he broke an engagement made for him when he was a youth with Cossutia of an equestrian but very rich family. He married Cornelia, the daughter of Cinna who had been consul four times, and from her Iulia was soon born. Nor could he be compelled in any way by the dictator Sulla to divorce her. Therefore he was deprived of his priesthood, his wife's dowry, and the inheritances he received as a member of the *gens* [*gentilicis hereditatibus*], and having been fined was considered to belong to the other party.

The issue for us is the meaning of these particular penalties. *Gentiliciae hereditates* is technical and precise. Caesar was deprived of his share of inheritances that came to him on intestacy as a member of the *gens*. He was not deprived of inheritances under a will or of any that might have come to him on intestacy otherwise as, for instance, from his father or as nearest agnate. Sulla's punishment is very specific. It will not do to treat *gentiliciae hereditates* as meaning his family estates in general.[361]

(London, 1952), no. 47, at p. 56; Michael H. Crawford, *Roman Republican Coinage* (Cambridge 1974), no. 258/1, at p. 1:254.

[359] Sydenham, *Coinage*, no. 1013, at p. 168; Crawford, *Coinage*, no. 458/1, at p. 1:471.

[360] See, e.g. Stefan Weinstock, *Divus Julius* (Oxford, 1970), pp. 80ff.

[361] See, e.g., H.E. Butler and M. Cary, ed., C. *Suetoni Tranquilli Divus Iulius*

How are we to read Suetonius's understanding of what Sulla did? Did he believe Sulla fined Caesar, almost by something like criminal actions, in amounts equal to the dowry Caesar received and to his *gentiliciae hereditates*? Or was Caesar somehow fined a particular sum that Suetonius extrapolated to make it equal to the dowry plus *gentiliciae hereditates*? Why would Suetonius think of *gentiliciae hereditates*, which can scarcely have been an everyday matter? *Gentiliciae hereditates* would come into play only in the unlikely event that there was no heir who took under a will and, for intestacy, no *suus heres* and no nearest agnate. And why would Sulla deprive Caesar of his position as *flamen Dialis*? If Caesar were a political enemy whom Sulla was eventually persuaded against his better judgment to allow to live, then Sulla's best choice was to keep him as *flamen Dialis*. This priest was very much subject to taboos. For example, he was forbidden to ride a horse or to see the army in battle array.[362] He could not spend a night outside the city without sin.[363] Thus, the *flamen Dialis* could not have a military career. Not only that, but political advancement was limited: Aulus Gellius reports that the *flamen Dialis* was rarely made consul because wars were entrusted to consuls.[364] As Weinstock puts it, Caesar "should have been grateful to Sulla for having saved him from this predicament."[365] Indeed, so restrictive was the position of *flamen Dialis* that the priesthood was not filled again until 11. B.C.[366]

But is Caesar to be regarded as a firm political enemy of Sulla at this time, at least in the eyes of Suetonius? I hardly think so. Suetonius's Latin *multatus diversarum partium habebatur* (having been fined he was considered

---

(Oxford, 1927) 44; *Suetonius*, trans. J.C. Rolfe Cambridge, Mass. 1964), p. 1:3; *Suetonius: The Twelve Caesars*, trans. Michael Grant (Harmondsworth, 1957), p. 9.

[362] Aulus Gellius *Noctes Atticae* 10.15.3f.; Plutarch *Quaestiones Romanae* 40; Aulus Gellius *Noctes Atticae* 10.15.14.

[363] Livy 5.52.13; three nights according to Plutarch *Quaestiones Romanae* 40; Aulus Gellius *Noctes Atticae* 10.15.4.

[364] Aulus Gellius *Noctes Atticae* 10.15.4.

[365] Weinstock, *Divus Julius*, p. 30.

[366] Dio Cassius 54.36.1; Tacitus *Annales* 3.58.2.

to belong to the other party)[367] implies that it was after or because of his punishment that Caesar was considered to be of the other party.[368] Caesar's offence may only have been that he was married to Cornelia, the daughter of L. Cornelius Cinna, Sulla's great enemy, who was killed in a mutiny in 84.[369]

When Sulla ordered Caesar to divorce Cornelia, he may only have wanted to prevent the marriage from strengthening a political alliance. Caesar, after all, would already be suspect because he was the nephew of Marius,[370] Sulla's other great enemy. If Caesar were already a clear enemy, Sulla would not have spared the man in whom he saw many Mariuses.[371]

What then was the nature and purpose of Sulla's punishment of Cesar? I would suggest that the answer is to be found in the three stated penalties, most obviously in the forfeiture of *gentiliciae hereditates*.

First, intestate succession was regulated under two provisions of the Twelve Tables: "If he dies to whom there is no *suus heres*, the nearest agnate is to have the estate. If there is no agnate, the *gentiles* are to have the estate."[372]

The order of intestate succession was thus: *sui heredes*, those who became free of paternal power by the death; failing whom, the nearest agnate; failing whom, the *gentiles*. Cicero defines the *gentiles inter se*:

---

[367] *Multare* (to fine) in the absence of something like *pecunia*, may also mean "to punish." My "having been fined" could also be translated "having been punished."

[368] The translation of Grant, "treating him as if he were a member of the popular party," seems inexact: *Suetonius*, 9.

[369] See, e.g., Appian 1.78; Livy *Epitome* 83; Velleius Paterculus *Historia Romana* 2.24.5; Plutarch *Sertorius* 6.1.

[370] Plutarch *Caesar* 1.1f.

[371] Suetonius *Divus Iulius* 1.3; Plutarch *Caesar* 1.2.

[372] *Si intestato moritur, cui suus heres nec escit, adgnatus proximus familiam habeto. Si adgnatus nec escit, gentiles familiam [habento].* The provisions are traditionally numbered *Tab.* 5.4.5: C.G. Bruns, *Fontes Iuris Romani Antiqui*, 7th ed. (Tübingen, 1909), p. 23; M.H. Crawford (whose reconstruction is slightly different), *Roman Statutes* (London, 1996), 2, p.641.

"*Gentiles* are those that have the same name." That is not enough.
"Who are born from free persons." Not even that is enough. "None
of whose ancestors served in slavery." Something is still missing.
"Who have never suffered change of civil status [*capitis deminutio*]."
Perhaps that is sufficient. For I see that Scaevola the pontifex added
nothing to his definition.[373]

How could this definition affect Caesar?

The *gens* to whose *hereditates* he would have claims was the patrician
gens Iulia. C. Julius Caesar bore the name. He had not undergone the
apposite *capitis deminutio*; for a male this would be adoption into another
family; for a female this would mean marriage *cum manu*. He was born of
free parents. So what was the issue? There is only one remaining ground for
excluding Caesar from inheriting as a *gentilis*: that he had a slave or former
slave among his ancestors! Could Sulla claim that Caesar had a servile
ancestor? If he did, Caesar would not be a *gentilis*, and hence he would not
be entitled to *gentiliciae hereditates*. Moreover, he would be a plebeian, not a
patrician. Freedmen normally took the name of their former owner, and there
were plebeians among the Iulii.[374] We may assume that the burden of proof
would be on anyone who claimed to be a *gentilis*.[375]

If we can consider this to be Sulla's approach -- to challenge Caesar's
title to be a member of the patrician *gens Iulia* -- then we can understand why
Caesar's right to other inheritances was not affected.

---

[373] *Topica* 6.29.

[374] See, e.g., Münzer in Pauly-Wissowa, *Real-Encyclopädie der classischen
Altertumswissenschaft* (Stuttgart, 1917), s.v. "Iulius." The number, of course, greatly
increased with Caesar's manumissions and grants of citizenship: see, e.g., Weinstock,
Divus Julius, p. 300.

[375] See, e.g. Alan Watson, *Rome of the Twelve Tables: Persons and Property*
(Princeton, 1975), p. 67f.

Of course, more is needed to substantiate a claim that this was Sulla's approach, at least in the eyes of Suetonius. This is provided by Sulla's other two punishments of Caesar.

Second, Suetonius says that Sulla deprived Caesar of his position as *flamen Dialis*, and I have already hinted Sulla would have done better to have maintained Caesar in that position. If Caesar was a Iulius but not a *gentilis* of the *gens Iulia*, however, he would not be a patrician and automatically could not be *flamen Dialis* because that priesthood was reserved for patricians.[376] Sulla would have had no choice: Caesar simply could not be *flamen Dialis*.

Caesar had been designated *flamen Dialis* in 87 or early 86 by Marius and Cinna after the suicide of the previous occupant, L. Cornelius Merula, who was a support of Sulla.[377] Whether Caesar was actually inaugurated is unclear. So is the nature of Sulla's deprivation of his office. For Velleius Paterculus it was because Sulla cancelled all the appointments of Marius and Cinna.[378] This may well be accurate. More to the point, Suetonius makes it appear that the deprivation was a personal act against Caesar.[379] This makes sense if Sulla's (supposed) claim was that Caesar was not a *gentilis* of the *gens Iulia*.

Third, Sulla deprived Caesar of his dowry from Cornelia. It is clear that this was basic to Suetonius's understanding of what was going on. Caesar's refusal to divorce Cornelia incurred wrath. No doubt under the circumstances Sulla simply wanted to deprive Caesar of the dowry, but what justification could he offer? It is, after all, a mark of tyrants often to make a show of legality for their behaviour.

During most of the Republic the control of good morals was the business of the censors. One matter of concern would be unsuitable

---

[376] Cicero *De domo sua* 14.38; Paul 151f.: cf. Georg Wissowa, *Religion und Kultus der Römer*, 2d ed. (Leipzig, 1912), pp. 491f.

[377] See, e.g., Weinstock, *Divus Julius*, p. 30.

[378] *Historia Romana* 2.43.1

[379] Plutarch *Caesar* 1.2 declares that Caesar was a candidate for the priesthood but that Sulla secretly and successfully opposed him. This does not seem

marriages. Some modern scholars believe that in the later Republic marriage between freeborn citizens and freed persons was void, but the better opinion (I think) is that such marriages were valid but regarded unfavourably both morally and socially.[380] Particular legal restrictions were introduced only by Augustus by the lex *Julia de maritandis ordinibus* of 18 B.C. I quote part of the law: "Whoever is a senator, senator's son, or grandson by a son, or great-grandson by a son and grandson, let him not knowingly and fraudulently have as a betrothed or a wife a freedwoman. . . . Let no daughter of a senator or granddaughter by a son or great-granddaughter by a son and grandson be knowingly and fraudulently betrothed or wife to a freedman."[381] I quote the law, though it is later than the period that concerns us, in the belief that it now put a legal ban on certain marriages that members of the Roman upper classes would earlier have considered thoroughly inappropriate.

Let us return then to Sulla's treatment of Caesar in Suetonius. If Sulla treated Caesar as a plebeian, the free descendant of an ex-slave (though perhaps far removed), then his marriage to Cornelia would be lawful and valid but disgraceful and could be subject to punishment. After all, Cornelia's father was no ordinary senator but had been four times consul. Sulla could not declare the marriage void, but he could directly or indirectly impose a fine. And what more appropriate fine could be imposed than deprivation of the dowry? A dowry was not necessary for the validity of the marriage, but it was certainly evidence of matrimonial intent. Its forfeiture would be seen by Caesar as a disgrace to him. Censors could impose fines.[382] Sulla did not abolish the office of censor, but he sidestepped it, and the functions of the office were fulfilled in other ways.[383] Our concern, of course, is not directly

---

to be accurate. Cf. Weinstock, *Divus Julius*, p. 30 n.2.

[380] For the argument see Watson, *Law of Persons*, 32 ff.; Susan Tregiari, *Roman Marriage* (Oxford, 1991), 44 n. 35.

[381] *D.* 23.2.44 pr.

[382] Cf. H.F. Jolowicz and Barry Nicholas, *Historical Introduction to the Study of Roman Law*, 3d ed. (Cambridge, 1972), 53.

[383] See, e.g., Theodor Mommsen, *Römisches Staatsrecht* (Leipzig, 1887; Munich, 1979), 2:336, 423, 427.

with the power of the censors but with steps Sulla might take with regard to marriages that traditionally would be regarded as disgraceful.

Sulla might even have conceived this form of spite against Caesar because his own marriage to Caecilia was regarded as a disgrace to the women. Plutarch tells us that Sulla belonged to a patrician *gens* that had been distinguished by only one consul who, moreover, had been dismissed from the senate in disgrace.[384] Sulla was born poor but acquired riches.[385] After successful military campaigns he was elected consul in 88.[386] He then married Caecilia, the daughter of the Pontifex Maximus Metellus. Plutarch records: "On the subject of this marriage many verses were sung in ridicule of him by the common people, and many of the leading men were indignant at it, thinking him, as Livy says, unworthy of the woman although they had judged him worthy of the consulship."[387] At the very least the passage indicates that, in the time of Sulla, Romans were greatly offended if an inferior male married a superior female, even if both were patrician. Plutarch is also recording the prevalence of political invective at the time.

That, then, is my interpretation of the three penalties imposed on Caesar according to Suetonius. The precise nature of the three penalties is best understood as meaning that Sulla treated Caesar not as a *gentilis* of the patrician *gens* Iulia but as a plebeian Iulius and, indeed, as the descendant of one who had been (as we shall see) a slave. For Caesar, with his reverence for his forebears with divine descent from Jupiter and Venus, princely descent from Aeneas, the creator of Rome, and from Ancus Marcius, the fourth Roman king,[388] no other insult could have been so great. It can be no surprise that afterwards Caesar was regarded as belonging to the other party. Of

---

[384] *Sulla* 1.1.

[385] See, e.g., Plutarch *Sulla* 1.1ff.

[386] Ibid.6.10

[387] Ibid.

[388] Suetonius *Divus Iulius* 6.1.

course, Sulla would also have a serious political aim: to diminish the dangerous young Caesar's prestige.

Faced with Caesar's refusal to divorce Cornelia, Sulla wished to punish him. And he did -- but in a possibly surprising way. In Suetonius's account he denied that Caesar was a *gentilis* of the *gens Iulia*. Very insulting, of course. Thereby he automatically and necessarily deprived Caesar of his position of *flamen Dialis*, thus opening up the possibility of a successful military and political career to Caesar. Why would he act in this way? Some explanation is urgently called for. Mine, is, of necessity, speculative but, I think, plausible.

The *gens Iulia* claimed descent from Venus, and Caesar was especially devoted to this genealogy. Sulla was of the old patrician *gens Cornelia*, which could not claim Venus as its *genetrix*. Yet Sulla, in contrast to other Cornelii, showed devotion to Venus. In 86/85, after his massive victory over Archelaus, he had inscribed on his trophies the names of Mars, Victory, and Venus, "believing that his success in war was due no less to good fortune that to military skill and strength."[389] The Romans regarded Venus as a deity of good fortune.[390] Still, her name on the trophies is surprising. Sulla also issued four coin types circa 82/81 -- one *aureus* and three *denarii* -- that portrayed the head of Venus with Cupid standing left holding a palm branch.[391] Sulla was the first of the Cornelia to depict Venus on his coins. Moreover, in the context of Sulla's adoption of the name Felix (Fortunate), Plutarch records that Sulla styled himself *epaphroditus* (favorite of Venus)[392] when writing on official business to the Greeks.

---

[389] Plutarch *Sulla* 10.5

[390] See, e.g., Wissowa, *Religion und Kultus*, p. 291.

[391] Sydenham, *Coinage*, nos. 760, 760a, 761, 761a, at 124; Crawford, *Coinage*, nos. 359/1, 359/2, at 1:373f.

[392] *Sulla* 34.2.

Sulla felt he had a particular connection with Venus.[393]   My suggestion then, speculative as it must be, is that Sulla had special respect for Venus but could not claim familial descent. When he was angered against Caesar who could -- rightfully in Roman terms -- claim descent from Venus, his response was jealously and vindictively to claim that, far from being descended from Venus,[394] Caesar was the descendant of a slave. In the Roman context of veneration of their ancestry, this would be a typical insult. Elsewhere Suetonius tells us that Mark Antony taunted the later emperor Augustus, saying that "his great-grandfather was a freedman, a money-changer."[395]   According to Porphyrius, the famous jurist Alfenus Varus (*consul suffectus* 39 B.C.) was either a shoemaker or the son of a shoemaker.[396] Even if Wolfgang Kunkel is correct that Porphyrius's meaning is that he was an enterprising business man whose slaves made shoes,[397] the intended insult from genealogy is patent. For the Romans of the time, the more outrageous the insult the better.[398]

Caesar's temple to Venus Genetrix was famous for its splendour.[399] At the battle of Pharsalus he had given "*Venus Victrix*" as his watchword and vowed a temple to her if he was victorious.[400] But he dedicated the temple to Venus Genetrix, not to Venus Victrix. There was a change from a rather impersonal form of the goddess -- not entirely so for a military commander -- to a highly personal one. At the very least the change shows Caesar's

---

[393] Lucretius's *De rerum natura* opens with an invocation to nurturing Venus, "*Aeneadum genetrix.*" "Mother of Aeneas and his *gens*." The poem is dedicated to Memmius, Sulla's son-in-law.

[394] Roman gentilician descent was through males, which becomes important in my section VI.

[395] Wolfgang Kunkel, *Herkunft und soziale Stellung der römischen Juristen*, 2d ed. (Graz, 1967), p. 29.

[396]   *Ad Horatii sermones* 1.3.130.

[397]   Kunkel, *Herkunft p.* 29.

[398] Cf., e.g., Amy Richlin, *The Garden of Priapus* (New Haven, 1983), pp. 96ff.

[399] Appian *Bellum Civile* 2.68; Dio Cassius 43.43.2f.

enormous pride in his claim to divine ancestry. But is there more? Lilly Ross Taylor suggests it indicates his new confidence.[401] I rather wonder whether Caesar, now the de facto ruler of Rome as Sulla had once been, still smarted under Sulla's slight and was insisting on his ancestry.[402]

But, it may be asked, did Sulla think that a claim of Caesar's servile origins would be plausible? Would people believe it? That, I think, rather misstates the issue. Sulla would have no such concern. His viciousness was well known, as was his sense of fun.[403] His intention would be to injure Caesar, especially in his pride. He would achieve that, even if no one believed his approach. Onlookers would remain silent. If Sulla showed contempt for Caesar, others would avoid being close to the young man.

How can one explain that Suetonius, Plutarch, and Velleius Paterculus do not say that Sulla's attack was to claim that Caesar was not a member of the *gens Iulia* because he had a slave ancestor? The answer must be that in the midst of Sulla's proscriptions this would be a minor affair. Not much attention would have been paid to it. Caesar was not such an important figure then. But why would Caesar not protest the contrary publicly and vociferously? The answer is that he could not. Sulla was after him to kill him, and Caesar was forced to go into hiding.[404] He could not respond to the challenge. Subsequently, it was better for Caesar to let the matter drop. It was politically wise not to notice publicly that his gentilician ancestry had been denied. It was much better simply to assert the descent from Venus by coins and the temple in the forum. Moreover, Sulla probably would not have proceeded against Caesar by any action at law. He would simply declare that Caesar was descended from a slave, deprive him of the office of flamen

---

[400] Appian *Bellum Civile* 2.68; Dio Cassius 43.22.

[401] Lily Ross Taylor, *The Divinity of the Roman Emperor* (Middletown, Conn., 1931), p. 63.

[402] Possibly Caesar had always intended to fulfill the vow to Venus Genetrix, but before the battle it was more politic to vow to Venus Victrix.

[403] Plutarch *Sulla* 2.2.

[404] Suetonius *Divus Iulius* 1.2. Moreover, Suetonius does not subscribe to a negative view of Caesar.

Dialis, seize property which he declared was wrongfully held by Caesar as coming from *gentiliciae hereditates*, and demand a sum equal to Cornelia's dowry.

A point that is probably overspeculative should be mentioned. Any charge by Sulla that Caesar had a slave ancestor would have been that one of his female ancestors had married a freedman Iulius.[405] No doubt such a charge could never be proved, but it could be made. Is it on this account that Caesar seems to have been over-sensitive when he divorced his second wife, Pompeia?[406] The sacrifice to the bona Dea was being celebrated when Clodius sneaked in and was discovered. Caesar immediately divorced his second wife Pompeia. Plutarch relates:

> Caesar immediately divorced Pompeia, and when he was summoned to testify at the trial he said he knew nothing about the matters with which Clodius was charged. His statement seemed strange, and the prosecutor asked: "Why then did you divorce your wife?" "Because," he said, "my wife ought not even to be under suspicion."[407]

Suetonius reports that Caesar did suspect Pompeia of adultery with Clodius.[408] Elsewhere he states boldly that Clodius was her lover,[409] as does Dio.[410]

---

[405] The charge could not be that a married female ancestor conceived as a result of sex with a slave, because the child would legally be presumed to be her husband's. Nor could the charge be that she was unmarried and had sex with a slave, because the child of an unmarried woman was not in the *potestas* of her father.

[406] Or is the divorce reflective of tension with Pompeius?

[407] *Caesar* 10.6.

[408] *Divus Iulius* 6.2.

[409] *Divus Iulius* 74.

[410] 37.45.2. Cicero simply records Clodius's presence in the house during the ceremony, and that Caesar divorced his wife: *ad Atticum* 1.13.3. But Caesar and Clodius were political allies. The story of Clodius's adultery with Caesar's wife may have been invented to discredit both men.

Only the approach I have taken in this chapter explains all three of Sulla's punishments of Caesar. None other can explain why the penalty regarding inheritances is restricted to *gentiliciae hereditates*. The removal of Caesar from his position as flamen Dialis can be explained otherwise, but the removal would then have been counterproductive and unnecessary. The "fine" of Caesar's dowry would otherwise have no apparent basis. My claim would, I think lack credibility only if it could plausibly be suggested that Suetonius was mistaken in his use of the term *gentiliciae hereditates* and that Sulla chose other punishments which by coincidence were particularly appropriate if Caesar were not a patrician, which could only mean that he had a servile ancestor.

The issue in front of us, the failure to treat technical legal terms technically, should not be restricted to the context of Suetonius. And it is important not just for law but also for an appreciation of society. Two instances spring to mind, with no need to provide scholarly apparatus. Thus, translators of Cicero frequently understand *hereditas* (inheritance) as "legacy" and take *legatum* (legacy) to mean "inheritance." But the position of a Roman heir or legatee was vastly different with regard to the performance of the *sacra* (religious duties of the deceased or the payment of debts of the deceased. Translators of the New Testament often take the Greek for *slave* to mean "servant," mischaracterizing the society.